PHILIPPIANS

Rejoicing and Thanksgiving

David Chapman

CHRISTIAN
FOCUS

David Chapman is Associate Professor of New Testament and Archaeology at Covenant Theological Seminary, where he has taught for the last 12 years. Previous to that he was involved in university campus ministry. He studied philosophy at Rice University, divinity at Trinity Evangelical Divinity School, and received his doctoral degree from the University of Cambridge. He is the author of *Ancient Jewish and Christian Perceptions of Crucifixion* (Mohr-Siebeck, 2006; Baker Academic, 2008). David is married to Tasha, and they have two daughters, Leela and Karis.

Unless otherwise indicated, all Scripture quotations are from The Holy Bible, English Standard Version, copyright © 2001 by Crossway Bibles, a division of Good News Publishers. Used by permission. All rights reserved.

Copyright © David Chapman

ISBN 978-1-84550-687-2

10 9 8 7 6 5 4 3 2 1

Published in 2012
by
Christian Focus Publications Ltd.,
Geanies House, Fearn, Ross-shire,
IV20 1TW, Scotland, UK.

www.christianfocus.com

Cover design by Alister MacInnes

Printed and bound by
Bell & Bain, Glasgow

MIX
Paper from
responsible sources
FSC® C007785

All rights reserved. No part of this publication may be reproduced, stored in a retrieval system, or transmitted, in any form, by any means, electronic, mechanical, photocopying, recording or otherwise without the prior permission of the publisher or a licence permitting restricted copying. In the U.K. such licences are issued by the Copyright Licensing Agency, Saffron House, 6–10 Kirby Street, London, EC1 8TS www.cla.co.uk.

Contents

Preface 5
Introduction 7
    Authorship 8
    Date and Place of Writing 10
    Occasion and Purposes 11
    Audience and Historical Context 12
    Theological and Ethical Themes 18
    Structure and Outline 27
1. Greetings (Philippians 1:1-2) 31
2. Thanksgiving and Prayer for the Philippians (Philippians 1:3-11) 43
3. The Advance of the Gospel (Philippians 1:12-18) 59
4. Paul's Focus in Life and in Death (Philippians 1:18b-26) 69
5. Christian Citizenship (Philippians 1:27-30) 85
6. Christian Unity (Philippians 2:1-4) 97
7. Christ's Example of Humility and Exaltation (Philippians 2:5-11) 117
8. Living as Children of God (Philippians 2:12-18) 149
9. Two Exemplars of Faithful Service (Philippians 2:19-30) 169
10. We Who Glory in Christ Jesus (Philippians 3:1-11) 187
11. Pressing on Toward Our Heavenly Citizenship (Philippians 3:12-21) ... 221
12. Standing Firm Together in the Lord (Philippians 4:1-9) 239
13. Of Gifts and Greetings (Philippians 4:10-23) 261
    Subject Index 277
    Scripture Index 281
    Abbreviations 285
    Selected Bibliography 287

Dedication

To Cecil and Mabelann Chapman, my beloved parents

Preface

For many years, this amazing epistle has captivated my attention. Teaching, preaching, and writing about Philippians has been a great source of joy, encouragement, admonishment, and instruction. It is a profound privilege and a great responsibility to study the Good News of Christ Jesus as found in the apostle Paul. My prayer is that the reader will better know and serve our Lord through considering anew Paul's letter to the church in Philippi.

A few words of orientation may be helpful. This commentary is designed for pastors and other ministry workers, as well as for every interested student of the Bible. It does not assume any technical knowledge (e.g., of systematic theology, Biblical studies, Greek, etc.). Yet it seeks to explain both the big picture of the letter and the details in each verse. Conscious of the many centuries of careful study of Philippians, I draw from the best of Christian scholarship and endeavor to make my conclusions understandable. I also consider it the duty of any commentator not merely to state opinions, but also to provide clear arguments for each interpretive judgment.

As I pen this commentary, I am conscious of two goals. First and most importantly, I hope to assist readers in understanding what Paul intended to convey to his initial audience in Philippi some two thousand years ago. The majority of the commentary is given over to this goal. Second, because the apostolic message also applies to Christians at all times and places, I aim throughout to illuminate some key transcultural applications. With that in mind and following the format of other volumes in this series, each section concludes with a few questions for personal reflection. Though writing in North America, with a British doctoral education, I seek to keep in mind the worldwide church, and I pray that this commentary will benefit many around the globe.

The translation cited is the English Standard Version. Yet as a commentator my own text has been the Greek, and throughout I have attempted to elucidate Paul's original Greek in ways understandable to those who know English. Occasionally, especially with issues concerning the original language, I have left more technical matters to 'Additional Notes' at the end of each section. These provide the curious with a bit more of a defense of positions taken in the main commentary.

One feature of Paul's letters that continues to impress me involves the way he employs similar themes throughout his epistles. While each letter has its own occasion and purposes and makes its own unique contribution, there remains, at the core, a striking theological consistency in his writings. Therefore, in the study of any one Pauline epistle, such as Philippians, it becomes vital to note its parallels with other letters; these correspondences help illumine his meaning in this particular letter. We also observe how Philippians links up with and contributes to Paul's broader literary corpus in order to better understand his thought-world and theology. Finally, given that recent critical scholarship has called into question the authenticity of some of Paul's New Testament writings, it is incumbent upon us (lay readers and academicians alike) to identify the various strong threads that link the earlier Pauline correspondence via Philippians with his later works (thus providing an inductive argument for their unity of authorship). For these reasons, I tend to highlight Pauline parallels more so than is typical of commentaries of this length.

This book is dedicated to my wonderful parents, Cecil and Mabelann Chapman, who affectionately raised me in the nurture and admonition of the Lord. My love for them is inexpressible. My dear wife, Tasha, and our delightful daughters, Leela and Karis, all deserve deep appreciation for how often they have had to endure my being holed up in my study. Tasha also kindly made helpful suggestions for improving this manuscript. Others have generously consented to read this work while it was in production. Among these, I would mention Cheryl Eaton for her exemplary editing skills, and Malcolm MacLean and Willie MacKenzie of Christian Focus for their longsuffering in waiting for this volume.

Introduction

The epistle to the Philippians accomplishes in four short chapters an amazing variety of purposes. This letter instructs, warns, admonishes, thanks, and encourages the church. It provides an opportunity to walk alongside the great apostle Paul and to learn from how he thinks, how he feels, and how he conducts his life. It expresses a deep-seated joy, even in the midst of spiritual opposition and physical challenges. Most of all, it directs the reader repeatedly to the Good News of Jesus Christ.

Commentaries typically begin by discussing such seemingly mundane issues as author, date, and occasion of writing. The reader might well ask why we should start here. Surely the author of the epistle has made himself known from the opening verse. Why do we really care what date it was written? And why do we need to discuss his purposes for writing if those will become clear as we read the epistle?

However, if our first responsibility in interpretation is to understand the author's intent in penning these words for his audience, then the more we know about the author and audience, the better informed we can be about his potential goals for this letter. Thus consideration of 'authorship' and 'audience' serves not merely as a defense of Pauline authenticity, but reminds us of who our author was and why he would write to a fledgling church in Philippi. Discussions of date, occasion, and purpose all orient us to the overall reasons this epistle was originally produced so that we can better recognize these motives when we meet them in the letter. And a preliminary analysis of the author's theological themes can sensitize us to the theological and ethical framework we shall later encounter as we proceed verse by verse. Therefore,

I would invite the reader to consider these matters earnestly prior to launching into the epistle itself.

Authorship

The opening words identify the author(s) as 'Paul and Timothy.' Nonetheless, it is clear that Paul has taken the lead throughout the writing process. After these opening words, Timothy quickly fades into the background, and Paul speaks directly to the readers. Indeed, Paul quite possibly co-listed Timothy as author in order to affirm his respect for Timothy in preparation for his upcoming trip to Philippi on Paul's behalf (see further the comments on 1:1). Thus, midway through the letter, Paul will say, 'I hope in the Lord Jesus to send Timothy to you soon' (2:19).

Outside of the opening verse, everywhere else the author actually refers to himself in the singular ('I, me, my, mine') rather than in the plural. In the Greek text there are 66 verbs and 54 personal pronouns all in the first-person *singular*. The only first-person plural references are occasions when Paul includes his audience as part of the 'we'. For example, in Philippians 3:20 Paul says, 'But *our* citizenship is in heaven, and from it *we* await a Savior.' Most often, Paul says things such as, 'Brothers, join in imitating *me*' (3:17). Therefore, we can rightly conclude that it is Paul's singular voice that resounds throughout the letter.

Despite the clear assertion of Paul's authorship from the opening of this epistle, his authorship has been questioned by some academics (especially in the nineteenth century). Nevertheless, Paul's role as author has been widely (and nearly universally) defended by contemporary scholars of all theological stripes. As will be witnessed throughout this commentary, the concerns of the letter overlap substantially with those of Paul's other epistles, and the autobiographical details cohere with other extant depictions of Paul's life (both in Acts and in his other letters). Moreover, this epistle was widely known in the post-apostolic church as coming from Paul's hand (e.g., in the writings of Irenaeus, Clement of Alexandria, and Tertullian; in the Muratorian Canon; and in the earliest manuscripts such as p[46]). The teachings of Philippians were influential among the first- and second-century church Fathers (e.g., Clement of Rome, Ignatius, Shepherd of Hermas, Justin Martyr, etc.), thus implying an early widespread distribution of the letter in Paul's name. The question of whether the text is a compilation of two (or more) letters from Paul has been an intriguing academic exercise, but the integrity of the manuscript tradition and the underlying continuity of thought between all the sections of the epistle rightly indicate that we are dealing with a single letter from Paul. Those wishing to pursue these issues further could investigate the introductions in the more technical commentaries by Peter T. O'Brien and Gerald F. Hawthorne.

The reader will likely perceive this letter to be one of the most introspective of Paul's epistles, with several long autobiographical sections that model sound Christian living to his recipients. It is these autobiographical references that provide the most detail about Paul and his situation at the time of writing. Most importantly, Paul has been imprisoned and is awaiting trial (1:13-14). The church in Philippi has sent him aid in the form of material assistance transported through the agency of Epaphroditus (2:25-30; 4:10-19), who ministered personally to Paul's situation. Paul is very grateful, and he writes in part to thank the church, whom he remembers prayerfully with immense fondness (1:3-7) and whom he wishes to see again soon (1:8, 26; 2:24; 4:1). At the same time, Paul indicates that he is content, even joyful, in his circumstances because of his eternal hope in Christ (1:18-26; 2:17). Paul sends this letter back with Epaphroditus, whose severe illness while in Paul's service had concerned both Paul and the Philippians; Paul, therefore, is eager for them to see Epaphroditus again in person (2:25-30). Eventually, Paul plans to send Timothy as his delegate to the church in Philippi in order to serve there and to report back about the situation in that church (2:19-24).

Paul also tells the story of his previous religious credentials in Judaism: he had been circumcised as an infant, could trace his ancestry through the line of Benjamin, and was trained in the Pharisee sect (3:4-5; cf. Acts 23:6; 26:5). He confesses that he had persecuted the church due to his zealous antagonism against the fledgling messianic movement (Phil. 3:6; cf. Gal. 1:13; Acts 8:1; 9:1-2). Now he views his former credentials as rubbish to be discarded in exchange for the joy of being a true follower of Christ. Indeed, Paul's current autobiographical reflections testify to his great passion for the gospel of Jesus Christ (e.g., Phil. 1:12-26; 3:7-16). Finally, his memories of traveling from Philippi to Thessalonica (4:15-16) align well with the history found in Acts 16–17.

Date and Place of Writing
The date of the letter closely connects to the issue of where and when Paul was in prison. Events mentioned in Philippians indicate that the occasion of this detention must have occurred a long time after Paul's second missionary journey (Phil. 4:10; cf. Acts 15:36–18:22), when he had first visited Philippi and Thessalonica (Phil. 4:15-16; cf. Acts 16:11–17:9). Paul appears optimistic for his own release (Phil. 1:25-26; 2:24), and this reminds us of Paul's last great period of imprisonment as depicted in the book of Acts following his third missionary journey (Acts 21:27–28:31). In that account, even the officials acknowledged that Paul had committed no crime, and they asserted that he could have already been released had he not appealed his case to Caesar in Rome (Acts 25:10-12, 18, 25; 26:31-32). This would indicate that Paul's imprisonment here in Philippians either took place in Caesarea (en route to Rome) or in Rome itself. Both locations are possible, but the latter is to be favored given the time required for all the events depicted in this book (which we will mention in a moment) and given the ease of sending Epaphroditus with gifts between Philippi and Rome.

Though later church tradition reports one final imprisonment after the events depicted in the book of Acts, Paul's situation during that later incarceration was a much more difficult one, and it eventually resulted in his death at the imperial command of Nero (cf. the pessimism for his release found in 2 Tim. 1:8; 4:6-8). However, the tenor of Philippians appears too optimistic to have been written during that time.

Some scholars have suggested that this letter could have been written from Ephesus, during an incarceration otherwise not mentioned in the book of Acts (though presumably during the events reported in Acts 19). While it is possible that Acts does not record all the occasions during which Paul was imprisoned (cf. 2 Cor. 6:5; 11:23), the detention depicted in this epistle appears to have been quite long and significant – at least long enough for the Philippians to have heard of Paul's predicament, gathered together a gift, and sent Epaphroditus, and also long enough for Epaphroditus to have made the journey, ministered to Paul, become gravely ill, and then recovered from his illness. Such a lengthy imprisonment would likely have made it into the pages of Acts, and there appears little reason to postulate otherwise. Moreover, the mention of the *praitōrion* ('praetorian guard') in Philippians 1:13, although it could designate the military headquarters of an imperial legate (e.g., Matt. 27:27; Acts 23:35), would here most likely refer to the imperial guard back in Rome. And a Roman location would also explain why Paul passes on greetings from 'Caesar's household' to the Philippians (4:22).

Therefore, many scholars have rightly concluded that the imprisonment mentioned in Philippians must be the one in Rome that occurred after Paul's third missionary journey. This can be dated to approximately A.D. 60–62. This would mean that Paul had already served as Christ's ambassador for at least 25 years, and that his first visit to Philippi had been just over 10 years before he penned this letter.

Occasion and Purposes

All of Paul's letters connect to the specific situations in the churches to which he writes, and he often composes them with a variety of purposes. In this case, the immediate occasion for writing involves Epaphroditus' travels to Philippi (2:25-30). Having been sent to Rome by the Philippian church with gifts for Paul, Epaphroditus now will return home after ministering to Paul and after a dire illness (2:30; 4:18). Paul plans to send this letter back to Philippi with Epaphroditus, providing Paul with an opportunity to express appreciation for Epaphroditus' work and to thank the church for their gifts and support during his imprisonment (esp. 4:10-19). Given the Philippians' evident concern for Paul, he affords them with evidence of his own joy and confidence in the Lord, even in the midst of his imprisonment and impending trial (1:12-26).

Moreover, this occasion also allows Paul to express his affection for the church (e.g., 1:7-8) and to mention his desire to send Timothy soon as his ministerial delegate to Philippi

(2:19-24). He uses the opportunity to instruct the Philippians by verbal directives and through his own apostolic example (see 3:17; cf. 1:12-26; 2:17-18; 3:3-16; 3:20-21; 4:11-13). Paul appears especially concerned about the possible divisions that are occurring in the church (4:2-3; cf. 1:27–2:11), and he writes to encourage church unity in the midst of potential challenges from persecution and from heretics (1:27-30; 3:2-3). Thus we observe that in a relatively short letter, Paul manages to cover a substantial amount of material.

Audience and Historical Context
Philippi stood as an important city in Macedonia on the famed Egnatian Way (a road that crossed Macedonia and connected it with Asia). Today, the remains of this ancient city are located in modern Greece, at the north end of the Aegean Sea. According to the book of Acts, Philippi was known in the first century as a 'leading city' and a 'Roman colony' (Acts 16:12).

The city had been formally founded by Greek colonists about 360 B.C., and then shortly afterwards, was conquered and fortified by Philip of Macedon (the father of Alexander the Great), who renamed it after himself. By the time of Paul, Philippi maintained an important connection with the nearby port of Neapolis (Acts 16:11).

In addition to serving as a vital commercial transit point, Philippi had been designated a Roman colony by Octavian (= Augustus Caesar) to commemorate his military victory there over the forces of Brutus and Cassius (42 B.C.). The city was thus permitted the title 'Colonia Augusta Julia Philippensis.' This imperial privilege permitted the urban citizens certain legal benefits (including reduced taxes), and it meant that Philippi had received a large influx of retired soldiers who settled in the city.

The colonists were granted Roman citizenship, thus adding to the importance of the city's populace. Much as the colonial status of Philippi brought certain imperial advantages to the city as a whole, so too did individual Roman citizenship grant legal and social benefits to those in Philippi who possessed citizenship (along with their families). Citizens of Rome enjoyed greater legal rights than non-citizens, and they could carry their citizenship as a badge of respect (cf. Acts 16:37-38;

22:25-29; 23:27). Paul will later play off this civic history by calling the Philippian church members to act as 'citizens of the gospel' and 'citizens of heaven' in contrast to any earthly Roman colonial citizenship (see comments on 1:27 and 3:20).

Archaeological discoveries in Philippi have confirmed from the first century the existence of a theater, a forum, various shops, tombs, and city gates. Portions of the marble-paved Egnatian Way have been identified. Also testifying to the ongoing significance of this city in the Roman world were later structures, including edifices such as pagan temples, a palaestra, an amphitheater, fountains, a library, a latrine, baths, and later Byzantine-era churches. Local church tradition assigns the prison site of Paul and Silas (in Acts 16:23-24) to a small stone crypt built over a cistern near the forum. (This is commonly shown to tourists today.) Civic inscriptions in Philippi, from about the time of the first century, are typically engraved in Latin, reminding us of substantive Roman influence in this Macedonian town. The presence of ancient temples to pagan gods (e.g., Apollo and Artemis) signals the paganism that surrounded the fledgling church in Paul's day.

As a Roman city, Philippi engaged in constant commerce. Local agriculture benefitted from the fertile land and natural springs, and many other commodities would have traversed the Egnatian Way. Although ultimately under the authority of the Roman Empire, local civic life was mostly governed by the city's economic elite, whose political influence coincided with their economic concerns and with their fiscal benefaction of the urban center. The wealthy would have been relatively few, although they engaged in patron-client relationships with those below (and above) them on the social scale. Many people possessed only very moderate means. Slaves were plentiful in antiquity, and most free householders owned a few slaves (and the wealthy owned many).

Roman pagan religion encouraged the ritualistic worship of a range of well-known deities alongside participation in the civic duties of the imperial cult. Individual families paid homage to their own 'house gods'. In short, the populace would have been captivated to religious practices that opposed Christian devotion to the one true God. Hellenistic philosophical thought was widely discussed in the gymnasiums and other places of intellectual debate. For example, the Stoics taught ethical ideals grounded in a desire to live rationally according to the reasoned soul that they believed governed the cosmos. Others would have been more attracted to Epicureanism, with its emphasis on community, alongside its teaching that life ended with death and that souls were not eternal. Such philosophical options abounded and provided the ethical teaching and metaphysical beliefs otherwise lacking in Roman pagan religion.

Yet Jewish people lived amid this pagan city, and some Gentiles found themselves attracted to such an austere monotheistic worship of God. Toward the beginning of Paul's first stay in Philippi, he makes contact in Acts 16 with a group engaged in Jewish worship outside the city walls. This indicates a Jewish presence in the area, and it reminds the reader that Paul often went to the Jewish places of worship first in his missionary work. Jewish believers (along with former Gentile 'God-fearers' and proselytes to Judaism) would have been prevalent in the early church. Their Jewish background provided a deep contact with the Old Testament Scriptures, as well as a heritage of Jewish worship practices. Paul himself drew on his Jewish heritage when he instructed Jews (and even converted Gentile pagans) in the way of the Lord. However, such Jewish influence in early Christianity may have made some church participants particularly susceptible to those who insisted that Gentiles be circumcised in order to participate fully in the life of the church (cf. Phil. 3:2).

The Philippians likely well remembered Paul's first ministry in their midst (cf. Phil. 1:5). Paul's initial contact with Philippi is recorded in Acts 16:12-40, during his second missionary journey. There, he had responded to a vision calling him to evangelize in Macedonia (16:9-10), and Philippi was his first major stop after crossing over from Asia. As mentioned earlier, it was in Philippi where Paul met women engaged in prayer on the Sabbath near a river outside the city gate (16:13). Scholars debate whether this episode depicts an actual synagogue outside the city or an outside venue set aside for a small Jewish prayer gathering (on the assumption that the Philippians possessed no synagogue). Lydia, who appears to have been a Gentile 'God-fearer' attracted to Judaism, was baptized along with her household after she heard the gospel. Lydia subsequently offered to host Paul and his colleagues in her home (16:14-15), and it was common for wealthy people in antiquity to practice such forms of hospitality.

Later, Paul cast out a demonic spirit from a fortune-telling slave girl, only to have her owners drag him to the forum in order to be judged by the civic magistrates (16:16-21). The legal accusation lodged against Paul and Silas was that they were Jews who advocated, 'customs that are not lawful for us as Romans to accept or practice' (16:21). The magistrates ordered Paul and Silas to be beaten and imprisoned overnight (16:22-24). Yet while they were singing hymns, a miraculous earthquake freed them from their bonds (16:25-26). Paul's willingness to stay in jail even after the earthquake, combined with his faithfulness to preach the gospel, led to the miraculous conversion of the jailer and his whole family (16:27-34). The next day, the magistrates learned of Paul's Roman citizenship and consequently apologized for their harsh treatment of him, though they still asked Paul to leave the city (16:35-39). Paul took one more opportunity to visit with Lydia and the other believers in Christ, then he left town to continue his missionary journey (16:40).

In addition to the record in the book of Acts, Paul also briefly references these events in a letter to the Thessalonian church. In that document, Paul recalls that he had been 'shamefully treated' and had 'suffered' in Philippi before arriving in Thessalonica (1 Thess. 2:2). Given that Paul had indeed once been imprisoned in Philippi (as the Philippians well knew), it is all the more significant that he wrote this letter to the Philippian church during a subsequent imprisonment in Rome.

We do not know much about Paul's continued contact with the Philippians after the events of Acts 16. He indicates in this epistle that they supported his missionary work when he continued on toward Thessalonica (Phil. 4:15-17; cf. Acts 17:1-9). During his third missionary journey, he traversed Macedonia twice (Acts 20:1, 3; cf. 1 Cor. 16:5). On the first occasion, he probably traveled through Philippi, and on the second, he definitely visited the city (Acts 20:6). In another letter, Paul readily champions the willingness of the

Macedonian churches to give to the needs of the saints, and it is quite possible that the Philippians generously participated in this alongside other Macedonian churches (2 Cor. 8:1-5). Paul clearly had deeper contact with the Philippian church than the book of Acts was able to depict. Thus in this epistle, Paul mentions other 'fellow workers' in Philippi who do not appear in Acts – especially Euodia, Syntyche, Clement, and an unnamed 'true companion' (Phil. 4:2-3).

Paul speaks appreciatively of how the Philippians had revived their concern for him during his present imprisonment (Phil. 4:10). They had not been given an opportunity for a long time to partner so fully with Paul, and he is clearly appreciative of how they sent Epaphroditus along with gifts to minister to his need. Indeed, as will be evident in the commentary below, Paul considers the Philippians to be his dear brothers in Christian gospel fellowship. He is certainly aware and deeply concerned about divisions within the Philippian church (4:2), and he may have learned of these divisions from Epaphroditus, but his awareness of these factions certainly indicates his ongoing interest in the church.

As noted above, Paul himself was 'imprisoned' while writing the letter (Phil. 1:7, 12-17). We need not imagine here some sort of dark dungeon, though Paul had experienced such adverse conditions previously in Philippi, Jerusalem, and Caesarea (see Acts 16:23-27; 22:24, 29; 23:35; 24:27; 27:1). Rather, the book of Acts represents Paul's time in Rome as an occasion of house arrest, where for at least two years prior to his actual trial before Caesar, he was permitted, at his own expense, to be chained inside a residence and guarded by an individual soldier (28:16, 20, 30). During that time, he could receive visitors, even in groups (28:30-31; cf. 28:17-28). Typically, imprisonment was not in itself a long-term punishment in Roman law, but instead, 'prison' was where one awaited a judicial verdict. Any sentence that led to a Roman citizen being delivered to a long-term removal from society usually involved 'banishment' and 'exile' to distant lands.

Paul writes three other letters while being incarcerated (and presumably awaiting trial). These are known collectively, along with Philippians, as his 'Prison Epistles' (see also Eph. 3:1; 4:1; 6:20; Col. 4:3, 10, 18; Philem. 1, 9, 10, 13, 23). In referring to these Prison Epistles, we should also mention again Paul's later imprisonment referenced in 2 Timothy (1:8, 16-17; 2:9); in that 'Pastoral Epistle' he is much less optimistic about the likely outcome of his trial (2 Tim. 4:6-8, 16). Paul's general attitude toward his imprisonments is to embrace their reproach as part of his apostolic call to spread the gospel. Indeed, such moments show forth Paul's weakness and thus exhibit the power of Christ through him (e.g., 2 Cor. 11:23-30; 12:9-10; 13:4). The personal humility and sacrifice entailed in his own imprisonment can also serve as an example for calling others to lead a humble life worthy of the gospel (Eph. 4:1-2).

The Philippian church itself faced opposition at the time Paul wrote this letter, though the details of this are not entirely clear. Paul speaks of 'opponents' of the Philippian church (1:28), who face destruction from God. He also passionately warns against the 'mutilators of the flesh' (3:2), and this speaks to those who would insist that Gentiles undergo circumcision. We cannot be entirely certain whether the categories of 'opponents' and 'mutilators' overlap, though I strongly suspect that the latter formed a subset of the former. The opposition Paul initially faced in Philippi (Acts 16) came from pagan businessmen, whose reliance on demonically inspired fortune-telling was undercut by the power of the gospel. Yet in the book of Acts, opposition to Paul's ministry during his second missionary journey in Macedonia and Greece also came from Jewish leaders in the community. Finally, the phrase 'mutilators of the flesh' appears to refer to Judaizers, who might insinuate themselves into the Christian communion. Thus the church potentially faced opposition from many quarters, and 1:28 refers to any such opponents of the gospel.

There is a lively academic debate about whether the 'mutilators of the flesh' in 3:2 refer to Judaizers or to Jewish (non-Christian) leaders. The issue (along with other options) will be discussed in the commentary on this verse. I will argue that Judaizers are more likely in view in 3:2 because Paul does appear earnestly concerned that this group may have real influence in attracting people in the church to their side (which would be unlikely if this were to refer to Jewish leaders from outside the church). In many of Paul's letters, we encounter the 'Judaizers,' who believed that a physical circumcision (combined with an adherence to law-keeping and to other traditional Jewish theological and social distinctives) was necessary for full membership in the messianic Christian church. There appears to be slight variations among these Judaizing elements (e.g., between those found in Galatia, Colossae, and Crete). Given those variations and the lack of detailed description in Philippians, we probably should not attempt to depict in detail the theology of those Judaizers who, Paul fears, may seek to insinuate their way into the Philippian church. We can, however, be certain that he was concerned about opponents to the gospel both within and without the church in Philippi.

These brief comments help to portray the context and circumstances that led to the writing of the letter. Other historical observations will be made as we progress through the letter. All of this is important as we place ourselves in the position of Paul's first readers in order to comprehend the significance of this epistle to his original audience, prior to applying its message to our various contexts today.

Theological and Ethical Themes

Although this letter does not set out to be a theological or ethical treatise, it does testify throughout to Paul's deep theological reflection and to his concern to instruct the church in proper Christian living. Nevertheless, Paul is writing to friends who know his theological teachings well, and therefore this epistle often serves more to prompt remembrance of Paul's Christian theology than to argue strongly for his positions. We shall consider below some of the key categories that emerge from a brief, inductive, theological study of Paul's letter. Naturally, much more detail will be found in the commentary to follow.

God in this letter is the ultimate source of grace and peace (1:2; 4:7), and He is addressed as the 'God of peace' (4:9). Both 'grace' and 'peace' have a huge theological background in Old Testament and New Testament thought, and this touches on a complex network of ideas associated in Scripture with God granting grace and peace. This reminds us that Paul assumes much of previous Biblical theology that had informed God's people throughout the ages about the one true God –

Introduction

a theology both he and his audience already knew from the Old Testament, from Christianity's Jewish heritage, and from early Christian instruction. Thus Paul does not seek to work out a complete 'doctrine' of God in this epistle, even if that doctrine is evident throughout.

However, in Paul's direct references to the deity in this letter, we obtain a profound indication of his broader theological understanding of who God is. To God the Christian turns in thanksgiving and in prayer (1:3ff.; 4:6). He deserves all glory and praise (1:11; 2:11; 4:20). God grants mercy to Paul and others (2:27), and He reveals truth (3:15). God supplies the needs of His people (4:19). It is this God who 'began a good work in you' and who will 'bring it to completion', thus testifying to the sovereign role of the deity in initiating and sustaining salvation (1:5-6; and see commentary on 1:28). God works in us for His good pleasure (2:13). Righteousness comes from God to those who believe in Jesus (3:9), and God is the one who summons Christians to His 'upward call' with its eschatological prize (3:14). In response to God's salvation, Christians desire to present pleasing offerings to Him (4:18). God is called our 'Father' (1:2; 4:20; cf. 2:15), and yet there is a special paternal relationship between God, the Father, and the pre-existing Son, Jesus Christ, whom the Father exalted from His humble state of voluntary humanity and death to reign over all creation alongside Himself (2:9-11). God and Jesus can be said to share the same form and to be equal (2:6). Further Trinitarian implications are noted below.

The *Christology* of this epistle is evident from the very opening words – Jesus is exalted as the Christ (i.e., the Messiah) and the Lord (1:1-2). The title 'Christ' occurs frequently in the epistle (thirty-seven times to be precise). It means the 'anointed one' and connects Jesus to the long line of Jewish messianic expectation that an eternal ruler would come from the Davidic line and govern His people in justice and mercy. The title 'Lord' refers to the sovereign rule of the messiah, and this title grants to Jesus the same exalted designation that the Lord God Himself receives throughout Scripture. As even these opening words intone, the deity of Christ is assumed throughout this letter and co-exists with clear indications of His humanity.

Jesus, alongside God the Father, blesses His people with grace and peace (1:2; 4:23). Like God the Father, Christ receives glory as His people boast in Him (1:26). The gospel is in truth the good news about Jesus Christ, and this good news certainly speaks about Jesus' salvific death and resurrection. Thus Christ is the one whose resurrection models the resurrection life that He has obtained for all those in His church (3:10-11). This good news envelops these great two historical moments of Jesus' death and resurrection, but it cannot be reduced to just those two events. Rather, the gospel connects the death and resurrection of the Messiah to the broader tapestry of the salvation-historical expectations of God's people throughout history – expectations that find their fulfillment in the whole of who Jesus is as the incarnate messianic deliverer, who humbled Himself unto death to atone for human sin, and who now sits exalted at the right hand of God the Father. This good news brings encouragement (2:1).

The implications of Paul's Christology in this epistle can be most fully discovered by reading 2:5-11. In that amazing passage, we witness the pre-existence of Jesus prior to His earthly ministry; indeed, Jesus existed in the form of God long before being born in Bethlehem. Yet He did not grasp onto such a privileged status, but He voluntarily gave that status over for the sake of others. Jesus, once in a position equal to God the Father, voluntarily took on human flesh, and Paul depicts this truth as the pre-eminent act of deepest humility. Paul represents this act in terms that strongly contrast Jesus' humanity with His deity – for to have taken on human form is (relatively speaking) to have become 'nothing' and to have taken on the form of a 'slave'. Nonetheless, this passage in no way suggests that Jesus relinquished His divine nature when He became human. What Jesus exchanged was the exaltation, glory, and status that came from being 'in the form of God'. By taking on His human nature alongside the divine, He permitted His former status to be diminished for the sake of the humans He came to save.

This act of humility is compounded by the manner of His death on a cross (2:8). Such humility is met with the highest commendation by God the Father, so that Jesus now is exalted beyond the whole of creation (2:9-11; also 3:21). The term

'Lord' thus denotes Jesus as the one who rules over all of creation. Jesus Himself continues in this age to embrace both divine and human natures. The categories that depict His present and future glorification prove Him to have returned to like status with God the Father (2:9-11). Yet He continues to possess a resurrection body and all other aspects of His humanity (3:21).

Paul calls Jesus 'Saviour' (3:20), and it is this Jesus in whom we must place our faith in order to be deemed righteous (3:9). For all those who have thus become citizens of heaven, the Lord Jesus will transform us into our resurrection bodies at the Day of Christ (3:21). It is knowing this Christ, who is the humble and exalted messianic Lord, that is the ultimate gain in our lives – or as Paul calls it, 'the surpassing worth of knowing Christ Jesus my Lord' (3:8).

The Holy Spirit receives mention at a few key junctures. The 'Spirit of Jesus Christ' assists Paul in the midst of his difficult plight, even bringing an anticipated deliverance from prison (1:19). The Spirit joins Christians in fellowship with one another (2:1). It is by the 'Spirit of God' that Christians are enabled to give true worship, in contrast to attempts to put spiritual confidence in our human flesh (3:3). Notably – and now we enter further into the Trinitarian mystery – the Holy Spirit is eternally related both to God, the Father, and to God the Son, and thus can be called both the 'Spirit of God' and the 'Spirit of Jesus Christ'.

Humanity presently exists in a world that has become crooked and twisted by human sinfulness. Christians continue to live in such a world and thus meet opposition, even while serving as lights to others (1:28-30; 2:15). Yet God reaches out through Christ to save a fallen humanity. Jesus Himself takes on human form and likeness (2:7-8), and this exhibits God's own salvific initiative to redeem for Himself a people formerly in the grips of sin. Paul's teaching here about Jesus' own humanity reminds us that God Himself created humans in His image (Gen. 1:26-28), and elsewhere Paul speaks of Christians being restored and renewed into that divine image through becoming conformed to the image of Christ (e.g., Col. 1:15; 3:10). In this theological context, we note that Jesus' resurrection body exhibits the truth that God redeems us in our humanity (even in all its physicality) en route to a more glorious inheritance in the coming fullness of the messianic kingdom (3:20-21).

Concerning *salvation*, Paul insists that we cannot attain our 'own righteousness'. That is, one cannot acquire a sufficiently righteous standing before God by keeping the law. Rather, any true righteousness before God must come to the believer from God through faith in Christ (3:9). This short declaration in 3:9 provides one of the most concise and clear statements of the gospel in all Paul's writings. Salvation is a gift from God through faith in Christ Jesus, and such salvation cannot be achieved from good works or from a personal zeal at law-keeping.

God sovereignly initiates salvation, for He is the one who 'began a good work in you' and who 'will bring it to completion' as well (1:6). As a consequence of such salvation, Paul depicts the church in Philippi as 'saints' – i.e., as those who have been deemed by God to be holy (1:1; 4:21-22). Salvation is the present possession of the believers in the church, and yet it must be lived out in such a way that it issues into good works from those who fear and trust God (2:12-13). Traditional theological categories have labeled this the process of 'sanctification'. It is important to note, in the midst of such Christian living, that God Himself is the one who 'works in you'. The 'working out' of salvation comes through the agency of God, who continues to 'work in' us unto His glory (2:12-13; cf. 1:6); He has begun our salvation and will complete it. Such Christian living can also be pictured in images of Christian perseverance, for believers are called to 'hold fast to the word of life' (2:16). This assurance of salvation is evident in the world in part by how the church stands together in the midst of persecution (1:28).

Ecclesiology in this book predominately assumes that church participants share in fellowship with one another. In such a 'fellowship', they are united in a voluntary corporate body that exists together to accomplish united aims. In particular, the Philippians are in a mutual fellowship for the sake of the gospel, and they have been since the first day that the good news came to them (1:5). They share this fellowship with Paul in multiple ways, including by participating in his defense and confirmation of the gospel in its public proclamation (1:7). Paul's frequent term for his fellow Christians is 'brothers', indicating that their fellowship issues forth into a family-like corporate belonging. Perhaps behind this, we should see Paul's doctrine of adoption into God's family, which is so prevalent elsewhere in his epistles (e.g., Rom. 8:15; Gal. 4:5; Eph. 1:5). In the midst of their fellowship, the church has leaders, and two church offices in particular are noted (namely, 'overseers and deacons' in 1:1).

Eschatology concerns Paul's teaching about the future life of the believer in Christ, and he often refers to the return of Christ as the 'day of Jesus Christ' or the 'day of Christ' (e.g., 1:6, 10; 2:16). In this eschatological Day, Paul anticipates the culmination of God's salvific work in the life of the believer (1:6). Yet as elsewhere in Paul, that salvific work has already 'begun' in the believer (1:6). Thus the future eschatological experience of a redeemed relationship to God through Jesus Christ and in fellowship with the Holy Spirit has already been inaugurated in the present life of the believer and in the current experience of the church community. While we strive for Christian moral perfection in this life (3:15), Paul himself does not expect that we will fully achieve that aim until we enter into resurrection glory (3:12). Nevertheless, Christians in this era await the full glory of the return of Christ and a consequent complete experience of communion with the Triune God. Also, in the 'Day of Christ', Paul expects himself to be granted a greater awareness of the fruit of his ministry as it has blossomed in the lives of others (2:16).

Paul mentions the 'Book of Life' that contains the names of the saints (4:3). Other Biblical passages also reference this eternal register of God's people, which lists those who shall be admitted to their everlasting reward. However, such a future age is not an ephemeral existence of bodiless immortal souls, nor is it a floating-on-clouds, playing-harps type of unearthly heavenly existence (as so often appears in popular media today). Rather, Paul looks forward to the physical resurrection of the dead (3:11) – that is to a resurrected bodily existence in Christ's presence on a New Earth. This resurrection is vouchsafed by the resurrection of Christ (3:10), in whose likeness we shall follow. Moreover, it is Christ Himself who will, 'transform our lowly body to be like his glorious body by the power that enables him even to subject all things to himself' (3:21).

Although the eschatological teaching of Philippians focuses on the future hope of the Christian, Paul also briefly mentions that the enemies of Christ face destruction (3:19), and that they will also be forced to acknowledge Christ's lordship in the end (2:10-11).

Paul is so confident of Christ's present reign over His kingdom, that even death itself simply brings him directly into what theologians call the 'intermediate' state of immediate conscious awareness of being in Christ's presence, even prior to the 'day of Christ' and the resurrection of the body (1:21-23). This indicates that believers who have already passed out of this life await the Day of Christ in a blissful state of being in Christ's presence. This has long been a comfort to those who face death themselves, and to those who grieve the loss of a loved one. Still, the future holds something even better than this intermediate state, as we join in the resurrection of our resurrected Lord (3:20-21).

Ethics and Christian living form a constant backdrop to Paul's instruction throughout this letter. Such ethics cannot properly be separated from Paul's understanding of salvation – for righteousness comes from God by means of faith in Christ (3:9). Thus Paul's ethic does not inform the means of salvation but speaks of the way that the saved ought to live. Here, as elsewhere in Paul, the gospel calls forth a people who will work out the salvation that God has already begun in them by engaging in proper Christian conduct in awestruck wonder of the sovereign God who Himself continues to will and to work in the believer (2:12-13).

Paul models an affectionate love for the church (1:3-4, 8). Indeed, Paul desires that Christian love be complemented by knowledge and wisdom, in order that all believers may follow the excellent, pure, and blameless ways of Christ (1:9-11). Christians are to meditate on the true, pure, honorable, just, lovely, and commendable thoughts of praiseworthy things (4:8). Paul's goal of Christian purity, even perfection, anticipates the Day of Christ (1:10). Yet prior to that Day, Paul does not consider himself to have achieved perfection, though it remains the ever-present goal he strains to achieve (3:12-16).

Introduction

While called to be active in this world (especially in the spread of the good news), Christians recognize a heavenly citizenship, rooted in the gospel (1:27; 3:20). This teaching appears at two key junctures in the epistle and contrasts with the earthly Roman citizenship that many in Philippi would have championed in their day. Thus Christian allegiances rightly focus on God and Christ, and any competing earthly loyalties must be held very loosely. Indeed, Paul introduces his whole ethical instruction in this letter with the general maxim: 'only live worthily as citizens of the gospel of Christ' (see comments on 1:27).

With its message of the crucified and glorified Christ, the gospel is indeed the central content of the Christian life. Christian fellowship involves mutual participation in the gospel (1:5). Paul's goal is to see the gospel defended (1:16) and advanced (1:12), and he calls others to cooperate with him in these endeavors (1:7). Christians strive together for the sake of the faith of the gospel (1:27; 4:15). One of the highest commendations Paul can give another person is that they have been a co-laborer in gospel service (2:22; 4:3).

Prayer forms a substantive part of the Christian life. Paul opens the epistle with prayer for the Philippians (1:3-11). He also invites prayers from the congregation (1:19). In their fellowship with one another, all members shoulder the responsibility of mutual prayer for each other. Prayer provides the means of lifting up anxieties to the Lord, through thanksgiving and petition, with the consequence being that believers receive the peace of God (4:6-7).

In this letter, Paul is deeply concerned for Christian unity. He specifically calls Euodia and Syntyche to 'think the same thing' (4:2, see commentary), but this call is also elsewhere delivered to the whole church (2:1-5). Such unity requires that each individual in the community practices humility, measured in how we look out for the interests of others and how we consider others to be more significant than ourselves (2:3-4). In this humble path, we are merely following the example set by our Lord (2:5-11). Many of the imperatives in this epistle assume a corporate church acting together. For example, it is together that Christians are called to 'stand firm' in the Lord alongside one another, even in the midst of persecution (1:27-30; 4:1).

The Christian life in this fallen world brings opposition and persecution. Suffering is a real consequence of commitment to Christ, yet Paul speaks of this as a gift from God (1:29-30). In the midst of such suffering, members of the church are to stand together and strive together for the faith of the gospel (1:27), knowing that the opponents of Christ will meet destruction and that the church will ultimately experience salvation (1:28). Paul himself exhibits endurance through such suffering (1:29-30; 1:12ff.).

Paul clearly commends those who provide for the needs of the saints. This is especially demonstrated by the Philippians as they partnered with him in his imprisonment for the sake of the gospel (4:10-19). Such gifts to others actually serve as sacrificial offerings that please God Himself (4:18). God supplies the needs of those who thus give generously to the work of the Lord (4:19).

Joy pervades this great epistle (with the noun 'joy' or the verb 'rejoice' appearing 14 times in this short letter). Paul models his own joyful approach to life, even in the most difficult of circumstances (e.g., 1:4, 18; 2:17). In those moments, he finds joy in the gospel and in the way others have responded to the Good News. In two key places, he commands Christians to rejoice *in the Lord* at all times (3:1; 4:4). This does not merely call believers to be happy, but it instructs the Philippians that the foundation for their joy in life must be grounded in Christ Himself and in the good news that announces His salvation and reign. When Christian contentment is truly rooted in the Lord Jesus, then such joy enables the Christian church to oppose heresies based on anything other than this wonderful gospel (3:1-3), and it encourages church members to find joyful unity together in the gospel (4:2-4).

The reader of Philippians will often observe that the notion of 'imitation' is fundamental to Paul's ethical instruction in this letter. When Paul speaks autobiographically, we should typically assume that he sets forth his own approach to life as a model for others to follow. Indeed, Paul commands the church to become 'imitators' of him (3:17). Believers are to practice that which they have learned and observed in the apostle (4:9). We perceive here, as elsewhere in Paul's writings, his recurring ethical motif: 'Be imitators of me, as I am of Christ' (1 Cor. 11:1;

cf. 1 Cor. 4:6; 1 Thess. 1:6; 2:14; 2 Thess. 3:7, 9). Paul also will commend other figures in the church as examples to follow (Phil. 2:29; 3:17; cf. 2:19-30).

Hence Paul's autobiographical ruminations in this letter provide opportunities for Christian instruction. His intense commitment to the spread of the gospel, even at personal cost to himself, is to be emulated (Phil. 1:12-18). He serves as an example as he engages boldly in service to Christ, abandoning even his own life to Christ's glory (1:20). Paul recognizes that dying is a means of gain, while living provides the opportunity for further earthly service (1:21-26). He models the truth that whatever gain we have achieved in this world, this gain must be counted as nothing in comparison to knowing Christ Jesus (3:7-11). Paul also portrays a contentedness in life that does not depend on material things. Whether in abundance or in need, he allows God to strengthen him (4:11-13), and Christians are to follow Paul in his exemplary approach to life.

In this brief section, I cannot presume to have fully reviewed all the many theological and ethical themes in this epistle. Yet it is my hope that this summary provides some initial categories for appreciating the complexity of Philippians. Indeed, these few pages would be useful were they merely to assist the reader to consider anew just how much Paul has to say in this short letter.

Structure and Outline
The Letter to the Philippians flows easily together as an epistle. However, it cannot be reduced to a single overriding argument or even to a comprehensive rhetorical form. It certainly contains the general components typical of Paul's letters: an introductory greeting and blessing, a thanksgiving, concluding greetings and benediction. Paul, however, also covers various topics as they occur to him throughout the letter. One striking feature concerns the number of first-person references Paul makes as he models the Christian life for his people. The variety in content has made for many different approaches to outlining the text. Below is my suggested outline, and I would invite the reader to improve on this.

The outline:

I. Greeting, 1:1-2

II. Thanksgiving and Prayer for the Philippians, 1:3-11

III. Paul Discusses His Imprisonment, 1:12-26
   A. The Advance of the Gospel Despite Paul's Imprisonment, 1:12-18
   B. Paul's Focus in Life and in Death, 1:19-26

IV. Exhortation Group 1: Striving Side-by-Side for the gospel, 1:27–2:18
   A. Christian Citizenship in the Midst of Opposition, 1:27-30
   B. Christian Unity and Humility, 2:1-4
   C. Christ's Example in Humility and Exaltation, 2:5-11
   D. Living as Children of God, 2:12-18

V. Two Exemplars of Faithful Service, 2:19-30
   A. Timothy – Paul Delegates His Spiritual Son to Serve in Philippi, 2:19-24
   B. Epaphroditus – A Minister to Paul on the Philippians' Behalf, 2:25-30

VI. Exhortation Group 2: Rejoice in the Lord Together, Even Amidst Opposition, 3:1–4:9
   A. We Who Glory in Christ Jesus: Paul Testifies to the Gospel's Surpassing Worth, 3:1-11
   B. Paul's Continued Example: Pressing on Toward Heavenly Citizenship, 3:12-21
   C. Standing Firm Together in the Lord, 4:1-9

VII. Paul's Joy in Response to the Philippians' Partnership and Gifts, 4:10-20

VIII. Closing Greetings and Benediction, 4:21-23

This outline indicates that the imperatives and direct exhortations to the Philippians are especially located in two extended sections (1:27–2:18 and 3:1–4:9) separated by descriptions of the ministerial service of Timothy and Epaphroditus (2:19-30). These sections are themselves located between two extended paragraphs in which Paul speaks in the first person – namely, Paul's personal reflections on his imprisonment (1:12-26) and his expression of appreciation for the gifts that the Philippians have sent (4:10-20). The whole is then framed by Paul's opening salutation, with its thanksgiving and prayer (1:1-11), and by his final greetings and benediction (4:21-23).

Some qualifications should be made to such an outline. First, Paul's discussion of Timothy and Epaphroditus (2:19-30) is not arbitrarily inserted in the middle of the letter but serves to exemplify (alongside Paul's own example) character traits he wishes the Philippians to admire and to imitate. Nonetheless, the transition from 2:18 to 2:19 is profound enough to consider 2:19-30, if not a digression, at least a division unto itself.

Second, while the sections toward the beginning and ending of this outline (1:12-26; 4:10-20) contain many references that Paul makes to himself, these are not the only such first-person references. Indeed, Paul also pens an extended section in 3:3-21 largely in the first person. In that section, verse 3:17 serves to remind us that Paul's personal reflections are really intended to model the kinds of exhortations he is otherwise commending in 3:1–4:9. It is for that reason that I have incorporated 3:3-21 into the 'Exhortation Group 2' division above. Of course, in light of Paul's call to 'be imitators of me', all of Paul's first-person references throughout the letter serve, in truth, as indirect exhortations to the church in Philippi.

writing from house arrest. You could pay to have guard to be house arrest.

> *Scripture were not written to us but for us.*
>
> *Speaking to ya'll.*

1

Greetings
(Philippians 1:1-2)

Paul and Timothy, servants of Christ Jesus, To all the saints in Christ Jesus who are at Philippi, with the overseers and deacons: ²Grace to you and peace from God our Father and the Lord Jesus Christ.

We may be tempted to breeze through such greetings in Paul's letters, but his brief introductions are packed with important information and signal broad theological motifs.

Ancient letters usually began with a salutation. Paul always identifies himself at the beginning of his letters and designates his intended audience. He also commonly employs such greetings to remind his readers of some key truths. In these opening two verses of the Epistle to the Philippians, such themes include: the submissive relationship of believers as servants/slaves to their Lord; the sanctifying work of Christ Jesus; and the grace and peace that comes from God the Father, and Lord Jesus the Messiah.

Paul and Timothy, servants of Christ Jesus (1:1)

Paul often jointly penned letters with his colleagues in ministry (see 1 Cor. 1:1; also Gal. 1:2), and frequently did so with Timothy (2 Cor. 1:1; Col. 1:1; 1 Thess. 1:1; 2 Thess. 1:1; Philem. 1). On Paul as author, see the introduction to this commentary. Timothy had been with Paul since early in his second missionary journey (Acts 16:1-3), when Timothy was identified as a disciple of Christ who had a good reputation in the church in Lystra and Iconium (in modern southern Turkey). Timothy was the son of a believing Jewish woman and a Gentile (literally, a 'Greek') father (Acts 16:1). As a result of his Gentile heritage, Timothy had not been circumcised as an infant, and Paul himself performed this rite on Timothy in order to increase his evangelistic effectiveness among the Jewish populace (Acts 16:3).

Elsewhere, Paul highlights the spiritual legacy Timothy had received in the Scriptures from his mother and grandmother (2 Tim. 1:5; 3:15). Timothy is known to have accompanied Paul during many of his travels in Asia Minor, Macedonia and Greece (Acts 16:1-3; 18:5; 19:22; 20:4). During this time, Timothy had been actively involved in the proclamation of the gospel (2 Cor. 1:19). Paul even designated Timothy as his apostolic delegate to nurture the churches of Macedonia and Achaia (Acts 17:14-15; 1 Cor. 16:10; 1 Thess. 3:2, 6) and later to minister within the church at Ephesus (1 Tim. 1:3). Paul also wrote at least two personal letters to Timothy to instruct him in his Christian life and ministry, both of which are in the New Testament canon.

Paul considers Timothy a 'fellow worker' (Rom. 16:21), a 'brother' in Christ (2 Cor. 1:1; Col. 1:1; Philem. 1), and a 'beloved and faithful child in the Lord' (1 Cor. 4:17; cf. Phil. 2:22; 1 Tim. 1:2, 18; 2 Tim. 1:2). Paul's reference to Timothy as a beloved child shows the trust and intimacy in their relationship, and it is illustrative of the way Paul had helped raise up Timothy in the gospel and in his ministry. Later, perhaps after Paul's death, Timothy even appears to have been imprisoned for the sake of the gospel (Heb. 13:23).

Yet despite the joint authorship suggested by this verse, it is clear that Paul remains the principal author of this epistle. Note the frequent first-person *singular* statements (i.e., I, me, mine) throughout the letter (e.g., 1:3, 7, 8, 9, 12, 16, 18, 19). Paul, as author, even states that he hopes to send Timothy to the Philippians soon (Phil. 2:19). Timothy was already well known to the Philippian church (Phil. 2:22; cf. Acts 16:1-12; 17:14-15). And by 'co-authoring' this letter with Timothy, Paul may have also wished to pave the way for their continued acceptance of Timothy as Paul's apostolic delegate when Timothy arrives in Philippi (see Phil. 2:19-24).

Paul labels Timothy and himself as 'servants.' There was Old Testament precedence for important representatives of God to be called a 'servant/slave of God'.[1] Indeed the whole people of Israel were supposed to act as servants of God,[2] as were any who followed the Lord (e.g., Ps. 34:22). The term 'servant' could also be used as a self-description of one who is in prayer to God (1 Sam. 14:41; 23:10; Dan. 9:17; and repeatedly in the Psalms), or simply to express submission to another in authority, such as to a king (e.g., 1 Sam. 17:34; 19:4; 22:14). Most commonly in the Old Testament, this word simply designates a 'slave.'

The Greek word for 'servants' (*douloi*) that Paul uses here actually referred in the first century to 'slaves'. Slavery was quite common in the Roman world, with a substantial portion of the populace being held as the property of others. Given that Paul was writing to people in a Roman colony/city, his recipients' first thoughts likely would have been of household slaves, who served within the home.[3] These positions could vary in importance, with some slaves having menial tasks and others being largely responsible for the economic well-being of the household. Despite position and responsibility, however, the universal truth of Roman slavery was that the slave was owned by another.

Thus, at the opening of this letter Paul designates himself as the personal property of Christ Jesus.[4] In his epistle to the Romans, Paul expands on this metaphor to speak of the Christian as one who has been transferred from the dominion of sin into the ownership of Christ (Rom. 1:1; 6:15-23; cf. Titus 3:3). Much as people of the Old Testament could envision their relationship to God as that of slavery in his divine service, Paul invokes this same humble title 'slave' to depict his service to Christ Jesus. As the result of Christ's work in purchasing him from sin and eternal judgment, Paul

---

1 For example, Moses (2 Kings. 18:12; Neh. 10:30; Mal. 4:4), Joshua (Josh. 24:29; Judg. 2:8), Samuel (1 Sam. 3:9-10), David (1 Sam. 23:10; 1 Kings. 3:6; Ps. 78:70), David's messianic heir (e.g., Ezek. 34:23; 37:24-25), Solomon (1 Kings. 3:7), various prophets (2 Kings. 14:25; Zech. 1:6; Ezek. 38:17) and priests (Ps. 134:1).
2 Ezra 5:11; cf. 1 Kings. 8:36; Isa. 42:19; 49:3; 63:17; Jer. 46:27.
3 Cf. Eph. 6:5-9; Col. 3:22–4:1; 1 Tim. 6:1-2; Titus 2:9-10; Philem. 16; also 1 Cor. 7:21-23; 12:13.
4 Also see Rom. 1:1; Gal. 1:10; 2 Tim. 2:24; Titus 1:1; cf. Epaphras in Col. 4:12.

considers his own will to be in complete submission to his Lord Jesus Christ. Yet, this same humble title also grants Paul great significance, for he is a slave of Jesus Christ: he serves the Lord of the universe. Oh, that we too could catch a vision for our roles as slaves of our exalted Lord!

Already at this point in the letter, Jesus is identified as the 'Christ'. This should not be passed over as if it were just another name. Rather, the word indicates Paul's firm conviction that Jesus is the Messiah, the promised deliverer who had been anointed by God. Much of the Old Testament story had held out the hope that there would be a king over Israel who, though in the line of David, would be a greater (even eternal) king on the Davidic throne.[5] In the centuries between the close of the Old Testament and the coming of Jesus, messianic belief had increased in many sectors of Second Temple Judaism (evidence of this can be observed especially in the Dead Sea Scrolls). The Messiah would succeed where David and his descendants had failed,[6] and he would establish the reign of God in the kingdom of God. Of course, Jesus had inaugurated the kingdom of God in a most surprising way – through His teaching, and via His humble death and exalted resurrection, rather than through military might. Yet, the eternal reign of the Messiah Jesus at the right hand of God, the Father, has indeed begun and will be consummated in the world to come (see especially Phil. 2:8-11).

To all the saints in Christ Jesus who are at Philippi, with the overseers and deacons (1:1)
The recipients of the letter are identified as 'saints'. Paul commonly employs this term to refer to Christians who receive his letters.[7] This designation 'saints' is the plural of the Greek word 'holy' (*hagios*). Hence, the word itself deems these people to be 'holy' and set apart for God. In the Old Testament, it could refer to those true followers of God (e.g., Pss. 16:3; 34:9; Dan. 7:18) who had been set apart as holy to their holy God (cf. Exod. 19:6; Lev. 19:2). Paul's use of 'saints' here refers both to the justified status of the believer and to the responsibility

---

5 E.g., 2 Sam. 7:12-16; 1 Chron. 17:10-14; Pss. 89:3-4, 20-37.
6 E.g., Pss. 89:38-52; 132:8-18; 1 Kings. 2:4; 8:25; 9:4-5.
7 E.g., Phil. 4:12; Rom. 1:7; 1 Cor. 1:2; 2 Cor. 1:1; Eph. 1:1; Col. 1:2.

each bears to respond to God's grace by living a holy life before Him. That Paul calls all Christians saints (even in this life) manifests his confidence in the ongoing sanctifying work of the Holy Spirit within all justified followers of the crucified and risen Christ. Paul writes to 'all' such saints in Philippi, emphasizing his inclusion of all members in the church as his recipients (cf. Phil. 1:4, 7-8) and perhaps reminding them of their unity in Christ (even in the midst of strife, see 4:2-3).

This particular group of saints dwells 'in Philippi.' Regarding the city of Philippi, see further the introduction to this commentary. Although founded in the fourth century BC, Philippi in the first century A.D. was a vibrant city in Macedonia, having been designated as a Roman colony (cf. Acts 16:12) by imperial commission to commemorate the victory of Augustus Caesar (Octavian) at the nearby battle of Philippi in 42 B.C. As a colony (Colonia Augusta Julia Philippensis), the city received special privileges, and many of its inhabitants could be said to be citizens of Rome. Paul and Timothy had first entered the city during Paul's second missionary journey (approximately A.D. 49; see Acts 16:12-40). Philippi served as Paul's first place of outreach in Macedonia. There the Lord opened Lydia's heart during a Sabbath service (Acts 16:14) and her household was converted (16:15). Paul exorcized the demonic spirit within a slave girl (16:16-18) and received, in turn, the wrath of her masters (16:19-23). Due to that incident, Paul was beaten and imprisoned. Although he had the chance to escape, Paul remained in the jail – and the jailer and his family were converted to Christ (16:23-34). Paul was released from prison, and the city officials apologized to him since he was a Roman citizen (16:35-39). Apparently he left the city shortly after this event (16:40). This letter testifies to Paul's ongoing connection to the Philippian church since his departure from the city.

These saints at Philippi are said to be 'in Christ Jesus' (also Phil. 4:21). This is a frequent phrase in Paul's writings, occurring in various forms and contexts more than 70 times. It broadly refers to the believers' salvific and sanctifying union with Jesus the Messiah.[8] In this epistle, the phrase is

---

8 E.g., Rom. 3:24; 6:11, 23; 8:1; 1 Cor. 1:2, 30; 2 Cor. 5:17; Eph. 1:3; 2:6-7, 10, 13.

used for the believers' glory/boast in Christ (1:26; 3:3; 4:19), encouragement in Christ (2:1), unity in Christ (2:5), peace that guards hearts and minds in Christ (4:7), and riches in Christ (4:19). Also Paul speaks personally of his chains manifest in Christ (1:13) and of his calling in Christ (3:14). Paul thus reminds the church from the very beginning of this great letter that the identity of its people is to be found in their union with the Messiah Jesus.

In addition to greeting the general populace of the church at Philippi, Paul especially highlights the 'overseers and deacons.' Elsewhere it is clear that 'overseers' and 'deacons' were positions of authority and service within the church.[9] While some translations render *episkopois* ('overseers') here as 'bishops' (e.g., King James, Revised Standard, New English Bible), others more correctly translate this Greek noun in keeping with its functional meaning, since *episkopos* in Greek simply signifies 'one who oversees' (e.g., the English Standard, New International, and New American Standard translations). In common parlance, *episkopos* could be used of people who had the responsibility of 'overseeing' political, military, or religious affairs.[10] After the New Testament era, by the early second century, at least some sectors of the church had transitioned their leadership structures to encompass three offices within a city church – a central bishop (*episkopos*) with multiple elders/priests (*presbyteroi*) and deacons (*diakonoi*). This arrangement is most evident in the writings of Ignatius of Antioch at the beginning of the second century.[11] However, prior to Ignatius one can witness a two-fold ecclesial structure (elder/overseer and deacon) in the post-Apostolic first century.[12] In the New Testament itself the terms for 'overseer' (*episkopos*) and 'elder' (*presbyteros*) were used interchangeably (compare Acts 20:17 and 20:28; also Titus 1:5 and 1:7). Moreover, in Paul's letter to the Philippians, rather than there being a single 'bishop', apparently there were many 'overseers' (*episkopoi*) in the one city of Philippi (the term *episkopois* is plural in Phil. 1:1). Thus here Paul knows

---

9 Esp. Acts 20:17-38; 1 Tim. 3:1-13; Titus 1:5-9; cf. 1 Tim. 5:17-20; 1 Pet. 5:1-5.
10 E.g., Num. 4:16; 31:14; 2 Chron. 34:17; Neh. 11:9, 14, 22.
11 E.g., IMag. 2:1; 3:1-2; 6:1; IEph. 1:3; 2:2; 4:1.
12 See 1 Clem. 42:4-5; cf. 1:3; 3:3; 44:1-6.

only of two official positions within the church at Philippi – 'overseers' and 'deacons' (compare 1 Tim. 3:1-13).

Paul does not elaborate in this epistle on the respective duties of the 'overseers and deacons'. Yet other passages in the New Testament directly address their roles more fully. Elders/overseers in Ephesus were responsible for overseeing and caring for the flock in their midst (Acts 20:28). Peter states that elders should 'shepherd' the flock of Christ, exercise oversight without domineering, and be an example (1 Pet. 5:1-4). Peter also indicates that younger people are to be subject to these elders (1 Pet. 5:5). Paul's letters likewise speak of the overseers/elders as caring for the church in a way similar to the 'managing' of their own households (1 Tim. 3:4-5). Such men are to be 'able to teach' (1 Tim. 3:2) and capable of giving instruction in sound doctrine (Titus 1:9). Paul also appears to assume that, while all elders 'rule' (or 'manage' – see *proistēmi* in 1 Tim. 5:17), some in particular are called to labor in preaching and teaching (1 Tim. 5:17). From these various passages it is apparent that overseers/elders were charged with the oversight of the churches in the first century – an oversight they discharged in part by being examples to their congregations and by teaching the Scriptures and doctrine of the church. Some (but apparently not all) focused especially on the teaching/preaching of Scripture.

The exact function of deacons in the first-century church is less certain. In the longest New Testament passage that directly describes the diaconate (1 Tim. 3:8-13), in contrast to the preceding passage on elders, there is a lack of descriptors indicating oversight or teaching responsibilities. Also the Greek word for 'deacon' (*diakonos*) often simply means 'servant.'[13] Thus it is traditionally assumed that while elders/overseers were charged with oversight and teaching, deacons had a subsidiary responsibility for caring for the practical daily lives of people in the church (perhaps similar to the role of the seven men set aside for such service in Acts 6:1-7).

It can only be a matter of speculation as to why Paul highlights the overseers and deacons in this epistle but does not do so in most other letters. Perhaps he simply wished

---

13 E.g., Mark 10:43; John 12:26; Rom. 15:8; 2 Cor. 6:4.

to honor their position or to model for the general church membership the honor they should be shown. Or maybe Paul wished these church leaders and servants to pay special heed to the matters he discusses in this letter.

Grace to you and peace from God our Father and the Lord Jesus Christ (1:2).
Paul always invokes 'grace and peace' on the recipients of his letters (cf. Phil. 4:23), especially at the beginning of each of his epistles.[14] In this, Paul is followed by other New Testament authors.[15] These opening invocations follow a fairly set pattern in Paul (with only slight variations found in Col. 1:2; 1 Thess. 1:1; 1 Tim. 1:2; 2 Tim. 1:2; Titus 1:4). However, one should not conclude from his consistency of expression that this invocation was without particular import to Paul. Rather, as we reflect on Paul's opening blessing of 'grace to you and peace', we observe that this Pauline expression indicates a distinctly Christian way of invoking God's grace and peace on others in lieu of more typical pagan Greek and Jewish expressions.

In everyday correspondence, Greek letters often began with the salutation *chairein* ('greetings,' or more literally 'rejoice'; see Acts 15:23; 23:26; James 1:1). Paul and other early Christians altered this standard salutation slightly to read *charis* ('grace'). This alteration is theologically important – God is the gracious God who gives all good gifts to His children,[16] especially the gift of salvation in Christ Jesus apart from any works-based merit on the part of those saved.[17] So this distinctively Christian opening salutation serves as an invocation of God's gracious blessing.

It is likely that Paul's mention of 'peace' follows the Jewish greeting *shalom* ('peace'; cf. Ezra 4:17; 5:7), which itself recognizes the blessings of peace that come from God. Old Testament benedictions invoke 'peace' on Israel (e.g., Num. 6:26), and this practice continues in benedictions in the

---

14 Rom. 1:7; 1 Cor. 1:3; 2 Cor. 1:2; Gal. 1:3; Eph. 1:2; Col. 1:2; 1 Thess. 1:1; 2 Thess. 1:2; 1 Tim. 1:2; 2 Tim. 1:2; Titus 1:4; Philem. 3.
15 1 Pet. 1:2; 2 Pet. 1:2; 2 John 3; Rev. 1:4.
16 E.g., 2 Cor. 9:8; cf. Rom. 12:6; 1 Cor. 1:4ff.; 2 Cor. 8:1ff.; Eph. 4:7.
17 E.g., Rom. 3:24; 4:16; 5:15-21; Gal. 2:21; Eph. 1:7; 2:8-9; 2 Tim. 1:9; Titus 2:11; 3:7.

Philippians 1:1-2

New Testament.[18] Elsewhere, Paul asserts that the 'God of peace'[19] has established such peace between Christian believers and God through the salvific work of Christ (Rom. 5:1).

Thus we observe that this opening, which in most ancient letters would be a simple salutation, has become, in Paul's hands, a benediction invoking grace and peace on the church. Moreover, Paul expresses the origins of such grace and peace. They come 'from God our Father and the Lord Jesus Christ'. This phrase, with its single preposition, expresses confidence that both these members of the Trinity are united in blessing the believer with grace and peace.

Paul's mention of the fatherhood of God (cf. Phil. 2:11; 4:20) is in keeping with the teaching of Jesus[20] and with the 'fatherhood' language found in Paul as well.[21] The fatherhood of God can refer to God as the creator of the world. More importantly, this speaks of a familial intimacy between Christians and God Himself. In a way analogous to God's adoption of Israel (Rom. 9:4, 8), Paul considers believers to have been given redemption and a promised adoption into the very family of God.[22] Yet beyond connotations of family intimacy, in a first-century context a father was also owed honor and obedience. Therefore, calling God 'Father' encapsulates the Christian's relationship with God as creator, savior, and sovereign.

Jesus is esteemed here as the 'Lord Jesus Christ'. Earlier in verse 1, we discussed the messianic meaning of the word 'Christ' (i.e., 'anointed one'). Here Jesus is also designated 'Lord.' In this letter, Paul often uses this word (*kurios*) in reference to Jesus (see 2:19; 3:8, 20; 4:23). To focus on one example, Paul declares that everyone in heaven and on earth will bow the knee to this risen Christ Jesus and confess him to be Lord (2:11). Certainly one cannot declare the crucified Jesus to be Lord without first asserting that he has also risen from the dead and now reigns at the right hand of God the

---

18 E.g., Rom. 15:33; Gal. 6:16; Eph. 6:23; 2 Thess. 3:16.
19 Phil. 4:9; Rom. 15:33; 16:20; cf. 1 Cor. 14:33; 2 Cor. 13:11; 1 Thess. 5:23; 2 Thess. 3:16.
20 E.g., Mark 14:36; Matt. 10:33; 11:25-27; 16:27; 23:9; 24:36; John 1:14; 3:35; 4:23; also e.g., Matt. 5:16; 12:50; 18:10.
21 Rom. 8:15; Gal. 4:6; cf. 1 Cor. 8:6; 15:24; Gal. 1:1; Eph. 2:18; 3:14; 4:6.
22 Acts 7:21; Rom. 8:14-17, 23; Gal. 4:5-7; Eph. 1:5.

Father as Lord and Master. The term *kurios* is also employed by Paul to speak of God, and this follows the practice of the Greek Old Testament Septuagint (e.g., Gen. 2:8; Exod. 3:4; and hundreds of other times). Thus the very label *kurios* applied to Jesus expresses His exalted, deific status. It also indicates the Christian's response of allegiance to our crucified and risen Lord!

Summary

This brief two-verse introduction to the epistle thus does much more than simply tell us who the author and recipients are. Rather, it serves as a subtle indication to the reader of so much of Paul's theology and purpose in writing. It designates Paul and Timothy as the willing slaves of their Lord. It reminds the readers of Timothy's relationship with Paul before they are asked to receive him as Paul's apostolic delegate. It calls the recipients 'sanctified ones', whose very essence is defined in their union with Christ Jesus. It indicates particular leadership and service roles within the Christian community. It depicts God as the Father, who has created, saved, and adopted us into His family. It identifies Jesus as the messianic heir, who rightly is worshipped as Lord. And this introduction reminds the readers that the source of all true spiritual blessing comes from the wondrous unity of Father and Son. That very blessing of grace and peace has now been invoked on his hearers, so Paul next turns to praying in thankfulness for them.

Questions for Personal Reflection:

1. In what ways can you relate to Paul's calling himself a servant/slave of God? What self-designations would you use to describe your own relationship to God?

2. Do you have a regular daily awareness that grace and peace flow to you from the Trinity? How can you grow further in that awareness? What are some practical ways that you can invoke that grace and peace on others as you interact with fellow believers?

Philippians 1:1-2

A few of the Study Questions in the following chapters intentionally overlap with some of the Questions for Personal Reflection. *This invites Bible study participants to share the fruit of their personal reflections with the broader group.*

STUDY QUESTIONS:

1. Take a very quick scan through all four chapters of Philippians. What stands out to you from this quick survey? What do you most hope to gain from this group study on Philippians? [handwritten: joyful, thankful, spread the gospel]

2. Paul's first arrival in Philippi is recorded in Acts 16. Read Acts 16:1-12, trace Paul's journey on a map (often good maps are found at the back of your Bible), and imagine together what such a journey would have been like in the first century (on foot or pack animal and via an ancient boat). Consider together God's providential leading in Acts 16:6-10. How might this have influenced Paul's understanding of the importance of his work among the Philippians?

3. Acts 16:11-18 recounts some early episodes in Paul's Philippian ministry. In what ways do you see God already at work in creating a church in Philippi? How is the city of Philippi described (note especially 16:12 and also 16:13)? Why might Philippi have been a strategic stopping point for Paul?

4. In Acts 16:19-40 Paul and Silas experience imprisonment in Philippi (cf. 1 Thess. 2:2). What aspects of this account are most striking to you? In his epistle to the Philippians Paul is writing from another prison, so how might that previous prison experience in Acts 16 resonate behind this letter (both in Paul's mind and also in the church back in Philippi)?

5. The introduction to this commentary deals with such matters as Paul's authorship of the letter, the date and place of its writing, Paul's purposes in writing, the audience, some aspects of the book's theology, and its structural features. Name some of the ways that these topics affect how we should approach

the book. If you have already read the commentary introduction, what items did you find most helpful from those pages?

6. What aspects of Christian theology inform Paul's very carefully worded introduction to his letter in Philippians 1:1-2? How does Paul depict himself (and Timothy), and why do you think he identifies himself in this way? How does he describe his audience? What do you observe about the blessing that he invokes?

saint
set apart

7. In what ways can you relate to Paul's calling himself a servant/slave of Christ Jesus? What self-designations would you use to describe your own relationship to Christ?

8. How can you (both individually and collectively) grow further in your regular daily awareness that grace and peace flow to you from the Trinity? What are some practical ways that you can invoke that grace and peace on others as you interact with fellow believers?

!

2

Thanksgiving and Prayer for the Philippians
(Philippians 1:3-11)

³I thank my God in all my remembrance of you, ⁴always in every prayer of mine for you all making my prayer with joy, ⁵because of your partnership in the gospel from the first day until now. ⁶And I am sure of this, that he who began a good work in you will bring it to completion at the day of Jesus Christ. ⁷It is right for me to feel this way about you all, because I hold you in my heart, for you are all partakers with me of grace, both in my imprisonment and in the defense and confirmation of the gospel. ⁸For God is my witness, how I yearn for you all with the affection of Christ Jesus. ⁹And it is my prayer that your love may abound more and more, with knowledge and all discernment, ¹⁰so that you may approve what is excellent, and so be pure and blameless for the day of Christ, ¹¹filled with the fruit of righteousness that comes through Jesus Christ, to the glory and praise of God.

This exuberant thanksgiving and prayer for the Philippians gives us great insight into Paul's tender relationship with them and into his aspirations for their growth in Christ.

Paul commonly follows his opening salutation with a section of thanksgiving. This is so often the case that the absence of such a section is more noticeable than its presence (as in Galatians). Each of Paul's opening thanksgivings is deeply theological and practically directed at the needs and strengths of the individual churches. Therefore, they deserve careful attention.

In this letter, Paul's thanksgiving speaks of his joyful and loving memories of the Philippian church, expressing confidence in the Lord's salvific work in their midst and remembering how they have assisted in the spread of the gospel (even standing by Paul while he was imprisoned). Paul then specifically prays for the church to grow in love and wisdom, with the goal of attaining the kind of righteous purity that brings glory to God. This whole passage flows easily, forming perhaps a single sentence in Greek (though possibly a full pause could be assumed at verse 8 and/or verse 9).

As you read through Paul's prayer, it is worth contemplating the people whom you lift up in prayer and why it is that you pray for them. Do we often express proper thanksgiving to the Lord for the Christian growth of others? What is our source of confidence concerning their spiritual growth (and our growth as well)? If we could pray for just one thing in the lives of others, what would it be?

I thank my God in all my remembrance of you, always in every prayer of mine for you all making my prayer with joy (1:3-4).

Paul's memories of the church in Philippi lead him into celebrative thanksgiving to God. The phrase 'I thank my God' appears elsewhere in Paul's letters (Rom. 1:8; 1 Cor. 1:4; Philem. 4). Paul expresses deep appreciation to God as the true source of the Christian salvation that has come to the Philippians, as the One who will continue to bring that good work to its climax in the eschatological future, and as the One who has moved the church to continue their fellowship with Paul in support of his evangelistic ministry.

That Paul thanks 'my God' speaks of his deep sense of personal relatedness to God. It also is evidence that, though Paul and Timothy are listed as co-authors (1:1), Paul himself is the lead author of this epistle. (Contrast this with *'we* thank *our* God' in Col. 1:3; 1 Thess. 1:2; 2:13; cf. 2 Thess. 1:3.) Such intimate language likely stems from Old Testament phraseology that expresses a personal relationship initiated by God (such as in the phrase 'the God of Abraham'). Thus Moses, Joshua, Ruth, David and others also call upon the Lord as 'my God'.[1]

---

1 E.g., Exod. 15:2; Deut. 26:14; Josh. 9:23; Ruth 1:16; 2 Sam. 22:3; Ps. 3:7.

Verses 3-4 repeatedly emphasize the frequency and extent of Paul's thanksgiving for the Philippians (note the use of words such as 'all', 'every', 'always'). The translation 'all my remembrance of you' correctly encapsulates the solution to an interpretive issue in the Greek. (See Additional Notes below.) Thus Paul gives thanks to God for the whole Philippian church because of his many fond memories of that Christian community.

Paul elsewhere speaks of his frequency in prayer and thanksgiving,[2] especially in prayer for the churches with whom he was involved in his mission.[3] Here he wants the Philippians to know not only that he is praying for them often, but also that doing so fills him with great joy. 'Joy' is repeatedly mentioned in this letter. It is clear that Paul rejoices greatly in his relationship with this church (1:4; 4:1, 10; cf. 2:2), and that he is eager for the Philippians to experience such joy in their relationships with God and with one another (1:25; 2:28, 29; 3:1; 4:4), even in the midst of suffering for Christ (1:18; 2:17-18).

...because of your partnership in the gospel from the first day until now (1:5).
When Paul refers to their 'partnership' (or 'fellowship' = *koinōnia*) with him, he is reminding them that they are engaged in a cooperative effort to reach others with the gospel. This perhaps should be seen against the backdrop of first-century pagan fellowship communities (such as trade associations, burial societies, etc.), which gathered together for the mutual benefit of members. Here, however, the focus is on the outward spread of the gospel worldwide and not just on the benefit of the participants. The Philippians have expressed their gospel-driven fellowship with Paul from their acceptance of the gospel (1:5-6), in their continued commitment to that gospel (1:6) even in suffering (1:29-30), and through their prayers, encouragement, and financial support for Paul's gospel work (1:7, 19; 2:25; see esp. 4:14-19).

The word 'gospel' designates the 'good news' that Paul has proclaimed throughout his ministry. In this letter, Paul

---

2 Rom. 1:9; 1 Thess. 1:2; 2:13; 2 Tim. 1:3.
3 E.g., Eph. 1:16; Col. 1:3; 1 Thess. 1:2; Philem. 4.

assumes his hearers already know what that gospel is, and thus he does not define the term. Instead, when he speaks in this letter about the gospel, it is to note the advance of this good news (1:12, 16), often at personal cost to himself (1:7, 12-13) and to others (1:14; 2:22; 4:3, 15). Nonetheless, Paul's thought in this epistle is consistent with his declaration of the gospel in his other writings.[4] Righteousness, he will assert, comes not from the accomplishment of works (even the good works found in God's law), but from faith in Christ Jesus (Phil. 3:9), who has died and been resurrected (2:5-11). This gospel provides us in the present with the eschatological hope of participating in the resurrection of the dead (3:11). Such a gospel also calls forth a people who, having received such grace, seek to live their lives in a way worthy of that gospel they have already received (1:27; 2:12-13).

The saints in Philippi have been in this gospel fellowship from 'the first day' when they received the good news. Perhaps Paul is reflecting back on the events described in Acts 16, when he first arrived in Philippi, and when Lydia and her household, followed by others (even Paul's own jailer), came to faith. Certainly he recalls the inception of their embracing this good news. Their sustained commitment to the spread of the gospel gives Paul confidence in their continued fellowship in this good news; yet ultimately he attributes his confidence in their salvation to God's sovereign work within them (1:6).

And I am sure of this, that he who began a good work in you will bring it to completion at the day of Jesus Christ (1:6).
Having referred in the previous verse both to the past (the beginning of their salvation) and to the present (their current ongoing partnership in the gospel), Paul now looks to their future. He expresses a confidence in God that speaks of his own trust in the Lord's sovereign hand to redeem those whom He has called. The impetus and sustaining power of the redeeming work is God Himself, who 'began' that work (v. 6) and who is the one who will bring their salvation to its completion at the return of Christ. Paul elsewhere expresses similar expectations in God accomplishing the salvation

---

4 E.g., Rom. 1:16; 1 Cor. 15:1ff.; Eph. 1:13; 2 Tim. 1:9-10; 2:8.

that He has already begun in the life of the Christian.⁵ This provides a hope and confidence to Christian believers because their relationships to the Triune God are preserved by God Himself. With this confidence, they can then pursue their love for God by growing in Christian wisdom with the goal of seeing Christ produce in them the fruit of righteousness (1:9-11).

Elsewhere, Paul typically speaks of Christians performing 'good works' in response to the salvation that God has already gifted them.⁶ In this verse, however, God is the one who has begun the 'good work' within the believer. Thus the reference here concerns not the works that a Christian performs, but the salvation that God has wrought within the Christian soul. God is the one who 'began' that work of salvation. Paul recognizes God as sovereign, not just of the future of their salvation, but also of its inception. God is the one who effectively calls people to a saving relationship with Christ Jesus. Yet God's sovereignty avails not just to the beginning of salvation (often theologically termed 'justification') but to all of Christian growth ('sanctification').

The Greek text might be better translated that God will 'bring it [i.e., this good work of salvation] to completion *until* the day of Jesus Christ.' The Greek preposition 'until' (*achri*) elsewhere in the New Testament universally refers to an action that is performed up to and until a certain moment. This is true both when a New Testament author uses a phrase such as 'until' a 'day',⁷ and when an author speaks of 'until' something is 'completed' at an eschatological moment.⁸ Paul does both here. This preposition then implies that God, who initiated the salvation of the Philippians, will continue to work to bring that salvation to fulfillment during this life in preparation for the eschatological return of Christ.

Paul's reference to the 'day of Christ Jesus' glimpses forward to the eschatological climax when Christ returns (e.g., 1 Cor. 1:8; 2 Cor. 1:14). It is thus equivalent to the 'day

---

5 E.g., Rom. 8:28-39; 1 Thess. 5:23-24; Eph. 1:11-14.
6 Compare Eph. 2:10; see also 2 Cor. 9:8; Col. 1:10; 1 Tim. 2:10; 5:10; 2 Tim. 2:21; 3:17; Titus 1:16; 3:1; cf. Acts 9:36; and contrast Titus 1:16.
7 See Matt. 24:38; Luke 1:20; 17:27; Acts 1:2; 2:29; 20:6; 23:1; 26:22; 27:33; 2 Cor. 3:14; there is a possible exception in Acts 27:33.
8 See Rev. 15:8; 17:17; 20:3, 5.

of Christ' and the 'day of the Lord'.⁹ Such language of the eschatological 'day' also invokes the common Old Testament theme of the 'day of the Lord.'¹⁰ Believers yearn for this day when the salvific work that God has started will reach its consummation as Christ returns to establish the New Heavens and the New Earth.

It is right for me to feel this way about you all, because I hold you in my heart, for you are all partakers with me of grace, both in my imprisonment and in the defense and confirmation of the gospel. For God is my witness, how I yearn for you all with the affection of Christ Jesus (1:7-8).
In these few words, we glimpse Paul's deep compassion for this church. Paul elsewhere openly expressed his love and affection for the churches under his care (e.g., 1 Thess. 2:7-8). He holds their welfare close to himself, and he yearns to be with them since he knows deep Christian fellowship with them.

The word translated 'to feel' (*phronein*) has cognitive aspects as well, denoting perhaps something closer to the English 'to have this opinion'.¹¹ 'Heart' (*kardia*) designates the seat of Greek physical, spiritual, and mental life. Paul can also speak elsewhere of the unity that comes from having someone 'in our heart' (2 Cor. 7:3). The word 'partakers' is a compound term in Greek (*sunkoinōnos*) that resonates with Paul's fellowship language from verse 5 (*koinōnia*). The basis for Paul's compassionate sense of unity with the Philippians comes from their mutual fellowship in God's grace. Paul again inclusively emphasizes that 'all' the saints in Philippi are highly esteemed by him since 'all' mutually partake of God's grace.

Paul has seen visible evidence of this fellowship in the expressions of solidarity the Philippian church has shown him in his ministry of defending the gospel, even when he

---

9 Phil. 1:10; 2:16; 1 Cor. 3:13; 5:5; 1 Thess. 5:2, 4; 2 Thess. 2:2; also 2 Tim. 1:12, 18; 4:8.
10 See for example: Isa. 13:6, 9; 58:13; Jer. 46:10; Ezek. 13:5; 30:3; Joel 1:15; 2:1, 11, 31; 3:14; Amos 5:18, 20; Obad. 1:15; Zeph. 1:7-8, 14; Mal. 4:5; also see Acts 2:20; 2 Pet. 3:10.
11 This word *phronein* evidences a large range of uses here in Philippians (2:2, 5; 3:15, 19; 4:2, 10).

was imprisoned. Paul later in the letter will also emphasize his calling as one involved in the 'defense' (*apologia*) of the gospel (1:16). The word 'confirmation' (*bebaiōsis*) similarly speaks to providing evidence for the authenticity of something (cf. Heb. 6:16). Paul, perhaps especially with his recent imprisonment in mind, is conscious that his proclamation of the gospel includes providing evidence for its truth.

To emphasize how strongly Paul holds this opinion of the Philippian saints, he invokes God as witness over his heart.[12] He longs to be with the Philippians again,[13] as does Epaphroditus later in this letter (2:25-26). Though Paul is still in prison and is unsure of the judicial verdict, he does express some confidence in his future release and ability to see the Philippians again (1:23-26; 2:24). Prison may have increased this longing to be with good friends, but ultimately Paul recognizes this yearning as stemming from an affection that flows from the Messiah Jesus. The word for 'affection' (*splanchna*) is a typical Greek metaphor that pictures human bowels as the seat of emotions (much as in English we often speak of the 'heart' as the seat of emotions). Thus Paul, in two verses (7-8), invokes two different Greek metaphors ('heart' and 'bowels' – we might say 'mind' and 'heart') to give weight to the depth of thought, emotion, and spiritual longing he finds within himself for the Philippian saints. This compassionate concern, stemming from his thanksgiving for their fellowship in gospel proclamation, then spills out into a prayer for the Philippians.

And it is my prayer that your love may abound more and more, with knowledge and all discernment (1:9).
Paul continues his prayer by transitioning from his reasons for thanksgiving to mentioning some of his key petitions on behalf of the Philippian church. Similar transitions from thanksgiving to petition occur in other Pauline epistles.[14] Paul employs a common Greek verb for prayer (*proseuchomai* – literally, 'And I pray this thing').

On translating this verse, see Additional Notes. The translation above helpfully indicates that this verse reports the

---

12 Cf. Rom. 1:9; 2 Cor. 1:23; 1 Thess. 2:5, 10.
13 Cf. Rom. 1:11; 1 Thess. 3:6; 2 Tim. 1:4.
14 Cf. Eph. 1:17; Col. 1:9; Philem. 6.

contents of Paul's prayer (rather than its purpose). However, the comma in mid-verse may be slightly misleading. Paul is not primarily praying for the Philippians to grow in love but for their love to increase in knowledge and discernment in the excellent things of God (i.e., 'and I pray this thing, namely that your love increase still more and more in knowledge and all discernment'). The next verse indicates that this love increases in knowledge and wisdom in order for them to live pure and blameless lives before God (vv. 10-11). This love is directed toward God, with the result being holy conduct. Therefore, the 'love' that is in view here focuses especially on the Philippians' love of God and of Christ (with perhaps only secondary application to their love for one another). Paul includes 'more and more' to express confidence that the Philippians have already begun in this process.

'Knowledge' (*epignōsis*) is a common word for cognition, though Paul typically only applies it to knowledge of God and His Son[15] or to knowledge of the things of God.[16] Paul also prays elsewhere for believers to increase in such knowledge (Eph. 1:17; Col. 1:9). This 'knowledge' certainly has both intellectual and experiential components. 'Discernment' (*aisthēsis*) appears only here in the New Testament, though it is related to a verb for 'to perceive' that is found in Luke 9:45. However, such 'discernment' is found frequently in the early Septuagint Greek translation of the Old Testament, especially in wisdom books.[17] This term thus conveys moral discernment and wisdom. The knowledge and discernment to be gained reaches its purpose in verse 10.

...so that you may approve what is excellent, and so be pure and blameless for the day of Christ, filled with the fruit of righteousness that comes through Jesus Christ, to the glory and praise of God (1:10-11).
The purpose of the Philippians' love increasing in such knowledge and discernment is so that they may walk in

---

15 Rom. 10:2; Eph. 1:17; 4:13; Col. 1:10.
16 Col. 1:9; 2:2; 3:10; 1 Tim. 2:4; 2 Tim. 2:25; 3:7; Titus 1:1; Philem. 6; though contrast Rom. 3:20.
17 Prov. 1:4, 7, 22; 2:3, 10; etc.; also note Exod. 28:3.

righteous Christian purity as those who love God and follow Christ.

To examine Paul's logic more closely, we note in the first clause of verse 10 that growth in knowledge and discernment ought to result in the Christian being able to judge that which is excellent. Paul employs identical wording in Romans 2:18, where he states that Jewish people have the advantage of knowing the will of God and are able to 'approve what is excellent' because of their instruction in the law; yet, in that context, Paul indicts his Jewish readers for not acting on that knowledge. Here in Philippians, however, Paul clearly assumes his readers, whose love of God is growing in knowledge and discernment, will act on their knowledge. Nonetheless, they must first 'approve' the 'excellent things' in order to properly respond in holiness.

'Approve' (*dokimazein*) is also applied by Paul to discerning the will of God (Rom. 12:2; cf. Eph. 5:10); to evaluating one's own self (1 Cor. 11:28), one's own works (Gal. 6:4), or the Christian heart of another (1 Cor. 16:3; 2 Cor. 8:22); and to proving the genuineness of one's love (2 Cor. 8:8). Such approval connotes a probing awareness of the truth. Here the word 'excellent' concerns those things that have differentiated themselves as being of the highest import in maintaining Christian holiness. Thus the Christian, out of an overflowing love for God, is to become an expert in comprehending the excellent, holy things of God.

This 'approving of what is excellent' itself has an intended result (*hina* clause) – namely, that these believers would be pure and blameless until the full establishment of Christ's kingdom. 'Pure' denotes something unmixed and sincere (2 Pet. 3:1; Wisd. 7:25). 'Blameless' indicates the quality of being without fault or offense (cf. Acts 24:16; 1 Cor. 10:32). Although neither of these Greek words is used in a religious setting in the Greek Old Testament Septuagint, perhaps Paul is alluding to the sacred purity associated with the worship of God in the Old Testament. It is clear that Paul sees 'pure and blameless' as being connected with Christian righteous living (note the connection with v. 11).

Paul again invokes the culminating goal of Christian living as being focused on the 'day of Christ'. As in Paul's previous reference to this day (1:6, see notes above; also 2:16), the 'day of Christ' looks to the time of Christ's return and the establishment of His eternal kingdom. The translation above '*for* the day of Christ' might better be understood as 'unto' (*eis*) the day of Christ. Thus the purity that Paul is speaking of here refers to ongoing Christian sanctification – living this life in light of the salvation that has already come through faith in Christ.

Pure and blameless conduct of the Christian stems from the 'fruit of righteousness' (cf. James 3:18). In the Old Testament, the phrase 'fruit of righteousness' appears roughly equivalent to justice (Amos 6:12), and the imagery of a fruit tree can picture the results of righteousness as a tree of life (Prov. 11:30). This fruit comes through Jesus Christ (see Additional Notes), and this reminds us that Paul is not speaking of a person generating his or her own works-righteousness (also see Phil. 3:9). Rather, this holy fruit comes out of response to the work of Christ in the life of the believer.

Combining verses 9-11, we learn that it is not enough simply to have a loving disposition toward God and others. That love must be combined with knowledge and discernment in order to be able to appraise how to live purely before the Lord. Similarly, knowledge and wisdom are not sufficient to assure a godly character, because such knowledge must be combined with a disposition of love toward God and a volitional effort to act on that knowledge. In short, Paul has very carefully delineated in these three verses vital aspects in the lives of Christians that must work together in order for them to achieve the 'fruit of righteousness'.

We conduct ourselves here in this life by letting our love for God, educated in the excellent things of God's Word, spill out into pure conduct in eager expectation of Christ's return. Moreover, Paul's perspective reaches out more broadly than our own human sphere of interest. Ultimately he is concerned for God's glory and praise. In the end, as those who love God, we are to conduct our lives with the goal of bringing praise, glory, and honor to Him.

Summary – Paul's Prayer and the Life of the Church

Paul has conformed his opening prayer to the specific needs and concerns of this congregation. He joyfully shares the depth of his affection for them as brothers and sisters in Christ. Part of his pastoral manner is to let them see his heart for them. He wants them to know of his frequent, joyful thanksgivings to God when he remembers them in prayer. He recalls their fellowship with him as they have often engaged with him in watching the good news of salvation spread abroad. Moreover, he expresses his confidence that God in His sovereign mercy will fulfill their salvation by bringing it to culmination at Christ's return. As Paul moves to specific prayer requests on their behalf, there is one overarching concern: that their love for God would be so educated in the wisdom of the pursuit of holiness that the result would be lives that are pure and blameless – lives that bring praise and glory to God. There is already in this opening prayer an eschatological expectation in Paul's words – he looks to God to complete the work of salvation in the lives of the Philippians in preparation for the return of Christ (1:6, 10). This eschatology is inaugurated in the life of the believer, in whom God has already begun the good work of salvation. There is also the clear assumption that Christian salvation stems not from our righteousness, but from the work of Christ. This salvation is all of God and leads to His praise and glory.

As twenty-first-century Christians, our hearts certainly resonate with Paul's prayer. When we minister to others in Christ's name, we should let them know our compassion and affection for them. We too should repeatedly turn to God in thanksgiving for them. Even if, like Paul with the Philippians, we can see areas of needed Christian growth (see esp. 4:2ff.), we must focus on the work of God in their lives to stimulate our thanksgiving. And we know with confidence that in all our lives, this work of salvation, which God Himself began, He will complete. We also can emulate Paul's passion for the spread of the gospel, which he proclaimed at great personal cost to himself, noting Paul's own focused attention to the defense and proof of the gospel's truth. Yet, it is important to remember that even the great apostle Paul needed others to be in fellowship with him. He was rightly dependent on their encouragement, their physical (even financial) support, and their prayers. Moreover, he looked to them to be agents of spreading this good news, and he undoubtedly saw it as his job to exhort, train and motivate others in their own work for Christ.

As we look more to our own selves, we should conduct our lives expectantly in light of the return of Christ, knowing that God Himself is at work in us to bring His work of salvation to its fulfillment. With similar dependency on the Lord, we can allow that eschatological outlook to inform our desire to be pure and blameless in this life. Not that such works will save us, since only Christ's death and resurrection shall avail to that end. Yet, as we respond to this gracious salvation, our love for God ought to be combined with knowledge and discernment in the things of God so that we live out the fruit of righteousness. All of this comes through Christ Jesus, and thus all of it should lead us to proclaim aloud the praise and glory of God.

Questions for Personal Reflection:

1. What are some ways you can grow in expressing heartfelt thanksgiving for other people in your life and in the church?

2. Do you have a personal sense that God 'who began a good work in you will bring it to completion at the day of Christ Jesus'? How would our lives change if we in the church were to more firmly rest on that confidence?

3. Reflect on how Paul prays that the Philippians' love would abound with discernment so that they may achieve spiritual purity (1:9-11). Do you possess an earnest love for God and others? Do you need to grow in knowledge and discernment of the things of God? Do you need to live out that knowledge in greater purity?

4. Read again the last two paragraphs of the summary above. Are there particular personal application points that strike you as you reread those words?

Philippians 1:3-11

STUDY QUESTIONS: *Gal was different*

1. Paul typically begins his letters with expressions of thanksgiving to God for the church to whom he is writing. Although opening thanksgivings also could be customary in letters elsewhere in the Graeco-Roman world, Paul, with great care, tailors his thanksgivings directly to each audience. Have the group members individually select another epistle of Paul and read silently through the opening verses of that epistle. As you read, observe the various ways that Paul often opens his letters with thanksgiving, and briefly share your findings with the group.

   Philemon
   Titus
   1 & 2 Timothy
   Colossian
   Eph
   Gal
   Roman
   1 & 2 Cor

   Rms 1:8
   1 Cor 1:4
   Philemon 1:4

2. List all the many ways that Paul speaks of the Philippian church members in 1:3-11. How would you summarize Paul's relationship to this particular church?

3. Paul describes the Philippians as in 'partnership' with him in the gospel (1:5). What does this mean? How have you and your church 'partnered' with others for the sake of the gospel (in your church, in your community, and around the world)? What ideas do you have for expanding those partnerships?

   work together · supporting

4. In Philippians 1:6 Paul states that he is 'sure' that 'he who began a good work in you will bring it to completion at the day of Jesus Christ.' What in your estimation does it mean to have this 'good work' brought to 'completion'? Why do you think Paul can express such confidence here? How does this encourage us in our own Christian walks? How would our lives change if we in the church were to more firmly rest on a similar confidence?

   salvation

5. Paul quite openly announces to the church that he holds them in his heart (1:7), he 'yearns' for them with the 'affection of Christ Jesus' (1:8), and he thanks God 'in all my remembrance of you' (1:3). Would you feel comfortable speaking in these terms about people in your church? Why or why not? How

can such language help bring together Christians into a greater sense of mutual fellowship?

6. Carefully note the sequence of clauses in 1:9–11. Describe in your own words what Paul is saying here.

7. In what ways does the prayer in 1:9–11 echo your own prayers for yourself, your family, and others you know? love abound in real knowledge & discernment

8. What are some ways you can grow in expressing heartfelt thanksgiving for other people in your life and in the church?

Additional Notes:

1:3 The ESV translation above correctly notes that Paul thanks God in 'all my remembrance of you'. The Greek text literally reads, 'I thank my God upon every remembrance of you.' The genitive 'of you' can technically either signify 'your remembrance [of me]' or '[my] remembrance of you'. Some have suggested that the first of these options connects well with the fact that the Philippians have given financial gifts (perhaps designated 'remembrances') to Paul's ministry, for which he is thankful (cf. 4:10-19). However, the overwhelming evidence in Greek from other occasions when 'remembrance' (*mneia*) is followed by a genitive indicates that 'remembrance of you' refers to Paul's remembrances of the church members in Philippi (compare Rom. 1:9; Philem. 4; also Eph. 1:16; 1 Thess. 1:2; 3:6; 2 Tim. 1:3). This is also most consistent with the possessive article (in the Greek) on remembrance, and with how Paul here speaks of *his* prayers for the church itself (1:4). The 'upon' in 'upon [my] every remembrance of you' is used here to state what causes such outbursts of thanksgivings (cf. *epi* with the dative in 1:5). In short, it is because of his fond memories of the Philippians that Paul gives thanks.

1:7 Technically the Greek can either read 'I have you in my heart' or 'you have me in your heart.' The first is preferable since it is Paul's compassion for the Philippians that is the central topic in this immediate context (see esp. 1:8). Also, the word order slightly favors 'I' as subject of the verb 'have'.

1:9 The first few Greek words in verse 9 literally state, 'and I pray this [thing] *that* your love may grow still more and more...' One can ask whether the word 'that' (*hina*) conveys the purpose of Paul's prayer ('I pray this *in order that* your love may grow…'), or whether it defines what Paul is actually praying (epexegetic – 'I pray this, *namely, that* your love may grow…'). Though the latter option is a less common use of *hina*, it is still possible and it makes the best sense of the passage. It is difficult to see how the 'purpose' of Paul's actions in 1:3-8 can be seen to grow their love; rather, he has shifted in the discourse from thanksgiving to praying that their love increases in knowledge and discernment.

Another question in the Greek text concerns whether Paul prays simply for the Philippians' love to abound, or whether he is asking for their love to increase in knowledge and insight. The issue concerns the relationship of the prepositional phrase 'with knowledge and all discernment' to the verb 'abound' (*perisseuō*). The verb *perisseuō* with the preposition *en* most often conveys what the subject is expected to increase in (Rom. 15:13; 1 Cor. 15:58; 2 Cor. 8:7; Phil. 1:26; Col. 2:7; cf. Sir. 10:27; 19:24). Hence, it seems likely that the Philippians' love is to increase in knowledge and insight. This also coheres well with the first purpose clause in verse 10 since that clause focuses on the Philippians' ability to recognize the excellent things they should follow and thus increase in purity and in the fruit of righteousness.

1:11 Concerning 'the fruit of righteousness *that comes through* Jesus Christ': the Greek has an articular prepositional phrase for 'that comes through Jesus Christ' (*ton dia Iēsou Christou*), and this article agrees in gender with the word 'fruit' (and not with the word 'righteousness'). Thus Paul states in 1:11 that the fruit comes through Jesus Christ; whereas in Phil. 3:9 it is righteousness itself that comes from God through faith in Christ. This is a helpful reminder that both our ongoing sanctification (1:11) and our justification (3:9) come solely through Christ.

3

The Advance of the Gospel
(Philippians 1:12-18)

¹²I want you to know, brothers, that what has happened to me has really served to advance the gospel, ¹³so that it has become known throughout the whole imperial guard and to all the rest that my imprisonment is for Christ. ¹⁴And most of the brothers, having become confident in the Lord by my imprisonment, are much more bold to speak the word without fear.

¹⁵Some indeed preach Christ from envy and rivalry, but others from good will. ¹⁶The latter do it out of love, knowing that I am put here for the defense of the gospel. ¹⁷The former proclaim Christ out of rivalry, not sincerely but thinking to afflict me in my imprisonment. ¹⁸What then? Only that in every way, whether in pretense or in truth, Christ is proclaimed, and in that I rejoice.

Having prayed for the Philippians, Paul continues to reflect on how the gospel is advancing, both through his imprisonment and the ministry of others. Had we been in Paul's shoes, we might very well have been wondering what God was doing. Why had Paul not been released? Was he being punished for having imprisoned Christians before he became a believer? Was it God's plan that Paul's final act of testimony should be that of a martyr?

Yet in all this, Paul sees God at work. The good news of Christian faith was progressing, even among the imperial guard.

Encouraged by Paul's example, others were proclaiming the gospel boldly. Even when some preached with impure motives (possibly wishing Paul harm), he could nevertheless rejoice that Christ was being declared to a watching world. Through this whole section, Paul models a joyful Christian response to suffering, persecution, and strife, and later explicitly calls on his readers to imitate him (3:17; 4:9).

We know from the book of Acts that Paul had been imprisoned before (even in Philippi) but only briefly (Acts 16:23ff.). Moreover, Paul had imprisoned others for their Christian faith (8:3; 22:4; 26:10) before his own spectacular conversion. Indeed, imprisonments were recurring events in the earliest church, often resulting in miraculous releases (5:18ff.; 12:4ff.; 16:23ff.). This time, however, Paul's imprisonment had lasted for a protracted period without miraculous intervention. He had languished in prison long enough for the Philippians to send him Epaphroditus, who ministered to him bravely before falling gravely ill (Phil. 2:25-30; 4:18).

First-century Roman law typically did not imprison convicted felons; this was deemed too costly, so other punishments were enacted. Instead, prisons were used to hold those awaiting a hearing prior to a verdict in their cases. Imprisonment could take on a variety of forms. On the one hand, a prisoner could be incarcerated in a dungeon built for that purpose (Acts 16:23ff.) or in an official facility attached to a military fortress or royal residence (Acts 21:37; 23:16, 35). On the other hand, a prisoner could be allowed the relatively pleasant confines of house arrest (Acts 28:16ff.). The book of Acts indicates that Paul experienced this whole spectrum of Roman imprisonment (contrast his severe beating and jailing in Acts 16:22ff. with his house arrest in Acts 28:16ff.). While we cannot be certain of the type of imprisonment Paul was experiencing as he penned this letter, it is likely that he wrote it during his (first) Roman imprisonment, which would mean he was under the less traumatic confines of house arrest. If this is so, then Acts indicates Paul was housed alone at his own expense, though chained and with a constant Roman guard (Acts 28:16, 20, 30), while awaiting an imperial hearing on whether he was a Jewish insurrectionist (for likely charges see Acts 24:1-6). Paul also could receive guests (Acts 28:17-31, esp. 28:30).

Moreover, we learn much about this imprisonment from his letter. The charges were serious, since Paul wonders whether he faces death (1:18b-26). Another indication of the severity of the charges is that he was in contact with the imperial guard (1:13). Yet, he was able to receive visitors (such as Epaphroditus mentioned in 2:25-30) and was allowed the opportunity to write this epistle. The matter most on Paul's mind was how his confinement had inhibited his goal of proclaiming Christ.

This somewhat introspective section continues through verse 26, but for thematic reasons, we shall treat verses 12-18 together. The last few words of verse 18 ('Yes, and I will rejoice') go syntactically and thematically with the next passage (1:19ff.), and will be examined in the next chapter.

I want you to know, brothers, that what has happened to me has really served to advance the gospel (1:12).
Here we glimpse Paul's perspective on his circumstances – he is more concerned about the gospel's advance than his own welfare. By sharing this with the Philippians, Paul intends to encourage them with his perspective, and he models a passionate concern for the gospel that they are to imitate.

'Brothers' (*adelphoi*) was a common first-century Christian expression that emphasized the family-relatedness of all believers in Christ's church.[1] It occurs several others times in Philippians (3:1, 13, 17; 4:1, 8, 21). Paul often connects 'brothers' with the concept of 'beloved brothers',[2] thus expressing endearment. Like other Greek generic masculine designations for groups of people, the word included all Christians in the church (male and female alike). The Greek idiom *ta kat' eme* ('what has happened to me') focuses on Paul's circumstances (cf. Eph. 6:21; Col. 4:7).

Paul speaks of the gospel's 'advance', referring to its movement toward an improved state (cf. Phil. 1:25; 1 Tim. 4:15). Paul's circumstances, especially his imprisonment, have led to the gospel's progression rather than its decline. Paul explains some aspects of the gospel's increase in the next two verses.

---

1 E.g., Rom. 1:13; 1 Cor. 16:20; Gal. 1:2.
2 1 Thess. 1:4; 2 Thess. 2:13; 1 Cor. 15:58; Phil. 4:1.

...so that it has become known throughout the whole imperial guard and to all the rest that my imprisonment is for Christ. And most of the brothers, having become confident in the Lord by my imprisonment, are much more bold to speak the word without fear (1:13-14).

Paul specifies two examples of how his circumstances have led to the gospel's advance: his imprisonment has caused the gospel to become known, and other Christians now proclaim it more boldly. Together, these two verses form two long parallel result clauses in Greek, stating the dual consequences of Paul's circumstances from verse 12. Thus it would be better to de-emphasize the period (full stop) in the translation at the end of verse 13.

In verse 13, the Greek literally reads, 'so that my chains have become manifest in Christ among the whole praetorium and all the rest.' There is some debate about what 'in Christ' modifies – 'chains', 'become', or 'manifest'.[3] Yet, this debate is somewhat inconsequential. The crucial matter Paul conveys is that his imprisonment itself has become a testimony to the gospel. Nevertheless, we cannot conclude from this verse alone that members of the praetorium (imperial guard) or 'the rest' have come to faith in Christ. Still, they are aware of Paul's imprisonment and of the way it testifies to his stand for Christ.

The 'praetorium' elsewhere in the New Testament typically refers to the Roman governor's headquarters in any one region.[4] This geographical designation here invokes all those who live and work in such a headquarters. The exact identification of 'praetorium' in this letter depends in part on where Paul is imprisoned. If in Rome, then it is likely that the praetorium refers to those in the emperor's own official retinue (hence the ESV above translates this as 'imperial guard'). Certainly, Paul's imprisonment has been officially recognized as being due to his proclamation of Christ. This he considers very important.

---

3 The last option seems most likely, due to Greek word order and to similar use of the preposition *en* elsewhere in Paul, see Rom. 1:19; 1 Cor. 11:19; also note 1 John 3:10.

4 Matt. 27:27; Mark 15:16; John 18:28, 33; 19:9; Acts 23:35.

Not just the 'praetorium', but 'all the rest' are aware of Paul's testimony in chains. Presumably, Paul is saying that not only are officials in the imperial administration aware that he is languishing in prison because of his Christian witness, but many others outside the official sphere also have become aware of his chains.

Moreover, Paul's imprisonment has emboldened other Christians to proclaim the gospel ('speak the word'). Using the word 'brothers' again (see above in verse 12), Paul speaks realistically of 'most' (not 'all') of these brothers being so emboldened. They have grown more confident, not in Paul, but because they have been persuaded 'in the Lord'. They have been 'persuaded in the Lord by my chains to dare even more to speak the word fearlessly'. As elsewhere, 'chains' metaphorically designates Paul's imprisonment.[5] He notes there is a real danger to these Christians. They must 'dare' to speak 'without fear'. In the midst of this danger, with the example of Paul and with their confidence of being 'in the Lord', these Christians are risking all to convey the gospel of Christ.

Some indeed preach Christ from envy and rivalry, but others from good will. The latter do it out of love, knowing that I am put here for the defense of the gospel. The former proclaim Christ out of rivalry, not sincerely but thinking to afflict me in my imprisonment (1:15-17).

Paul is under no illusion, however, that everyone who proclaims Christ does so with sincere motives. He is aware that some announce the gospel largely because they are jealous of him; others do so with a sense of fellowship in his proclamation of the gospel. This passage has often confounded readers. How is it that someone could proclaim Christ, but do so in a way intending to harm Paul? Yet, even in our modern context, we witness divisions in the church and various factions (even within missions groups, parachurch organizations, or denominations) wishing to win converts to their side of the church rather than converts to the church

---

5 Phil. 1:7; cf. Acts 20:23; 26:31; Col. 4:18; 2 Tim. 2:9.

universal. Paul's attitude here can provide helpful instruction as we reflect on such matters.

The word for 'preach' (*kērussō* in 1:15) refers to the proclamation of the message of Christ (see 1 Cor. 1:23; 2 Cor. 11:4). It is typical Pauline shorthand for sharing the good news of salvation found in Christ's death and resurrection. For Paul, this message is so rooted in the person of Christ that Jesus Himself is the focal point of all such proclamation.

Two categories of people are mentioned – those who proclaim Christ from 'envy and rivalry' (vv. 15, 17), and those who do so 'from good will' (v. 15) and 'out of love' (v.16). We can rightly ask, 'envious of whom?' Or, 'out of love for whom?' The context in verses 16-17 indicates that these groups act either out of envy *of Paul* or out of love *for Paul*. Note how those preaching Christ 'out of love' in verse 16 do so knowing that *Paul* is put here for the defense of the gospel. Likewise, those who proclaim Christ 'out of rivalry' do so to afflict the imprisoned apostle (v. 17).

'Envy' (*phthonos*) in verse 15 suggests that some are jealous of Paul. 'Rivalry' or 'strife' (*eris* in v. 15) points to a desire to engage in quarrels with him. Elsewhere such envy and strife is a characteristic of the fleshly nature.[6] Out of envy, the Jewish leaders delivered Christ to be crucified (Matt. 27:18; Mark 15:10). Quarreling had disrupted the Corinthian church (1 Cor. 1:11; 3:3; 2 Cor. 12:20). Such envy and strife can even be the motive for false teaching (1 Tim. 6:4; Titus 3:9).

However, since Paul here rejoices that the gospel is being spread even by the envious group (1:18), his concern does not appear to be that they are preaching a false Christianity. Rather, he notes their impure motives ('not sincerely' or 'not purely' in 1:17). The word for 'rivalry' in 1:17 (*eritheia*), which is different from the Greek word in 1:15 also translated above as 'rivalry' (*eris*), probably has the broader meaning of 'selfish ambition'. In verse 17, it appears that this rival faction was actually hoping to somehow add to Paul's afflictions. How they intended to do so is a matter of speculation, though perhaps they were hoping to establish a rival anti-Pauline faction within the church – a group that would have allegiance to its own set of leaders.

---

6 Rom. 1:29; Gal. 5:20-21; cf. Rom. 13:13; Titus 3:3.

On the other hand, there were others with purer motives. These are described as people of 'good will' (*eudokia*; 1:15), who are kindly disposed toward Paul. Their love for him helped motivate them in the proclamation of the same gospel (1:16). Even Paul's imprisonment, as shameful as it would have been in the first century, did not dissuade them from love for him, since they recognized his chains to be a mark of his willingness to *defend* the gospel (on *apologia*, 'defense,' in 1:16, see comments on 1:7). While the rival faction likely took advantage of Paul's imprisonment to spread the gospel and gain adherents to their side, these people of good will were instead motivated out of love for Paul. The question then is: how would Paul respond to these two groups? More pointedly, we could ask: How would we react if we were in his place?

What then? Only that in every way, whether in pretense or in truth, Christ is proclaimed, and in that I rejoice (1:18).
Ultimately, Paul's response is simply to rejoice in the spread of the good news. While he might yearn for this proclamation to be entirely out of pure motives and in loving relationship with him, he is still able to take joy in the fact that his Lord is being made known to the world. That is not to say that Paul, given the opportunity, would not have sought to correct the rival group, for he does not hesitate to warn against contentious factions elsewhere (see esp. 1 Cor. 1:10–4:21; 2 Cor. 10:1–13:10). And in Philippians, he does clearly label these rivals as those with impure motives (1:17) who act on pretense (1:18). However, here in this letter, he is not addressing these opponents. Rather he is writing to his beloved church in Philippi and modeling how to reflect on such matters. Christ is proclaimed. Even if others personally injure us in the process, we should rejoice that Christ is being exalted.

'Proclaimed' here is a common word used for the verbal spreading of the gospel (*katangellō*).[7] The phrase 'in every way' refers specifically to the two ways of announcing Christ mentioned in 1:15-17 and summarized in this verse concerning those who proclaim Christ out of 'pretense' and those who preach him out of 'truth.'

---

7 Cor. 9:14; 11:26; Phil. 1:17; Col. 1:28.

'Truth' (*alētheia*) is an everyday Greek word for truthfulness, here applied to those who have honest motives. 'Pretense' (*prophasis*) is an antonym for truth; and Paul thus insinuates that his rivals had alleged good motives, but in reality had much different designs. Two illuminating illustrations of 'pretense' found in the New Testament concern: (1) the scribes, who make the pretense of long prayers while they also 'devour widow's houses' (Mark 12:40; Luke 20:47); and (2) the group of sailors, who, abandoning their passengers, sought to flee an imperiled ship while pretending to save it (Acts 27:30). Paul, in contrast, is careful elsewhere to state that he does not preach the gospel out of a pretense for greed (1 Thess. 2:5). In light of this last reference, Paul may even be alluding in Philippians 1:18 to his rivals as those who are seeking their own greedy aims. In any case, Paul clearly labels these rivals as those of impure and pretentious motives.

Nevertheless, despite such rivals, Paul again in this letter, openly states his 'joy' that Christ is proclaimed. The verb 'rejoice' is also found in Phil. 2:17-18, 28; 3:1; 4:4, 10 (cf. the cognate noun in 1:4, 25; 2:2, 29; 4:1). As elsewhere, Paul's joy is not encumbered by his own circumstances (see esp. 2:17-18). He thus models throughout the epistle his admonition to 'rejoice in the Lord always' (4:4; cf. 3:1). And he reminds us all that our pre-eminent concern should be not for our own welfare, but for Christ's glory.

Conclusion
Again, we might ask ourselves, 'How would we have responded in Paul's circumstances?' Imprisoned and unable to publicly announce Christ, Paul finds opportunity for the gospel's advance. Rivals outside also proclaim Christ, with the pretense of good motives, but in reality out of envy and selfish ambition. Yet, even here Paul can rejoice that Christ is being made known. Do we face opposition for the sake of Christ? Why or why not? If we do, are we able to rejoice that Christ is exalted even in those times?

Questions for Personal Reflection:
1. In what ways have you personally experienced the gospel advance (in your life, in the lives of others,

Philippians 1:12-18

and around the world)? Have there been special challenges along the way? How have you witnessed God use even those challenges to His glory?

2. What would it take in our lives for us to be 'more bold to speak the word without fear' (1:14)?

3. Have you observed Christian ministries engage in rivalries against one another? How have you reacted to this in the past? Compare and contrast your thoughts on this with Paul's words in verses 15-18. How can we work to transform our churches and other ministries to be more unified in working toward a common goal?

4. Also note the reflection questions in the conclusion above.

STUDY QUESTIONS: *Gets news on the outside.*

1. Read through 1:12-18. What can we learn from these few verses about Paul's situation at the time he was writing? From a quick skim through the rest of Philippians, what else do we know about Paul's condition? *in prison. advanced gospel. joyful. pressing on towards goal. Christ centered*

2. Paul spends considerable space in this letter modeling his approach to the Christian life. What do we learn in these verses about Paul's focus in life? *on Christ*

3. How do you imagine that Paul's imprisonment helped others in the church 'become confident in the Lord' so that they were 'much more bold to speak the word without fear' (1:14)? What are some experiences in your life (or in the lives of others) that have emboldened you in a similar way to 'speak the word'? *his example shine as lights in the world*

4. Paul depicts two groups of people in 1:15-17. How does he describe them? How does he respond to each group? What do verses 1:15-18 reveal about Paul's character and about his focus in life? *blameless/ innocent or crooked and twisted*

5. When have you encountered people who appear to minister to others out of selfish motives? Have you

observed Christian ministries engage in rivalries against one another? How have you responded to these Christian ministries in the past? How would Paul's words here help us relate to such people? On the other hand, are there proper limits to our charitable toleration of self-seeking ministers or of divisive ministries?

4

Paul's Focus in Life and in Death
(Philippians 1:18b-26)

[18]Yes, and I will rejoice, [19]for I know that through your prayers and the help of the Spirit of Jesus Christ this will turn out for my deliverance, [20]as it is my eager expectation and hope that I will not be at all ashamed, but that with full courage now as always Christ will be honored in my body, whether by life or by death. [21]For to me to live is Christ, and to die is gain. [22]If I am to live in the flesh, that means fruitful labor for me. Yet which I shall choose I cannot tell. [23]I am hard pressed between the two. My desire is to depart and be with Christ, for that is far better. [24]But to remain in the flesh is more necessary on your account. [25]Convinced of this, I know that I will remain and continue with you all, for your progress and joy in the faith, [26]so that in me you may have ample cause to glory in Christ Jesus, because of my coming to you again.

What is the purpose of life? How can I endure when life seems too much? What happens when I die? Is there any point to it all? These, and many more, existential questions haunt the modern world. Voices in popular media claim to know secrets to coping with life, while others say life is just a sham. Some find solace in family and friends, others bury themselves in work or pleasure-seeking, and still others chase after popular philosophies, self-esteem psychologies, or the bewildering array of new spiritualities. Many assume that the search for meaning in life is fruitless, so it is best to make a good show of it for our brief time on earth.

These deep questions of life have been encountered throughout human history. Fascinatingly, most of the modern answers to these existential conundrums were anticipated in Paul's own day. The Epicureans pronounced that a person was a mere assemblage of atomic particles, which existed together for a brief time and then was gone (to face neither the perils of hell nor the joys of heaven, but merely to cease to exist); thus one must simply enjoy this momentary life while one can. The Stoics retreated into the life of the mind, despising the fluctuations of emotion, and assumed that their reason would be caught up in the great pantheistic mind/logos that governed the cosmos. Cynics challenged others not to think too highly of themselves, but simply to glory in their own self-identity. Indeed, a fuller list of philosophical and religious options from the first century might remind the reader of the maxim, 'There is nothing new under the sun' (Eccles. 1:9).

Paul does not directly present this paragraph as a solution to these great philosophical issues. Yet, in this passage we do discern Paul's own focus in life – what sustained him through his hard life, and what he anticipated upon his death. Paul models for us a truly Christ-centered spirituality. To die is to spend eternity with Christ. To live is to spend fruitful time in spreading the gospel of Christ. Both options are so full of joy that Paul is torn as to which is best. Yet, he concludes, somewhat sacrificially, that the Philippians truly need him around; for that reason, with confidence in the Trinitarian God, Paul assumes that he will continue in this mortal life.

Yes, and I will rejoice, for I know that through your prayers and the help of the Spirit of Jesus Christ this will turn out for my deliverance (1:18-19).
Paul again announces his joyful confidence in the midst of his difficult situation (cf. 1:18; 2:17-18). In the first part of verse 18, Paul affirmed his joy that Christ is being proclaimed, regardless of the other evangelists' motives (see the previous chapter). Here, in some contrast to verse 18 (see Additional Notes), Paul immediately moves on to rejoice confidently in the future outcome of his own imprisonment.

Although in verses 21-24 Paul acknowledges the possibility of his own death, in verse 19 (as also in vv. 25-26) he speaks of a confidence that he will be delivered from prison. Paul typically uses the word for 'deliverance' (*sōtēria*) to designate eternal 'salvation'.[1] Elsewhere in the New Testament, however, this noun can refer to deliverance from a more immediate situation.[2] The context here implies that Paul has in mind his current circumstances in prison, rather than his eternal state. Yet Paul would attribute such a release from prison to the sovereign hand of God, and thus he readily speaks of such release as a God-sent salvation in language that evokes his broader salvific confidence in God.

This projected release from prison, coming as it does from God's hand, will occur through the instrument of the Philippians' prayers and through the work of the Holy Spirit. Paul assumes an intermingling of human response and divine action. Prayer works. It works because God's children have the ear of the God of the universe. Moreover, the believer is never alone – the Holy Spirit serves as a constant help in times of trouble.

Just as Paul engages in constant and joyful prayer on behalf of the Philippians (1:4, 9), so the church in Philippi has been praying for Paul. Paul wishes to encourage them to persevere in prayer (4:6). And he attributes efficacy to their prayers on his behalf (cf. Philem. 22). Paul often entreats the churches to pray for his ministry.[3] The mutuality of this is striking. All Christians are to pray for one another, and Paul models this both in his prayer life and in his call for others to pray.

'Help' (*epichorēgia*), both in the noun form and in its cognate verb, depicts the 'support' or 'supply' that enables, for example, a human body to be nourished.[4] The Spirit, Paul affirms, will meet the needs of the hour. He refers here to the Spirit as the Spirit of Jesus the Messiah. His interchangeable descriptions of the Holy Spirit as the 'Spirit of God'[5] and as the 'Spirit of Jesus Christ' (cf. esp. Rom. 8:9) testifies to the deity of all the members of the Trinity.

---

1 E.g., Rom. 1:16; Eph. 1:13; Phil. 2:12; 1 Thess. 5:9; 2 Tim. 2:10.
2 E.g., Acts 27:34; cf. Acts 7:25; Heb. 11:7.
3 Rom. 15:30; 2 Cor. 1:11; Col. 4:3; 1 Thess. 5:25; 2 Thess. 3:1.
4 Eph. 4:16; Col. 2:19; for other uses, see 2 Cor. 9:10; Gal. 3:5.
5 Phil. 3:3; cf. e.g., Rom. 8:14; 1 Cor. 2:11; 2 Cor. 3:3; Eph. 4:30.

...as it is my eager expectation and hope that I will not be at all ashamed, but that with full courage now as always Christ will be honored in my body, whether by life or by death (1:20).

Paul employs two roughly synonymous expressions ('eager expectation' and 'hope') to express his intense hopefulness in God. Perhaps this hope is most intoned in the less common term 'eager expectation' (*apokaradokia*). (Compare Romans 8:19, where creation itself eagerly longs for the salvific revealing of the adopted children of God.)

The juxtaposition of shame and honor in this verse is quite striking. Public honor was a significant facet of Roman life in the first century, with public shame serving as its polar opposite (see Additional Note). A person of rank would seek the accolades of popular approval and avoid any sense of public ridicule. From the outset, we could think that Paul's imprisonment was itself a shameful event in his life. Yet he is confident in his ultimate vindication. Probably this involves release from prison (as in 1:19 and 1:25-26), but this verse also serves to transfer us from his expectation of temporal deliverance to an additional dimension of Christ being honored regardless of the immediate consequence for Paul.

Paul likely surprised his readers with this sentence. After his confident affirmation that he himself would not be put to shame, it is natural for the reader to assume that Paul is about to assert the opposite – namely that *Paul* would be honored. Yet, with a sudden shift in subject, he instead declares that *Christ* will be honored. This underlines the theme of this paragraph: Paul is more concerned for Christ's glory than his own.

Paul expects Christ's honor to result from Paul himself functioning as Christ's representative; thus he can bring honor to Christ in this life. Elsewhere Paul knows himself to be Christ's 'ambassador'. His actions can bring glory to Christ, as can those of other Christians (Rom. 15:6-7; 2 Cor. 9:13). Paul even speaks of his sufferings as 'filling up what is lacking in Christ's afflictions' (Col. 1:24). Indeed, those who suffer with Christ also will be honored with him (Rom. 8:17). Whatever happens to Paul in his earthly life, Paul intends to honor Christ.

'Honored' (*megalunō*) generically refers to something being enlarged (Matt. 23:5; 2 Cor. 10:15), but often it is used of 'honoring' God[6] and 'honoring' the Lord Jesus (Acts 19:17). Paul expects Christ's glory to be magnified in his own life and death. When Paul speaks of Christ being honored 'in my body', he is certainly referring to the time before his death, but he may also be implying that Christ will be honored by Paul's own physical suffering. Whether in life, or in death, Paul longs for Christ to be glorified.

In addition to the juxtaposition of shame and honor in this verse, there are other antonymous pairings. Paul emphasizes that he will 'not at all' be ashamed (literally he 'will be ashamed *by nothing*'); and this contrasts with his 'full courage' (literally '*all* boldness'). Such boldness stems from Paul's confidence in his sovereign deliverance by God. There is also a temporal contrast in this verse between 'always' and 'now'. Because Paul has such a long track record of seeing Christ honored in his life ('always'), he can look expectantly for the same to occur in this current circumstance ('now'). Perhaps the most striking antonymy is between 'life' and 'death' at the end of the verse. Even in Paul's death, Christ can, and will, be honored. So he need not fear death, since his concern is Christ's glory, and he need not flee from the joys and pains of this life, because also in those, Christ can be glorified through him.

For to me to live is Christ, and to die is gain (1:21).
Church history continues to resonate with the impact of these few, simple, timeless words. Herein the Christian's focus in life is summarized: Christ's glory is the purpose of life, and death brings eternal solace in His presence.

We should note that this verse begins with a logical connection to the preceding sentence ('for'). Rather than a stand-alone philosophical epigram, the verse itself undergirds the viewpoint Paul is expressing throughout this passage. Christ will be honored in Paul, whether in his life or death, because Christ is the very meaning of the apostle's life and the joyful hope of his death (1:20). Similarly, the verses that follow this sentence (especially verses 22-26) help

---

6 Luke 1:46; Acts 10:46; also 2 Sam. 7:22, 26; Ps. 34:3 [LXX 34:4].

us unpack what Paul means by this simple, yet profound, statement in verse 21. 'To live is Christ', because life permits Paul to engage in 'fruitful labor' on Christ's account (v. 22) – labor that includes the upbuilding of the church in Philippi (vv. 24-26). 'To die is gain', because death brings Paul rejoicing into the very presence of Christ (v. 23).

Are you looking for purpose in life? Are you fearful of the specter of death? Find purpose and solace in these words of the apostle.

If I am to live in the flesh, that means fruitful labor for me. Yet which I shall choose I cannot tell. I am hard pressed between the two. My desire is to depart and be with Christ, for that is far better. But to remain in the flesh is more necessary on your account (1:22-24).

Paul here wrestles with the question of which is better: life or death. Both are so good that he can hardly state a preference. This is particularly striking, given where Paul currently resides. Having been severely treated in the past, now he languishes in prison. Death is a real possibility; and, even if he is released, it is unlikely that Paul could anticipate a luxurious and easy life. Many people from the outside would bemoan Paul's circumstances. Yet, because of the Christ-centered focus he expressed in verse 21, thoughts of both life and death bring joy to him.

Paul helpfully clarifies that 'life' here means 'life in the flesh' – that is, life in this present world (also 1:24). Although 'flesh' can have negative associations in Paul (contrasting 'fleshly' in opposition to the 'spiritual'; e.g., Rom. 8:4ff.; Gal. 5:16ff.), Paul often employs the term 'flesh' to refer simply to physical flesh and blood.[7] Elsewhere, Paul speaks with confidence about 'eternal life';[8] it is thus apparent that, unlike the Epicureans of his day, Paul does not imagine that death leads to the eternal cessation of life and the end of conscious awareness. Moreover, Paul also expects that the believer will receive a resurrection body in the final judgment (Phil. 3:20-21; 1 Cor. 15:35ff.). Therefore, 'in the flesh' here simply designates the mortal body of this present life, as opposed to the state of

---

7 Rom. 1:3; 4:1; 2 Cor. 4:11; Gal. 2:20; Eph. 5:29; Col. 1:22; 1 Tim. 3:16; Philem. 16.
8 E.g., Rom. 5:21; 6:22-23; Gal. 6:8; 1 Tim. 6:12; Titus 3:7.

Philippians 1:18b-26

being with Christ (the 'intermediate state'), which a believer experiences upon death and prior to the final judgment and bodily resurrection of believers.

This present life affords the Christian the opportunity of being Christ's servant on earth. Paul expresses this as 'fruitful labor'. He often employs the metaphor of a tree bearing fruit (see 1:11; 4:17). Here the fruit is the result of Paul's labors on behalf of the gospel (see Additional Notes). Here, as elsewhere in this letter, Paul envisions his life purpose to be labor in Christ's service. The gospel so enthralls him that his very reason for being is to bring glory to Christ. Thus Paul models a purposeful Christian life.

In whatever labor the Lord has called you to do, there is fruit there that can bring glory to Christ. Certainly this involves our participating in the active spread of the gospel, but it also includes conducting all parts of our lives as those who seek Christ's honor. We can see this worked out practically in Paul as we consider his ethical instruction.

Paul's ethics are concerned with bringing all of life under Christ's lordship. Consider the long ethical passages in his letters (e.g., Rom. 12–15; Eph. 4–6; Col. 3–4, etc.), the corrective instructions detailing good Christian life in a pagan society (e.g., 1 Cor. 5–15), and the lists of spiritual fruit (e.g., Gal 5:16-25). In such places, the apostle addresses our conduct in our families, in our work, and in society at large. He speaks to our loving and encouraging others in the body of Christ, our godly lives, and our prayers on behalf of others. He refers to how we should use (and not use) our money, our bodies, and our minds. All are to come under Christ's lordship, and all are to bring glory to Him. And this can be done in the workplace, in the home, and (even as for Paul) in prison. This last example indicates that our physical circumstances can hardly restrict the goal of Christian living. Surely there are immense labors for us to do on Christ's behalf in this life, and ample fruit to be found in them.

Although Paul contemplates the possibility of his own death, and even uses the word 'choose', we need not imagine that Paul actually anticipates he will be asked to decide his own fate (let alone wonder whether he is considering suicide). Rather, the future-tense verb 'will choose' should be understood in the sense of, 'which I would choose if the choice were mine.' The grammatical possibility for this stems from the way in which the future tense in Koine Greek increasingly takes on the function of a subjunctive. More importantly, when Paul speaks of his deliverance from prison in this context (see vv. 19, 25-26), he recognizes that it is ultimately God who will release him. The apostle does not believe himself to truly have the final decision on his fate, but he anticipates that God still has a purpose for him in his mortal body.

Nonetheless, Paul very much desires the Philippians to know that he does not fear the outcome of the court's decision. A judgment of death would actually be a better outcome for Paul personally than his release. Given that Paul is about to express his own confidence in his release (vv. 25-26), we can understand his discussion in one of two ways. He is either hedging his bets in the event that he has misread the situation, and martyrdom is his fate, in which case he wishes the Philippians to know he is content with this outcome. Or he is simply taking the opportunity his imprisonment affords to instruct the church at Philippi on how to approach death. The latter view seems more likely, since Paul does indeed express great confidence in his release (vv. 19, 25-26). In addition, if this is Paul's first Roman imprisonment (resulting from the charges initially brought in Jerusalem, see Acts chapters 21–28), then Roman law appears to be on his side, as he would likely know (see e.g., Acts 23:29; 25:10-11; 26:30-32).

When Paul acknowledges that he is '*hard pressed* between the two,' he employs a verb (*sunechomai*) that indicates a strong pressure placed on someone. Jesus uses this same verb in Luke 12:50 when he speaks of how His salvific mission to be crucified presses upon Him. Paul can speak of the love of Christ 'pressing us' into ministerial action (2 Cor. 5:14 – often translated as 'the love of Christ *controls* us'). If this decision were truly left up to Paul, it would be a very difficult choice indeed, for he is pressed between two excellent opportunities.

Death, Paul states, is actually the option that would bring him more personal bliss. That alternative is what Paul, left to his own devices, would 'desire'. He speaks of such death in two ways: 'departure' and 'being with Christ'. The former metaphorically pictures death as a 'release' or a 'return'. This verb (*analuō*) can be found outside the New Testament in other contexts speaking of death (cf. Wisd. 16:14), but mostly it describes people returning from something, such as from a wedding party (Luke 12:36) or from war. It thus depicts death as a mere moving on to another state, much as how in English we will speak of someone as having 'passed on'.

More importantly, Paul portrays death as an opportunity to be 'with Christ'. Given how often Paul reminds readers that they are 'in Christ' in this present life, we should not assume the converse of this statement (i.e., that in this life we are 'without Christ') – quite the contrary! Indeed, in this present life, believers are identified as having already participated in Jesus' death and resurrection, and thus as those who are (both now and in the future) 'with Christ' in his death and resurrection (e.g., Rom. 6:8; Col. 2:13, 20; 3:3-4). Paul is indicating, however, that there will be a fuller experience of Christ's presence in the eternal life of the believer after death.

Paul also appears to assume that he will enter into this experience of being 'with Christ' immediately upon his death, even before the last judgment and the resurrection of those in Christ. This would refer then to what theologians call the 'intermediate state' – a time of joyful conscious awareness of being in Christ's presence even before the final state of resurrection life on the new earth.[9]

Paul describes this presence with Christ as 'far better'. His language is quite emphatic. The Greek takes a comparative ('better' – *kreisson*), adds to it a further comparative ('more' – *mallon*), and compounds that expression with the adjective 'much' (*pollōi*). The result literally reads: '[for] that is much more better.' Clearly death is to be desired by the believer. Far from fearing death, it should be welcomed because the opportunity to be in Christ's presence means that release from these mortal bodies affords a far greater joy than any happiness in this life.

Nonetheless, while in this mortal body, the believer has a purpose, and that should be sufficient to enable us to welcome life (even a life of suffering). Paul recognizes a necessity to remain in mortal flesh. His ministry among the

---

9 Also 2 Cor. 5:6-10; cf. Luke 23:43; Heb. 12:23; Rev. 6:9-11; 7:9-10.

churches, including the church in Philippi, means that there is still work for him to do that will produce fruit for Christ's glory. When Paul states that remaining in the flesh is 'more necessary,' he intends the comparison to imply that it is more important that he lives for the sake of others than that he personally experiences the bliss of death in Christ's presence. That this necessity was 'on your account' is a concept more fully explored in verses 25-26.

Convinced of this, I know that I will remain and continue with you all, for your progress and joy in the faith, so that in me you may have ample cause to glory in Christ Jesus, because of my coming to you again (1:25-26).
From these two verses we learn that Paul hopes his continuing presence in this mortal life will advance the faith of the Philippians, will give them cause for joy in that faith, and will result in their giving glory to Christ.

Paul is 'convinced' (*peithō*) that it is necessary for him to remain alive at this time (1:24). He has periodically used throughout this epistle the verb *peithō* in the perfect tense to refer to being persuaded of something (1:6, 14, 25; 2:24; 3:3-4), though a variety of terms can be used to translate this verb into English. In this verse, Paul expresses that he is persuaded of this simple truth: the Philippians (and others) need him.

Because of this truth, Paul confidently predicts the outcome of his imprisonment. He will remain alive. By compounding two cognate verbs (*menō* and *paramenō* – 'remain and continue'), Paul emphasizes the deep conviction he has that he will carry on in this life. This reminds us of the confidence Paul has previously expressed that the Lord will deliver him from his imprisonment through their prayers and through the support of the Holy Spirit (1:19).

Paul states a central reason for him to remain in this life – 'for your progress and joy in the faith'. Through the use of a single article in Greek, Paul unifies the 'progress' and 'joy' of the Philippians into a single goal. Yet both components are important. Paul wishes to facilitate the progress of the Philippians in the faith – to help them grow as good citizens of the gospel (1:27) so that their faith pervades their individual and corporate lives. (On 'progress' [*prokopē*], also see 'to advance [*prokopē*] the gospel' in 1:12.) We have already noted how important 'joy' is in this letter (see above on 1:4, 18). Here Paul emphasizes that the Philippians themselves are to experience joy in their faith, especially as they progress in that faith and as they glorify the power of Christ, who will grant Paul release from prison.

It is sometimes suggested that Paul conceives faith as an internal, subjective disposition of believing rather than as a coherent belief-set. But the article ('*the* faith') here implies that this is a false disjunction.[10] In this one letter, Paul can speak of 'faith' both as believing in something (3:9) and as a belief-set itself. Here 'the faith' clearly is used as shorthand for the 'the faith of the gospel' (as in 1:27). It is the message of Christ's death and resurrection, its meaning of salvation for sinful people, and the consequences that this message should bring in this life (as well as in the life to come). The proper disposition of a Christian to this message is one of believing in it, and so 'the faith' is both the object of what is believed and the disposition that is properly involved. In short, 'the faith' is the Good News, and trust/belief is what is required to rightly respond to and appropriate that gospel.

Yet, the Philippians' progress and joy in the faith, which is furthered by Paul's continuing in this life, also has an intended outcome – namely, that they may 'glory in Christ Jesus.' Literally the Greek reads 'so that in me your boast may abound in Christ Jesus.' While 'boasting' is often used negatively in Paul's writings (e.g., Rom. 4:2; 1 Cor. 5:6), those cases typically concern boasting in the wrong things (e.g., boasting in good works, or boasting in licentiousness). There are other times when 'boasting' (*kauchēma*) is viewed positively (e.g., Phil. 2:16 – see more extensive comments on this verse; also 2 Cor. 1:14; 5:12; 9:3). Here the believers' greatest reason for satisfaction in this life is to be focused on Jesus the Messiah. Such a boast in Christ Jesus indeed will overflow in Jesus' praise because Christ will have brought Paul, released from prison, back to visit the Philippian church. Thus Paul anticipates that his own emancipation from jail will result in the Philippians giving glory to Christ as they magnify their boasting in Christ.

---

10 Also 1:27; cf. e.g., Rom. 4:14; 1 Cor. 16:13; 2 Cor. 13:5; Gal. 1:23; Col. 1:23; 2 Tim. 4:7.

Confident of this and cognizant that his presence will also advance their faith and give them joy, Paul looks to God as the one who will deliver him from prison and from execution.

Summary
This section continues Paul's somewhat introspective reflections on his own imprisonment. These reflections, though personal, were intended to edify the church at Philippi. They provide a perspective on Paul's chains, which undoubtedly helped to alleviate concerns for him back in Philippi. Moreover, Paul here models a Christian approach to matters of life, suffering, death, and Christian witness.

Whereas the preceding section (1:12-18) focuses on the present realities of Paul's confinement and how his imprisonment has caused the gospel to flourish, this passage transitions to his contemplation of his own future: whether he will be freed from chains or executed. Just as Paul has rejoiced in his present circumstances because the gospel is being proclaimed, he now expresses joy in what God has yet in store for him. Rather than his being put to shame, whether the next day brings death or life, Paul is confident that Christ will be exalted in him.

Death is a real possibility for the incarcerated apostle. But such a release from this mortal life actually means moving on to a fuller experience of presence with Christ. Such an 'intermediate state,' awaiting the final judgment and bodily resurrection of believers, is actually to be desired since it will be spent with Christ. So Paul shows no fear or apprehension at this prospect.

Yet Paul is confident that God will deliver him from prison. That confidence rests on the support of the Holy Spirit, on the prayers of the Philippian saints, and on Paul's belief that his release is necessary for the sake of the church. Indeed, his liberation will result in the progress of the faith of the gospel among the Philippians and in their joy. That progress and joy in the faith will in turn bring glory to Christ, for the Philippians will find even greater reason to boast in Christ when they again have Paul with them. Because their progress and joy in the gospel is so important, Paul knows what God will have him do – Paul will remain, and Christ will be glorified.

Herein lies the focus of the Christian life as modeled for us by the apostle – to seek, whether in life or death, the glory of Christ. With such a focus, death holds no fear. Indeed death, though not something to be pursued, produces reason to rejoice, for death brings us into the presence of our beloved, exalted Lord.

Have we brothers and sisters in Christ who have passed on? Then we can rejoice for them that they are with Christ, even while we grieve our own loss of their presence. Are we faced with our own mortality? Then let us hold fast in confidence that our release from mortal flesh brings us into the presence of Christ. Yet this mortal life has supreme value. Whatever we do unto Christ, we bring glory unto Him. There is fruit-filled labor waiting to be plucked. Even if we are bound in chains and suffering for the gospel, or even if we are simply going through our everyday lives, we must concentrate on the advance of the gospel, on the joy of the Christian faith, and on the magnification of Christ's glory.

Questions for Personal Reflection:

1. If your friends, family, and co-workers were asked what they perceive to be the most important goals in your life, what would they list?

2. What gets you out of bed in the morning? Or helps you get through the day? What brings the most excitement and joy to your life? Can you truthfully say, 'To live is Christ'? Why or why not?

3. When you contemplate death (either yours or that of a close friend), what most comes to mind? How would your day-to-day life be different if you were to live as if, 'My desire is to depart and be with Christ, for that is far better' (1:23)?

4. What is there in this life that is necessary for you to do for the sake of the faith of others (cf. 1:24)? Are there people in your life whose 'progress and joy in the faith' is encouraged by your ministry to them (cf. 1:25)? Consider some ways you can reach out even more to others.

Study Questions:

1. Read through this passage together. As Paul continues to model the Christian life, here he reflects on his imprisonment and on the question of whether it will lead to his death or to his release. How would you describe the overall mood of this passage?

   [margin: rejoice, hopeful]

2. What outcome do you think Paul anticipates from his imprisonment (and why)?

   [annotation: Jesus Christ this will turn out for my deliverance.]

3. How would you depict the relationship between the Philippians' prayers and the help of the Holy Spirit (1:19)? What can we learn from this?

4. Observe the honor and shame terminology in 1:20. What do you think it means for Paul when he states his desire that 'Christ will be honored in my body'? How can this be true of us?

   [annotation: he will bring it to completion]

5. One of the most famous sayings from Philippians is found in 1:21. What does this mean in context? In what ways can you personally relate to this statement, and in what ways can you not?

   [margin: bound to Christ]

6. What do these verses say about how Paul views his ministry?

7. Return to the 'Questions for Personal Reflection' section on this passage and share your answers with the group if you are comfortable.

Additional Notes:

1:18-19 The opening words of this paragraph (translated in the ESV as 'Yes, and') actually represent 'but also' in the Greek (*alla kai*) – 'But I also will rejoice.' Thus there is a contrast implied in the Greek text that can be missed in most English translations. While in prison, Paul, on the one hand, rejoices that Christ is being proclaimed (v. 18), and, on the other, he rejoices in his own anticipated deliverance (vv. 19-20). Both thoughts bring joy to the apostle.

1:20 In recent New Testament scholarship, some argue adamantly that the first-century Mediterranean world was an 'honor/shame' culture, more concerned about the perceptions of others than about a personal internal sense of guilt. But this seems at times to involve an over-appropriation (and frequently, an over-simplification) of highly dichotomistic sociological categories. Nevertheless, ancient literature and inscriptions certainly do testify to the importance of 'honor' in first-century Graeco-Roman culture (and in Jewish culture as well). Hence this juxtaposition of shame and honor terminology here provides an indirect cultural critique of Roman values.

1:22 The Greek expression translated 'fruitful labor' is most literally rendered 'fruit of work' (*karpos ergou*). There remains some debate about how to translate 'of' after 'fruit' in Paul – 'fruitful work' or 'work that produces fruit' (technically known as a debate between an attributed genitive and a genitive of producer). It seems to be the case, however, that (apart from genitives which refer to people, see Rom. 6:22) the genitive after *karpos* consistently expresses in Paul that which produces the fruit (1 Cor. 9:7; Gal. 5:22; Eph. 5:9; Phil. 1:11; cf. Matt. 3:8; Mark 12:2; Luke 1:42; 3:8; 20:10; Heb. 13:15; James 3:18; 5:7). So, the reference above is that of the 'fruit' produced by Paul's labor. That is to say, the 'fruit' is the result of Paul's work on behalf of the gospel. Nonetheless, the debate is a minor one, since both translations convey the sense that Paul's life in this mortal body results in his work on behalf of the gospel.

Handwritten notes:

Stay dependent on the Lord...
 failure can come when we don't rely on God.

Christ is worth dieing for.

Prayer –

Phil 1:21

Bonnie – Brother-in-law Alex 88 in hospital (salvation?)
Spiritual understanding

(Tim) Brother-in-law Christian has cancer
Jewish Dr. – witness

Julie — graduation went well. Redemption with daughter

Marcia — Kids - a lot of changes. Moving
Heather being deploy Andrew Sept. probably
China sea

Lucy – removal of gall badder Jay. not a lot of energy.

Rebecca – physical healing, emotional, graduation complete

Kristina – husband (Tim) home for Chines. Suprise visit from son.

Tiffany – Interview thursday. new teaching job. Family would get alone.

Linda – Scheduling for Pres meeting and hymn sin
new kitchen details

5

Christian Citizenship
(Philippians 1:27-30)

²⁷Only let your manner of life be worthy of the gospel of Christ, so that whether I come and see you or am absent, I may hear of you that you are standing firm in one spirit, with one mind striving side by side for the faith of the gospel, ²⁸and not frightened in anything by your opponents. This is a clear sign to them of their destruction, but of your salvation, and that from God. ²⁹For it has been granted to you that for the sake of Christ you should not only believe in him but also suffer for his sake, ³⁰engaged in the same conflict that you saw I had and now hear that I still have.

As Paul has been called to suffer for the sake of the gospel, so too the Philippians must endure opposition in this life. In the preceding verses, Paul modeled the Christian life through his own self-reflections. Now he shifts to directly addressing the situation in the Philippian church in light of the believers' relationships to Christ and their contact with Paul. He commends them to be good citizens of the gospel and to stand together in unity, even in the midst of resistance to their faith.

Only let your manner of life be worthy of the gospel of Christ (1:27a).
In verses 24-26, Paul transitions from his introspective tone in verses 12-23, referring more specifically to the letter's

recipients in the church at Philippi. In those preceding verses, Paul anticipated his own future release from prison, expecting that the Lord would return him to Philippi for the sake of the church's progress and joy in the gospel. Believers will consequently boast in Jesus and bring glory to Him. Now, in verse 27, Paul instructs the church directly. His overarching theme, which serves as an umbrella for his ethical and doctrinal instruction found in the many verses yet to come, is 'be a good citizen of the gospel'.

In order to more precisely understand the words, 'let your manner of life be worthy', we should observe that the ESV footnote provides a more literal translation of the Greek: 'Only behave as citizens worthy of the gospel of Christ...' The Greek imperative here is *politeuesthe*, and you can perceive its connection to citizenship by observing that *polis* is the Greek word for 'city' (note the similar letters in the beginning of the verb *politeuesthe* and the noun *polis*). By extension, the verb speaks of people properly fulfilling their duties as citizens of their own city or country.

Surprisingly, here Paul connects the Philippians' citizenship not to any physical country of origin, but to the gospel. The Christian's ultimate allegiance is to the kingdom of God, and Christian conduct requires us to be good citizens of God's realm and rule.

The book of Acts recalls Paul applying this verb to his own conduct (Acts 23:1). Such metaphorical usage is not unique to Paul, since many intertestamental Jewish sources also connect 'behave as citizens' with proper conduct in keeping the Jewish law (see Additional Note). Paul will return in Philippians 3:20 to speaking of Christians as those whose 'citizenship' is in heaven. And in another epistle Paul proclaims, 'So then you are no longer strangers and aliens, but you are fellow citizens with the saints and members of the household of God...' (Eph. 2:19).

Citizenship carried significant import in the Graeco-Roman world, especially as Rome grew to envelop the whole Mediterranean. At first, Rome granted citizenship only to residents of the city of Rome or its immediately surrounding territories in Italy. However, as the Roman Empire expanded, it permitted more and more people outside Italy the privilege of citizenship, especially in return for duties (such as military service) that a person had performed on its behalf. Paul, we learn in Acts (22:25-29; 23:27), was a Roman citizen from birth, probably because his father had been granted citizenship for some undisclosed reason. Roman citizenship came with certain privileges and honors, including a legal status superior to that of the non-citizen. Paul was once unjustly beaten and imprisoned in Philippi; the magistrates only recognized the seriousness of this injustice once they learned he was a Roman citizen (Acts 16:37-38). About the time this letter was written, Paul's own legal appeal to Rome was likely predicated, at least in part, on his Roman citizenship.

The Philippians too would understand the import of citizenship in Roman society. Not only had they seen a living example through how Paul had been treated in their midst (Acts 16:37-38, mentioned above), but citizenship likely took on a special meaning in this Roman colony. As noted in the commentary introduction, Philippi had been refounded as a colony to honor the victory of Octavian (later Augustus Caesar) and Antony against Brutus and Cassius. The establishment of the Roman colony included a large influx of military retirees, who had received citizenship in appreciation for their service. And the colony itself garnered special legal and fiscal dispensations just as though its inhabitants were living in Italy. Many authors have thus suggested that there would have been great civic pride in this city, focused both on Philippi's special colonial privileges and on the Roman citizenship that many of its leading citizens would have possessed.

In the midst of this first-century context, Paul takes up the concept of citizenship and redirects the reader from his or her allegiance to Rome or any other earthly authority. Rather, the Philippians are to conceive of themselves as citizens of the Good News. They are to be caught up in the significance of Christ's advent, life, death, resurrection, and heavenly rule. This is the basis for their identity corporately and individually. We need not assume, however, that this involved a complete rejection of any engagement in civic affairs, for some in Paul's ministry apparently continued to play leading roles in society (cf. Erastus in Romans 16:23). But Christian citizenship in the gospel does speak to the central focus and identity of the Christian life.

That focus is indeed the Good News. Christians are to be 'good citizens of the gospel'. Paul has already referred often to the gospel (Phil. 1:5, 7, 12, 16). It bears repeating that this gospel is the good news of the Messiah, the Davidic King long promised to the Jewish people, who has come to give his life on behalf of sinners, who was raised so that those who believe in him may experience resurrection life, who now reigns over all, and whose kingdom will ultimately expand to bring all things under his direct authority. That good news outshines any claims of earthly powers. It undermines any pagan religion, even those that deify the Roman state and its Caesar. And it provides meaning and hope in life, even in the midst of suffering and opposition. Given the glories of this good news, then citizenship in Christ's kingdom inevitably calls for allegiance beyond any earthly rule.

This citizenship is to be lived out in 'worthy' conduct. Paul elsewhere can use this term 'worthy' to speak of good Christian behavior as 'walking in a worthy manner' (Eph 4:1; Col. 1:10; 1 Thess. 2:12). Christian conduct must conform appropriately to the message of the gospel. Christians are to be good citizens of Christ's kingdom. The following verses instruct the Philippians what such gospel citizenship entails (especially verses 27-28).

> ...so that whether I come and see you or am absent, I may hear of you that you are standing firm in one spirit, with one mind striving side by side for the faith of the gospel, and not frightened in anything by your opponents. This is a clear sign to them of their destruction, but of your salvation, and that from God (1:27-28).

Paul here calls for unity in the church in the midst of opposition in society. This focus on Christian unity continues into chapter two of the letter, and it reminds us of how important it is for Christians to live together in one body.

Earlier in this chapter, Paul wrestled with the question of whether he would ever see the Philippians again. He acknowledged his current absence from them and yearned to come to them (1:8, 25-26). Yet, even while imprisoned, Paul kept in touch with the churches. And he wants to continue to hear good reports from Philippi, whether he is able to visit them in person or languishes in prison (or is called to minister elsewhere). Paul is not averse to motivating this church in part by their desire to please the apostle, who first introduced them to the gospel, and who thus serves as their father in the faith.

Paul desires to hear that this church is unified, and its members are confident in their salvation. He wants to know that they 'stand firm in one spirit'. Paul elsewhere directs the churches (and the individuals in them) to 'stand firm'.[1] This metaphor represents one who confidently holds his ground, even in times of opposition. This does not mean that anyone 'stands firm' through his or her own strength, since Paul expresses that God Himself enables Christians to 'stand' (Rom. 14:4). The Christian life involves holding fast in the faith (1 Cor. 16:13; cf. 2 Thess. 2:15), with the knowledge that we are standing in the Lord (Phil. 4:1; 1 Thess. 3:8) – that is, for Him and by His strength. In the next verses, Paul will acknowledge opposition to the gospel in Philippi (1:29-30), and thus he well knows that his Christian recipients are called to stand their ground when faced with opposition in this world. The Christian does not run and hide when faced with attacks on the faith, nor is he or she to capitulate to other doctrines and to societal pressures. We are to hold fast confidently to the gospel, and yet redemptively to engage the culture around us.

Christians, however, do not stand alone as individuals. Rather, the call here is a corporate one – the whole church is to stand together in Christian unity ('in one spirit'). One question naturally arises concerning the meaning of 'one spirit': does Paul refer here to the Holy Spirit or to the corporate solidarity of spiritual connectedness? That is, should we translate this as 'in one Spirit' or as 'in one spirit'? The question is complex, for although Paul talks often of the Holy Spirit (e.g., Phil. 1:19; 3:3), he also speaks of human beings as possessing their own 'spirits' (Phil. 4:23; cf. 1 Cor. 15:45). In the next clause, Paul acknowledges the Philippians to possess a common 'soul' or 'mind' ('with one mind striving side by side'), and so this may

---

1 1 Cor. 16:13; Gal. 5:1; Phil. 4:1; 1 Thess. 3:8; 2 Thess. 2:15.

indicate that here 'in one spirit' refers to a collective spiritual unity (cf. 1 Cor. 6:17). However, Paul also talks elsewhere of Christians being in the 'one [Holy] Spirit' (1 Cor. 12:9, 13; Eph. 2:18; 4:4), and shortly Paul will refer to being in fellowship with the Spirit (Phil. 2:1 – see notes on this verse). It therefore seems that in this verse Paul calls Christians to stand together in the 'one Holy Spirit'. Nevertheless, whether one understands this as 'spirit' or 'Spirit,' certainly Paul emphasizes the collective unity of the church.

The rest of verses 27-28 in Greek connect to the verb 'stand firm' by means of adverbial participles ('striving' and 'not being frightened'). These phrases thus expand on the notion of what it means to 'stand firm.' Standing firm requires that the church (positively) works together in unity for the faith, and that (negatively) they do not fear worldly opposition to the gospel.

In penning 'with one mind striving side by side for the faith of the gospel', Paul employs the Greek verb *sunathleō* (translated above as 'striving'; cf. 4:3). The careful reader will observe that this is an athletic or military metaphor (*sun* – 'together' combined with *athleō*, 'compete in a contest'). Paul is instructing these Philippian believers to compete together in this world on behalf of Christ. The victory they are seeking must be a corporate one.

The notion of 'together' in the verb is emphasized by the phrase 'with one mind.' This depicts the 'soul' (*psyche*) as a collective agreement of mind and intent in the church. In chapter two, where Paul continues this emphasis on church unity, he will again call the church to be 'of one mind' (*sumpsychoi*, 2:2). The apostle so strongly emphasizes this theme of unity that we dare not miss the point: Christians must stand together in this world and compete for the faith together.

The context of competing together concerns 'the faith of the gospel'. As earlier (see notes on 1:25-26), 'the faith' here refers to the object of belief (the Christian faith which is in 'the gospel') and connotes the disposition of entrusting oneself to that gospel. The good news of Jesus' death and resurrection is worthy of our trust; and it is worth fighting for!

Yet in this world there will be those who rise against this gospel. Certainly 'your opponents' refers to human antagonists (such as those who generated Paul's sufferings, as well as those who bring sufferings upon the Philippians, see 1:29-30), but 'your opponents' likely would include even spiritual animosity from demonic forces (such as the 'principalities/ authorities,' 'powers' and 'spiritual hosts' of Eph. 6:12; cf. Eph. 2:2; 3:10). Whatever comes at the Christian in this life, we are not to be frightened by such hostility. Greek lexicons will also suggest the translation 'intimidated' or 'terrified' for the word 'frightened' (*pturō*).

The Christian church can confidently engage opposition in this world – but why? Because the gospel is the only means of salvation. And when Christians collectively refuse to be antagonized by worldly opponents, that stance signifies that their salvation, which is 'from God', is their security in the present. Moreover, such Christian steadfastness also points their opponents to the final days – the eschatological judgment when Christ puts all things under His lordship (2:10-11). This judgment will mean 'destruction' for the opponents of Christ. And that judgment will culminate fully the 'salvation' of the church – a salvation that is evidenced in the present by the church's unified stance on the gospel.

[handwritten annotation: *give freely* or *give graciously*]

For it has been granted to you that for the sake of Christ you should not only believe in him but also suffer for his sake, engaged in the same conflict that you saw I had and now hear that I still have (1:29-30).

These verses connect via an inherent logic with the verses that precede them (note the opening word 'for' or 'because'). Paul has just called the Philippians to stand together in spiritual communion and in common purpose, in order that they may contend together for the gospel in their society, even in the midst of social (and spiritual) antagonism. Having mentioned the opponents of the gospel, Paul now further addresses the sufferings the Philippians have endured and will continue to undergo.

One striking feature concerns the verb 'granted' (*echaristhē*). Paul speaks of the sufferings of the church as a gift! The Greek is actually a bit awkward to render into English; perhaps a more literal translation would read: 'Because this thing on behalf of Christ has been given to you...' Paul repeatedly emphasizes that these are sufferings 'on behalf of Christ'. Just one line later, Paul will again state that the sufferings the church endures are 'for his sake'. It is not just any suffering in life to which Paul refers. These are sufferings that result from persecution by the opponents of the church, and thus these are sufferings endured for the sake of Christ.

Though contextually Paul is emphasizing Christian suffering, he actually indirectly affirms two 'gifts' to the church. One gift is that they 'believe in him'. This is certainly continuous with the disposition of faith in Christ found throughout Paul's letters. Yet, it also is an indirect indicator that he envisions the very possibility of faith in Christ as itself a divine gift. It is all from God's grace – the gospel itself, and our ability to believe in Christ.

The second gift involves suffering for Christ's sake. What a striking thought! Paul views suffering in this life as a gift! The nature of the sufferings to which Paul is referring is more clearly outlined in verse 30. The Philippians are privileged to suffer the 'same' conflict (that is, the same kind of sufferings) that he himself has endured. Paul applies the word 'conflict' (*agōn*) elsewhere to opposition to his ministry (1 Thess. 2:2); it is the same term he uses when he says 'fight the good *fight* of faith' (1 Tim. 6:12; cf. 2 Tim. 4:7). Paul has known opponents of the gospel, both human and demonic. This is the same battle in which the Philippians are called to 'stand firm' and 'strive together,' not being 'frightened' by their opponents (Phil. 1:27-28).

The church at Philippi witnessed Paul's sufferings first hand (1:30). Its members 'saw' him jailed after being beaten (Acts 16). They likely 'heard' of the continued opposition to his message that he endured shortly afterwards in places such as Thessalonica, Berea, Athens, and Corinth (Acts 17–18). And they certainly currently 'hear' that he resides in jail due to his proclamation of the gospel (Phil. 1:12ff.). Thus, by his apostolic example, Paul prepares this church to face similar persecution.

Summary

It can be uncomfortable to speak of suffering on behalf of Christ, but the notion of Christian suffering will repeatedly engage us in this epistle. For some brothers and sisters in Christ today, such suffering is a daily reality as they confront perils to life and limb in societies that contend against the Christian faith. As I write, I am especially cognizant of fellow believers in certain Islamic countries, and of others in societies where animism and magic is the norm. For other Christians, especially in the 'Christian West,' the notion of deep persecution (including the danger of death) appears quite remote. In such contexts it becomes easier to consider Christian 'sufferings' to be anything negative that life brings (e.g., medical issues, financial loss, difficulties at work). Yet though our Lord does indeed help us engage in such everyday struggles of life, Paul refers here specifically to opposition resulting directly from one's commitment to Christ. While some may wish to downplay Paul's words, he is definitely calling the church to be prepared to suffer for the sake of the proclamation of the gospel.

Paul approached his own sufferings by rejoicing (see esp. 1:18). He knew death would bring him into Christ's presence, and that life (even a difficult life) meant gospel-centered labor resulting in fruit to Christ's glory (1:19ff.). What was most important to Paul was the spread of the gospel – both its proclamation to those who have never heard it, and its pervasive spread within the lives of believers as they progress in faith (1:12-14, 24-26). Paul's exemplary response to his circumstances has already served as a model for those Philippians who are now enduring the 'same conflict.' They well know what Paul has undergone, and they are likewise called to stand firm, to contend together, and not to fear their opponents.

All of this falls under the banner of those whose manner of life is worthy of the gospel – that is, of those who live as citizens of the good news of Jesus Christ. The message of Jesus' own sufferings – as well as of his life, death, resurrection, and eternal rule – this is the basis for Christian identity. Even though we are indeed 'citizens' of our various nation-states, in reality our most fundamental commitment is to Christ and to His gospel. Our motivation must be to conduct ourselves in such a way that our thoughts, actions, and person show the world what citizenship in Christ's kingdom looks like. That citizenship will likely bring us into direct conflict with opponents whose commitments lie contrary to the gospel. In those circumstances, Paul directs the Christian church to stand together – to be unified for the sake of the gospel.

Questions for Personal Reflection:

1. How are you impacted by the phrase: 'Only live worthily as citizens of the gospel of Christ'? Where else (other than the gospel) have you been tempted to let your identity be found? How do you think our Christian citizenship in the gospel ought to relate to our earthly allegiances to our own cities or countries?

2. Where do you see evidence in your local church of people 'striving side by side for the faith of the gospel'? Where have you observed such evidence in the worldwide church? How have you in the past worked alongside others for the sake of the gospel (both at the local and world levels)? Name some specific ways you, together with others, continue to further the church's mission.

3. When have you witnessed opposition to the gospel (both locally and worldwide)? Describe some of these occasions. How can you best confront the suffering that you personally face due to your allegiance to Christ? What are some ways you can encourage others to stand firm in the midst of such opposition?

STUDY QUESTIONS:

1. Paul now transitions to directly addressing the Christian behavior of the Philippian church. Do you think Paul's close personal relationship with that church would have made these words sound differently to them than they sound to us today? Try to put yourself in the position of the original audience

and hear this passage as they would have heard it. What stands out to you from their perspective?

2. Quickly skim the commentary section on 1:27a. Note that the commentary suggests that a more literal translation of this verse would begin 'Only behave as citizens worthy of the gospel of Christ…' How would this notion of 'citizenship' have sounded in Philippi in the first century? How does this idea of being 'citizens of the gospel' help you understand Paul's directive in this verse?

3. Where else (other than the gospel of Christ) have you been tempted to let your identity be found?

4. How do you think our Christian citizenship in the gospel ought to relate to our earthly allegiances to our own cities or countries?

5. As Paul continues in 1:27, he instructs the church corporately to 'stand firm in one spirit, with one mind striving side by side for the faith of the gospel, and not being frightened in anything by your opponents.' Picture together how this would look in a church setting. How would you describe such a church from the perspective of those outside the congregation? How would this look and feel from the church members' perspectives?

6. How does such church unity help the membership of a church endure persecution?

7. Where do you see evidence in your own local church of people 'striving side by side for the faith of the gospel'? Where have you observed such evidence in the worldwide church? How have you in the past worked alongside others for the sake of the gospel (both at the local and world levels)? Name some specific ways you, together with others, continue to further the church's mission.

8. Paul speaks of such unity as a 'sign of destruction' to the church's opponents and as a 'sign of salvation' to the church. What does he mean by such language?

9. Paul depicts suffering and persecution as a gift from God (1:29), much as faith in Christ is a gift from God. Why do you think he speaks in these terms? What kind of suffering is he talking about in this context? Do you conceive of such suffering as a gift?

10. When have you witnessed opposition to the gospel (either locally or worldwide)? Describe some of these occasions. How can you best confront the suffering that you personally face due to your allegiance to Christ? What are some ways you can encourage others to stand firm in the midst of such opposition?

Additional Notes:

1:27 'Only' (*monon*) appears first (i.e., in the clause initial spot) occasionally in Paul (Gal 2:10; 5:13), though this mention here in 1:27 is the example in Paul with the greatest rhetorical flair. Paul is focusing the Philippians' lives on one thing: living as good citizens of the gospel.

1:27 The imperative *politeuesthe* is translated above as 'let your manner of life be worthy' (or better rendered as 'be a worthy citizen'). This is from the verb *politeuomai*, which is also found in various works of Jewish literature roughly contemporary to the time of Paul (e.g., Josephus, *Ant.* 12.142; 2 Macc. 6:1; 11:25; 3 Macc. 3:4; 4 Macc. 2:8, 23; 4:23; 5:16; and Esther 16:15 [in the Greek A-text = 8:12p]). These Jewish texts all speak of Jewish people conducting themselves according to God's law (including God's law as interpreted by the rabbinic teachers of the day; cf. Josephus, *Vita* 12). The Jewish people are to be good citizens of God's law. From this we learn that Paul's metaphorical use of *politeuomai* was likely already widespread in his day. Such cases connect 'being a good citizen' with that which was most to govern their lives (i.e., in Jewish contexts, with the law). Though *politeuomai* certainly speaks to one's 'manner of life,' we should not assume that it has lost its overtones of good citizenship. Thus Christian citizenship is firmly connected with the Good News that governs our lives – the death, resurrection, and everlasting Lordship of Christ Jesus.

6

Christian Unity

(Philippians 2:1-4)

¹So if there is any encouragement in Christ, any comfort from love, any participation in the Spirit, any affection and sympathy, ²complete my joy by being of the same mind, having the same love, being in full accord and of one mind. ³Do nothing from rivalry or conceit, but in humility count others more significant than yourselves. ⁴Let each of you look not only to his own interests, but also to the interests of others.

Building on his call for Christians to respond in unity to persecution (1:27-30), Paul now emphasizes the need for Christian unity. The structure of this passage is clear. In verse one Paul reminds the Philippian church of the deep corporate benefits of their Christian calling. In light of those benefits, he then emphatically directs church members to walk together in unity (2:2-4). This will require that all members humble themselves for the sake of the greater whole. Christ Jesus then serves as the greatest model of humility, whose example we must follow (2:5-11).

Since the unity theme here was first announced in 1:27-30, it seems a bit artificial to treat this paragraph by itself (note also that verse 1 begins with 'so' which connects this passage to the preceding). Moreover, verses 5-11 belong together with this passage, for Christ is the true exemplar of humility. Yet, these four brief verses are weighty enough to require focused attention; and, given the immense import of the Christological themes in 2:5-11, we will examine that paragraph separately in the next chapter. Still, we should recognize the connections between these four verses with their overall context. This call to unity was no mere abstraction for Paul. He will invoke the same Greek terminology when he later refers to the dissension in the church between Euodia and Syntyche (4:2-3). Factions are beginning to form in the Philippian church, and Paul desires to reverse that trend. Indeed, he is well aware of dissensions in other churches he has founded (the Corinthians being a principal example), and so he is rightly concerned about the dangers that disunity brings. Dissensions cut at the heart of Christian fellowship. They weaken the church's ability to respond to an adversative world (1:27-30). And such prideful disunity dishonors the example of our Lord Himself, whose humility caused Him to relinquish the privileges of deity in order to die on our behalf (2:5-11).

So if there is any encouragement in Christ, any comfort from love, any participation in the Spirit, any affection and sympathy (2:1)
First, contemplate the little word 'so' (*oun* – perhaps better translated 'therefore'). This reminds us of the connection between this passage and the preceding (1:27-30). In the previous four verses, Paul encouraged good Christian citizenship, but with a focus on the need for Christian unity in light of external opposition to the church. He also connected the persecution of the Philippians with his own sufferings, thus emphasizing their mutuality of Christian fellowship. These themes resound again in 2:1-4. Paul again calls the church to unity, though this time not in opposition to external threats but in light of the very real danger that prideful dissensions within the congregation could tear it apart. Paul also appeals to their mutual fellowship with one another and with him, including their desire to increase his own joy (2:2), in order to motivate them to unity.

While the overall purpose of verse 1 is clear, there are certainly questions about the particulars. In general, Paul here is writing a series of conditionals ('if' clauses) that he takes to be true. These truths then ground his resulting instruction in verse 2. The main issues concern: What is the implied source of 'encouragement', 'consolation', etc.?

Although the translation above (the ESV) employs the word 'if' only once in translating the verse (undoubtedly to show the conceptual connectedness of all the 'if' clauses), the Greek emphasizes four different (but related) conditionals: 'So *if* there is any encouragement in Christ, *if* any comfort from love, *if* any participation in the Spirit, *if* any affection and sympathy...'

Paul definitely considers these conditionals ('if' clauses) to be true of the Christian life. There is encouragement in Christ. There is comfort from love, and participation in the Spirit. There is indeed affection and sympathy. We can prove Paul's affirmation of these conditionals not so much from the structure of the conditionals themselves (see Additional Notes), but from the theology of Paul and from his use of the word 'any'. Four times, Paul employs 'any' (*tis* or *ti*) to emphasize something like 'any ... at all'. We could well translate, 'so if there is *any* encouragement *at all* in Christ (and there is), if *any* comfort *at all* from love (and there is)...'

Furthermore, in order to provide theological evidence that Paul believes the 'if' clauses to be true, we observe that he certainly affirms elsewhere that there is indeed 'encouragement' [*paraklēsis*] to be found 'in Christ'. God Himself is the 'God of encouragement' (Rom. 15:5; cf. 2 Cor. 1:3; 2 Thess. 2:16), the Scriptures are sources of encouragement (Rom 15:4), and encouragement comes through mutual edification in the church (2 Cor. 1:4), including through those who are specially gifted for the task (Rom. 12:8; 1 Cor. 14:3). It hardly needs to be argued that Paul also envisions the Christian life as one lived in love, spiritual comfort, fellowship, affection, and sympathy.

But herein lies the interpretive rub. Is Paul assuming that these benefits in verse 1 stem directly from God Himself (i.e., it is God that encourages, comforts, etc.)? Or is Paul insisting that such benefits come from the mutual fellowship of believers with one another? After all, when we listed sources of Christian encouragement in the preceding paragraph, we found evidence in Paul's own writings that God is the 'God of encouragement' and that fellow believers encourage one another. Similarly, many of the other Christian blessings listed in verse 1 (love, comfort, fellowship, affection, and sympathy) also stem both from our direct relationship with God Himself (in Christ through the Holy Spirit) and from our relationships with one another in the church. Yet, even as we recognize this interpretive dilemma, we must allow the possibility that these two questions frame a false dichotomy. Could not such benefits (encouragement, comfort, and all the rest) come both directly from God and through God's people?

As we seek to grapple with these questions, it appears important that we note the connectedness between verses 1 and 2 in this context. Verse 2 clearly focuses on human interaction within the church, so it makes some sense that verse 1previously acknowledges the mutuality of their fellowship with one another. Believers provide encouragement, con-solation, affection and sympathy to one another in the Christian community; therefore, they ought also to be unified in mind and love. A human origin of these Christian blessings thus cannot be ruled out.

Nevertheless, the encouragement they receive is also found 'in Christ' – that is, in union with Him. Such encouragement stems from the God of encouragement, but also flows through their mutuality of participating together in union with Christ. Similarly, when the text mentions their 'participation in the Spirit' (better translated 'fellowship of the Spirit' as mentioned below), we can envision both a vertical and a horizontal dimension – church members are both connected in fellowship with God through the Spirit and in mutual fellowship with one another. The other blessings (consolation, love, affection, sympathy) can similarly be said to ultimately stem from God, but also refer to how the individuals in the church respond to one another.

Therefore, Paul is reminding believers of the many benefits they have in their Christian fellowship – benefits that stem directly from God but also flow through mutual loving relationships within the church body. In light of these benefits, Paul will call for Christian unity. It is important to note that such benefits provide consolation in times of external persecution (thus connecting us with verses 1:27-30), but they also highlight the mutuality of congregational Christian life in corporate union with Christ (thus reminding us of the need to remain in congregational Christian unity, as per Paul's appeal in 2:2ff.).

Before we proceed to the next verses, there is more we can say about each item listed in these conditionals. The word here translated 'encouragement' (*paraklēsis*) can also be variously translated 'exhortation, comfort, consolation'; here it focuses on the emboldening of another person for action or on the offering of comfort to another person. Thus it involves instilling someone with courage or cheer. This encouragement is found 'in Christ' – a phrase we have already met and discussed in Philippians 1:1, 13, 26. This indicates that the encouragement is rooted in the mutual connectedness of being in the sphere of Christ's lordship, fellowship, and blessing.

The second conditional mentions 'comfort from love', with 'comfort' (*paramuthion*) implying that Christian love provides consolation to the Christian community. There is an obvious overlap in meaning between such consolation and the 'encouragement' found in Christ in the previous conditional (indeed the Greek cognates of *paramuthion* and *paraklēsis* are often found connected together – see also 1 Cor. 14:3; 1 Thess. 2:12; 5:14). Here the consolation stems from 'love' (in the Greek genitive case). Again the question arises: is this comfort from God's love, or from the mutual love in the Christian community? And again the answer that most commends itself is 'both'. Just as the Philippians are mutually in Christ and thus receive encouragement both from communing with Christ and with one another, so the love that God has poured out on them in Christ overflows into a mutuality of love for one another.

'Participation in the Spirit' could be more literally translated 'fellowship of the Spirit'. The word 'fellowship' (*koinōnia*, above translated as 'participation') refers to a close association that involves mutual interests and sharing with one another (see BDAG, s.v.). This is not merely fellowship in the subjective sense (in which a person emotionally feels he or she is enjoying the company of others), but it implies a more objective formal association/group. Christians belong to such an association, and that has the consequent consolation of meaning that we face this life (with all its joys and sorrows) together. Moreover, this particular association or fellowship is 'of the Spirit'. Given that Biblical Greek originally had no capitalization, immediately we must ask: Is that fellowship with the [Holy] Spirit (with a capital 'S'), or is this a fellowship of human souls/spirits (with a lower-case 's')? The mutuality of souls and minds in the congregation commended in verse 2 could be used to support the latter option (a fellowship of a unity of human 'spirit'). However, Paul elsewhere speaks of Christians as those in fellowship with the Holy Spirit (as is certain in 2 Cor. 13:13). Christian fellowship is certainly a joint association of human believers in Christ called by His gospel (Phil. 1:5). However, Christians are also mutually in fellowship with the very God of the universe, with His Son (1 Cor. 1:9; cf. 10:16; Phil. 3:10), and with the Holy Spirit (cf. 1 John 1:3, 6, 7). In sum, Paul says, 'if there is any formal mutual association of Christians with the Holy Spirit (and there is)...'

In the final conditional 'if' clause, Paul refers to 'affection and sympathy'. He has already mentioned his 'affection' toward the Philippians (see notes on 1:8). The Greek word *splankna* portrays the seat of emotions, and hence the affection that stems from a fondness toward others. In Paul's writings, the term is otherwise used of human fondness for another person.[1] On the other hand, Paul employs the word here translated 'sympathy' (*oiktirmoi*) elsewhere to refer to God's merciful and compassionate demeanor towards His people (Rom. 12:1; 2 Cor. 1:3), which is to be emulated as Christians act compassionately toward one another (Col. 3:12). It again appears likely that these blessings in the Christian community of 'affection and sympathy' stem from God, whose fondness and compassion for His children flows into a mutuality of affection and sympathy for one another.

In sum, this verse reminds the Philippian church of the many great blessings they have in their congregational fellowship in Christ. These blessings stem from the Trinitarian God, whose encouragement, consolation, love, fellowship, sympathy and affection has been poured out on the community. Yet, the community itself, as a mutual association of Christ's followers, also imitates their God in encouraging, consoling, and loving one another. With such bounteous congregational benefits, it only makes sense that the believers in Philippi stand together, not only united against their persecutors but also unified in putting off all prideful dissensions in their midst.

---

1 2 Cor. 6:12; 7:15; Phil. 1:8; Col. 3:12; Philem. 7, 12, 20.

Today, we too should remember how God blesses the church with such great gifts. And, if we have experienced any small taste of such affection, fellowship, love and consolation, then we too must champion the unity of the church and put off all prideful dissension.

...complete my joy by being of the same mind, having the same love, being in full accord and of one mind (2:2).
This verse continues one long sentence in Greek from 2:1-4. Since the conditionals of verse 1 are undoubtedly true of the church, Paul now admonishes the congregation to Christian unity.

Although the ultimate call is for Christians to be united in mind, heart and soul, the imperative to the Philippians is actually to 'complete my joy'. Paul elsewhere invokes this verb 'complete' (*pleroō*) to refer to filling up someone with joy (Rom. 15:13; 2 Tim. 1:4), as well as filling someone with (among other things) knowledge (Rom. 15:14; Col. 1:9) and comfort (2 Cor. 7:4). Earlier we encountered the Greek word when Paul prayed that the congregation would be 'filled with the fruit of righteousness' (1:11).

We have already noted that 'joy' is a recurring theme in this epistle (see notes on 1:4 and 1:18). Paul makes his prayer for the Philippians with joy (1:4). He even refers to the Philippian church as his 'joy and crown' (4:1). He already rejoices in the Philippian church, and now he asks its members to fill his joy to overflowing.

Paul is certain of the love the believers of this church have for him, and so he knows that their love for him is an effective way to motivate their unity – together they will seek to bring joy to their father in the faith, to the apostle who founded the church, and to the man for whom they all have such affection. In related ways, Paul elsewhere can encourage others in their Christian walks through their desire to bring joy to their beloved apostle.[2]

This verse is actually a bit more complex in Greek than proper English style will allow translators to put into modern English. After the imperative ('complete my joy'), there is

---

2 See Rom. 15:32; 16:19; 2 Cor. 2:3; 7:7, 9, 13, 16; 1 Thess. 2:19-20; Col. 2:5; 2 Tim. 1:4; Philem. 7.

a central purpose, followed by three modifiers. The Greek could be represented graphically something like this:

> Complete my joy
>   in order that you think the same thing
>   having the same love
>   [being] fellow-souled
>   thinking the one thing

The purpose clause spells out how the Philippians can increase Paul's joy. The ESV translates this clause 'by being of the same mind', although literally the Greek reads: 'in order that you think the same thing'. The purpose clause here functions in a slightly unusual way to provide the necessary outcome (and hence the presumed manner) of increasing Paul's joy.

Notice that each of the three modifiers emphasizes the initial call to unity. How do you 'be of the same mind' or 'think the same thing'? Well, you participate in a mutual love, with a sense of mutuality of soul, and focusing your thoughts together on the same single thing. Notice also the almost complete overlap between the purpose clause ('think the same thing') and the last of the three modifiers ('thinking the one thing'). This repetition serves to emphasize the initial call to unity of mind.

Significantly, the call to unity in the purpose clause ('think the same thing') is identical to the Greek later in Philippians 4:2, where the Greek literally reads, 'I entreat Euodia and I entreat Syntyche *to think the same thing* in the Lord.' The level of correspondence between these verses indicates that, even here in 2:2, Paul is already introducing a call to Christian unity that has specific import in the current divisions at Philippi between these two women. In other words, as noted earlier, this is not a hypothetical call to Christian unity at Philippi. There is a real, on-the-ground urgency to Paul's directive.

Paul often calls for unity in the churches. He even employs these same Greek words ('think the same thing') in Romans 12:16 and 15:5. Also note 2 Corinthians 13:11, where he says: 'Finally, brothers, rejoice. Aim for restoration, comfort one another, agree with one another [lit. 'think the same thing'], live in peace; and the God of love and peace will be with you.' Quite possibly there were divisions that existed in these churches as well, with disharmony between Jew and Gentile believers in Rome and factional divisions at Corinth (see especially 1 Cor. 1:10). Nonetheless, for Paul, this mandate serves as an important theme in his Christian ethics: churches are to be unified in their thinking.

What this looks like is spelled out in the three modifying clauses that concern all aspects of human life together – mind, heart, and soul. As to heart, Christians are to have the 'same love'. There is some ambiguity here as to whether this refers to love for Christ/God or to love for one another (if we must choose, the former seems a bit more likely). What is certainly evident is that Christians should resonate even in their deepest affections. Their souls should share in the communal bond, and together they should think unified thoughts.

Sometimes we fear this level of unity. 'Thinking the same thing' could sound a bit too much like communal 'group think', which appears vaguely irrational, even dangerous. Surely there is room for discussion and debate. And indeed, there likely should be. Paul was certainly one to contend for his viewpoints among his fellow believers, all the while arguing both from Scripture and from the Good News of Christ's death and resurrection. Truth cannot be sacrificed simply to create some artificial peace. Yet there comes a point at which unity should be the prevailing virtue – when, after the discussion and careful sharing of views, the church mutually agrees, out of love for Christ and a desire to serve one another, to live and minister alongside one another in full harmony for the sake of Christ and the spread of the gospel.

I am reminded as a Western Christian of my first visit to an African church in Ghana. At that time, the church meetings in my local home church in the United States were quick, decisive, and businesslike – they operated based on Robert's Rules of Order and on a simple vote of the majority. All it took to win the vote was a strong voice, the right connections within the church, a knowledge of aggressive democratic political machinations, and a belligerent stubbornness that said, 'It must be done my way.' To the victor (and to his or her allies) went the spoils, while the minority was left fuming in the corner. Little surprise that my home church eventually split, leaving wounds among many that have not truly healed to this day.

By contrast, many of the churches we saw in Ghana operated based on consensus. There would be no decision until all in the church agreed. Everyone ultimately had to vote the same way. Hours of discussion were often held concerning seemingly simple matters as people listened to one another, negotiated, and prayed together. A decision sometimes had to be delayed a few days until a consensus could be reached. Yet although the process was much less efficient than a simple application of Robert's Rules, the resulting consensus allowed for much more (and much deeper) concord than my own church had experienced. Now, I am not so naïve as to believe that all went smoothly in this Ghanaian church. Political alignments existed under the surface, decisions could at times occur at an excruciatingly slow pace, and the church was still made up of sinful human beings seeking to have things their own way. Nevertheless, it did cause me to wonder whether my Western drive for efficiency and for majority rule at times ended up generating disunity, and thus could even on occasion be at odds with the gospel.

In any case, whatever our church system, we must seek to be of 'one mind', 'fellow-souled', and 'loving the same thing'. This certainly applies to the church at the local level. Each congregation should actively seek a unity of purpose and an atmosphere of loving communion. And as individual Christians, we must honestly ask ourselves whether we are contributing to the unity of the church, whether any of our actions or attitudes have injured the peace of the church, and whether our desire to 'have it our way' has created dissension in the communion of saints.

Of course, the history of Christianity also makes us aware of the great divisions between our various denominations and church bodies. Sitting in my home office, I can quickly think of more than a dozen different Christian denominations within a few miles from my house. Here is a partial list: Lutheran (at least three different denominations), Episcopalian (at least two different alignments), Presbyterian (at least four different groups), Methodist, Baptist (three or more varieties), Chinese Baptist, Evangelical Free, Church of Christ, Christian Church, Assemblies of God, Pentecostal, Roman Catholic, and Greek Orthodox. Each has its own history, theological emphases, and rituals. Of course, one solution has been attempted repeatedly throughout church history – that of unifying Christianity by building congregations loosely connected but not aligned with pre-existing denominations. This often ends up, however, generating new denominations (whether in name or essence), and I can also think of a half-dozen examples of those churches just down the road. In any case, the drive to not align with a denomination is itself a result of disunity and a refusal to cooperate with others. Parachurch bodies compete on university campuses or at athletic venues for the same students. Seminaries train students in specific traditions. These divisions make apparent the great distance between the current state of the church (especially in the West) and Paul's call to unity among the Christians in Philippi.

Nonetheless, some of these divisions, at least at their inception, certainly appear (even in retrospect) to have been necessary. Whenever the gospel becomes obscured in a church, or the leadership becomes immoral and entrenched, or the debates become intractable, or the mission of the church is lost, reforming movements tend to arise. Such was the case when Martin Luther stood his ground before the Roman Catholic Church and the Holy Roman Emperor at Worms. And yet, with his decided appeal to conscience and to the individual understanding of Scripture, Luther also opened the Protestant churches to increasing fights and divisions based on similar appeals to conscience and to divergent Biblical interpretations. Certainly there can be no room for heresy, which undermines the gospel. Yet even among the orthodox, theological differences exist concerning such matters as the precise meaning and practice of the sacraments, the question of the sovereignty of God and the free will of humankind, the import and enumeration of spiritual gifts, the correct relationship between the church and a nation-state, and the proper internal governmental structure of the church (just to name a few key issues). The contrary option of a magisterium of scholars or churchmen that controls and coerces the uniformity of the church has repeatedly resulted in authoritarian suppression, dangerous theology, and capitulation to syncretism with worldly paganism and political systems – all under the banner of church unity.

Whether a church based on individual conscience or a church based on an authoritative clergy, both paths have their grave dangers.

How ought we negotiate these complex realities? First, we must embrace the call to unity (both in our local churches and in our global relationships). Second, we must also regretfully allow that there are times when division is necessary. Certainly Paul himself, and his contemporaries and successors, took courageous stands for truth (consider, for example, the stand Paul makes in his letter to the Galatians). In particular, they were willing to separate themselves (with great sadness) from advocates of heresy that cut at the very root of the gospel of Christ.[3] Third, we must be very, very slow to seek division, and we must look for opportunities for a return to unity. Fourth, our own attitude through it all must be one of humility – and it is to this last point that Paul turns in the next verse. These are some principles – consistent I think with Paul's overall approach to such matters. It demands great wisdom, and (I should hasten to add) immense love, in order to best live out these principles in our own sinfulness and in the midst of a church made up of fallen people (albeit redeemed souls in the process of sanctification). Yet we all must engage this call to concord in our churches and in our own spheres of relationship; there we must all seek the peace and unity of the church.

Do nothing from rivalry or conceit, but in humility count others more significant than yourselves. Let each of you look not only to his own interests, but also to the interests of others (2:3-4).

Any unity in the church demands some give and take, some willingness to compromise. That willingness requires us to be open to not getting our own way. In short, it demands humility. This is Paul's great insight here (influenced undoubtedly by our Lord Himself). So he calls for Christian humility, and looks to Christ as the great exemplar of such humility (2:5-11).

The great enemies of a united church are rivalry and conceit. 'Rivalry' (*eritheia*) is the term Paul used earlier to describe the

---

3 E.g., 1 Cor. 5:5; 1 Tim. 1:20; Jude 3-19; 2 John 7-11; Rev. 2:2, 14-16.

motives of those who were preaching the gospel with the goal of adding to his travails in prison (Phil. 1:17). It essentially refers to 'selfish ambition', and is among the list of traits that are the opposite of the fruit of the Spirit (Gal. 5:20). Paul cautions about such selfish ambition bringing God's wrath, especially when combined with disobedience (Rom. 2:8). James, too, considers disorder in the church to stem from such selfish ambition (James 3:14, 16). Elsewhere, when Paul is concerned about disunity in Corinth, he lists the hostility that stems from such rivalry among the other markers of such disharmony: 'quarreling, jealousy, anger, hostility [*eritheia*], slander, gossip, conceit, and disorder.'

The meaning of 'conceit' here clearly overlaps with rivalry and selfish ambition. The term *kenodoxia* has two components: *kenos* ('empty') and *doxia* ('glory'). Thus the old King James translation understood this as 'vainglory'. By Paul's day, the word had been used for centuries after these two stems had first been put together to form *keno+doxia*, so one might wonder whether the etymology is determinative here. Nevertheless, the continued use of *kenos* compounds in Paul's Greek likely still conveyed that sense of futility (or emptiness) that such conceited pursuits entail. Perhaps the English word 'vanity' best maintains similar connotations.

What unites 'rivalry' and 'conceit' is a deep desire to have things 'my way'. 'My way or the highway', as the saying goes. If we all seek to have things our own way, then rivalry and quarreling is the natural outcome. Paul's cure is to call for a community of humble Christians who look out more for the interests of others than for their own glory.

Such 'humility' is a recurring theme in Paul's writings, especially in the context of relationships in the church. He directs the Ephesians, 'with all humility and gentleness, with patience, bear with one another in love' (Eph. 4:2; cf. Rom. 12:16; also see 1 Pet. 5:5-6). To the Colossians, he charges (Col. 3:12-14): 'Put on then, as God's chosen ones, holy and beloved, compassion, kindness, humility, meekness, and patience, bearing with one another and, if one has a complaint against another, forgiving each other; as the Lord has forgiven you, so you also must forgive. And above all these put on love, which binds everything together in perfect harmony.' Oh, that our churches were indeed marked by such character!

This humility calls forth a mindset that considers others as 'more significant than yourselves'. Rather than seeking our self-interest and vain conceits, we must discipline our minds to put the needs of others and the concerns of the church before our own. Many English translations add 'only' or 'merely' to the Greek text ('Let each of you look not *only* to his own interests'), in part because it is likely that the second clause in verse four contains the word 'also' ('but *also* to the interests of others'; see Additional Note). Yet since Paul's original Greek does not include the word 'only', the Greek is starker and puts heavy emphasis on the need to focus on other people's interests.

When English translations use the word 'interests' they are actually trying to render a Greek phrase that is even more generic: 'their own things' versus 'the things of others' (the Greek merely adds articles to substantivize both 'their things' and 'things of others'). An overly literal translation of verse 4 would thus read: '…each not looking to their own things but each also looking to the things of others.' Therefore, in a sense the Greek is not limited to merely the 'interests' of others, but to all matters that concern other people. In short, our focus is not to be on ourselves, but on how we can serve others.

Can this be taken too far? I was recently asked in a church about the difference between appropriate self-denial and self-abuse. In the American vernacular, does this text call us to become 'doormats' for other people to step on? In answering this question we must acknowledge that this issue is not Paul's concern here. He does not address the appropriate limitations on his directive, thus we should be careful to distinguish our advice on this matter from apostolic mandate. Still, wisdom may help us discern some qualifications.

First, Paul's words here have their first referent in putting off discord in the church. While other applications may be appropriate, and Christians should be appropriately humble in all aspects of life, Paul's directive especially seeks to achieve a unified Christian church. Therefore, discernment must be exercised to know when the call to 'count others more significant than ourselves' applies outside of situations involving Christian unity. Second, it is clear that Paul is talking about a volitional putting off of one's own interests for the sake of others. This does not give sanction for the kind of self-abuse that goes beyond one's own willful commitment to others and substitutes instead a co-dependent subjugation of oneself to the abuses of others due to one's own psychological inability to set up appropriate boundaries. Third, the self-denial here is oriented toward the spiritual benefit of others and the building up of the Christian church. We should not unthinkingly assent to the desires and demands of others, rather we must conscientiously seek other people's best interests and the unified growth of Christ's church. Sometimes this means we must 'stand up' to others for the sake of their long-term best interests (whether they understand our good motives or not).

Nevertheless, while we acknowledge that some boundaries may be appropriate concerning the self-denial that Paul requires, we must not blunt the force of this command. In order for Christ's church to reflect the unified fellowship we are called to have in the Spirit, we must each contribute humbly toward the good of everyone else in the church. Certainly, this provides a strong cure to the dangers of discord and disunity within a Christian assembly. If we would all practice humility and consider others' interests to be more important than our own, then we would much more readily achieve a unity of mind, heart, and soul in our congregations.

Summary
Paul here begins with known truths of the Christian life. As Christ's followers, we together have the privilege of encouragement and comfort from the Trinitarian God and the joy of community with one another. The Spirit has knit us together in fellowship with the God of the universe and with each other. There is thus indeed affection and sympathy poured out from God upon, and within, the Christian church.

If God has privileged us to be united in Christian communion, then how should we conduct ourselves in our churches? Naturally, we should be unified in loving fellowship together with our heavenly Father, brought into one family by the death and resurrection of His Son, and filled with the Holy Spirit in Christ. For Paul, to see the Philippian church in such unity would fill him with joy. Yet he knows that the seeds of disharmony have taken root (4:2), and so he motivates these Christians to unity through their desire to bring joy again to their earthly father in the faith, the apostle Paul.

Such unity is not a mere outward show without effect on the inner lives of believers. Rather, it comes from the commitment of each individual to a collective agreement of heart, mind, and soul. In order to achieve such concord, each must put off his or her self-interests and vain conceits, and all must humbly seek the interests of the others in the community.

Theologically, we could rightly reflect on the Trinitarian nature of God Himself: how the Father, the Son, and the Holy Spirit exist in unceasing love and unity with one another. That is what holiness looks like; and that is what we, who are being recreated in His image, reflect when we are in unity with one another. Moreover, if the sum of the law is love (Rom. 13:9-10), and if love is thus the principal Christian virtue, then certainly a peaceful, unified harmony will be the result as Christians, out of love for one another, consider others to be valued and cherished.

How would your church look differently if this characterized God's people?

Questions for Personal Reflection:

1. What are some occasions in your Christian experience where you have found encouragement in Christ? Comfort from love? Fellowship in the Spirit? Affection and sympathy? How do these moments contribute to your desire to see Christ's church unified?

2. Paul instructs all the members in the church to 'think the same thing', to 'have the same love', and to be 'fellow-souled'. What do you find that is inviting about these commands? Is there anything that scares you about such a deep call to unity of thought, soul, and love? What would this look like in your congregation if it were really to happen? How close is your local church to achieving this level of unity? How have you helped the church reach this goal? And where have you stood in the way?

Philippians 2:1-4

3. How would you describe humility? In what ways have you recognized church disunity to have its roots in self-interest and a lack of humility among the members?

4. Where do you personally struggle to be humble? Give some examples of times you have been able to consider others to be more important than yourself. Are there occasions where one must stop considering others and look out for ourselves instead? Discuss.

Study Questions:

1. Paul continues his appeal to church unity. In what ways do you see verses 2:1-4 fitting together with 1:27-30? With 2:5-11? *same love and one mind* *Based on Christ*

2. In verse 2:1 what does Paul mean by 'encouragement in Christ'? By 'comfort from love'? By 'participation in the Spirit'? By 'affection and sympathy'?

3. Name some of the ways that you have found these descriptors in 2:1 to be true in your life and in the life of your church. How do these experiences contribute to your desire to see Christ's church unified?

4. In 2:2 Paul talks about the church having the 'same mind', the 'same love', 'full accord', and being of 'one mind.' How do these phrases interrelate? *unity, same priority and goals. God glorified*

5. How do you personally react when you are directed to be of the 'same mind' with someone else? Is this an easy concept for you to swallow, or does it seem hard at times? Is there anything that scares you about such a deep call to unity of thought, soul, and love?

6. What do you find inviting about these commands in 2:2? What would this look like in your congregation if it were really to happen? How close is your local church to achieving this level of unity? How have you helped the church reach this goal? And where have you stood in the way?

7. What are some practical steps that you can take to promote this kind of deep church unity? How can you as a group help encourage your church (or churches) to this end?

8. Name some ways that rivalry and conceit can inhibit church unity. Feel free to share personal stories where you have seen churches damaged by individuals with tendencies toward rivalry and conceit.

9. How does humility, and looking out for the interests of others, promote church unity? Can you name some 'success stories' where individuals acting in humility have helped to build up the unity in a church or Christian group?

10. Humility has long been central to Christian ethics, yet our own struggles against pride often seem insurmountable. What has been most helpful to you as you seek to grow in humility in Christ?

11. In light of your discussion of this passage and the previous passage (1:27-30), name some reasons why Paul commands the church to be unified. How important do you believe this command is relative to other ethical instructions in Scripture?

peace and *purity* of the church.

Additional Notes:
2:1 This series of conditionals in verse 1 are known as 'first-class conditionals' in Greek (since the Greek word *ei* is used in the 'if' clause). Some may mistakenly argue, merely on the basis of identifying these as first-class conditionals, that these 'if' clauses must certainly be true. In reality, however, first-class conditionals as a whole merely assert something for the sake of argument ('if' this is true, 'then' that follows); only the context can provide evidence as to whether the 'if' clause is indeed correct. Here, as is argued above, the context does inform us that these conditionals are true (both because of Paul's overall theology and because of his repeated use of the word 'any').

The complexities of interpreting the conditionals in verse 1 are well represented in O'Brien's 1991 commentary (pp. 166-76). He does a fine job of summarizing the wealth of different interpretive positions on this passage. His thoughts (and those of Fee, among others) inform some of the interpretive decisions above.

One issue not fully considered above concerns whether the opening clause ('if there is any encouragement in Christ') could refer to Paul's own word of exhortation/encouragement to the Philippian community (i.e., the exhortation of his epistle itself). Many commentators hold this position (which O'Brien refutes). Certainly, *paraklēsis* can be used to refer to a verbal appeal. More often, however, *paraklēsis* ('encouragement' or 'comfort') in Paul stems from sources other than preaching or exhortation (cf. Rom. 15:4, 5; 2 Cor. 1:3, 4; 2 Thess. 2:16). Combined with the other three conditional clauses in verse 1, it appears most likely that Paul is referring to some privileged comfort the church has long experienced in Christ. As argued above, this encouragement comes from the God of all comfort who also gifts His people to comfort one another.

Also worthy of consideration is Fee's suggestion that the 'affection and sympathy' in the last clause refer to *Paul's* affection and sympathy for the Philippians (see Fee's 1995 commentary, pp. 178-9, 182). Fee distinguishes here between references to the Trinity in the first three clauses ('encouragement' comes from Christ, 'consolation of love' from the Father, and 'fellowship' from the Spirit) and a presumed reference to Paul in the last ('affection and sympathy' come from Paul). This has two advantages and one significant drawback. The first advantage is that it connects with Paul's appeal to the Philippians to 'complete my joy' in verse 2 – the Philippians are motivated by Paul's affection and sympathy for them in order to return joy to him. The second is that it highlights the Trinitarian nature of the first three clauses (drawing on a parallel with 2 Cor. 13:13). The significant drawback, however, is that it requires Paul's language to lack 'rhetorical precision' (in Fee's own words, p. 178), shifting abruptly from a focus on the Trinitarian God to a focus on Paul without any actual indicators in the text. Paul's conceptual leap would thus be quite confusing. It seems preferable to think that Paul knew what he was doing as he moved from clause to clause, and that he expected his audience to follow. It is more likely that Paul draws on benefits that are both Trinitarian in origin and part of the mutual fellowship within the church. In this way, because the fellowship of the church is also with Paul, he can connect this mutual fellowship in Christ to his appeal that the Philippians complete his joy in 2:2.

The interested student can pursue the complex discussions of this verse in larger commentaries on the Greek text (especially in O'Brien's fine work). Virtually all commentators agree that the broader purposes of Paul in this verse are clear: Paul is appealing to the truth of Christian benefits in verse 1 in order to commend church unity in verse 2. This much is certain. And with this, we can give thanks to God that we, as Christians, possess encouragement in Christ, consolation of love, fellowship with the Spirit, and affection and sympathy.

2:4 In the clause 'but *also* to the interests of others,' there is some variation in the Greek manuscripts. Many Western manuscripts (including the Old Latin translation) omit the word 'also', which would put heavy emphasis on personal self-abandonment for the sake of other fellow believers. However, a large number of Greek manuscripts, from a variety of locales and families, do include 'also', so we think it likely that this word goes back to Paul himself.

Prayer May 15

Joyce - sick

Last ELL today

Julie and baby for two weeks.

Zach - follow up interview for new job.
wet sell

Marsha - int. licensing went through
High School launch all the prep is happening n

Unity in Christ — encouraging and modeling

Bonnie - friend Dot - moved into nursery facility fell
broke bones in pelvic area.

Prespitary this week

7

Christ's Example of Humility and Exaltation
(Philippians 2:5-11)

⁵Have this mind among yourselves, which is yours in Christ Jesus, ⁶who, though he was in the form of God, did not count equality with God a thing to be grasped, ⁷but made himself nothing, taking the form of a servant, being born in the likeness of men. ⁸And being found in human form, he humbled himself by becoming obedient to the point of death, even death on a cross. ⁹Therefore God has highly exalted him and bestowed on him the name that is above every name, ¹⁰so that at the name of Jesus every knee should bow, in heaven and on earth and under the earth, ¹¹and every tongue confess that Jesus Christ is Lord, to the glory of God the Father.

A missionary friend of mine recently wrote about an experience her team had among the Inapang people of Papua New Guinea. They presented a drama of the story of the cross in one of the villages, and during the discussion afterward, one of the men said of Jesus, 'We men, we wouldn't do that. If we had that power and our enemies wanted to kill us, we would show off our power and burn them all up. He is God. He isn't like us men. He didn't do it that way. He died willingly for us.'

That simple, yet profound, statement gets at the very essence of this passage. 'He died willingly for us.' Jesus' death atones for our sin, and simultaneously, His sacrifice provides the perfect example of humility that every Christian is called to imitate.

In the preceding context of this passage, Paul focused on church unity (1:27–2:4). He has already recognized that, in order for a church to be unified in mind, love, and spirit (2:1-2), each member must practice humility toward every other (2:3-4). Such humility considers others to be more significant (2:3) and looks out for their interests (2:4). Who best models that kind of humility? Our Lord and Savior.

Yet while Paul is grounding his call to church unity in the humility of the Messiah, he can hardly restrain himself from expounding on the great Christological truths of who Jesus is, what Jesus has done, and the glory that awaits Christ's return. The humility of Christ also serves as the encouragement to all His followers of the great eschatological truth that exaltation follows humility. This is not an exaltation that is self-glorying or self-reveling. Rather, all things are done ultimately for the glory of God the Father (2:11). Yet our Lord Himself instructs us that the 'first will be last, and the last will be first' (Matt. 19:30; 20:16; Mark 9:35; 10:31; Luke 13:30). Those who serve the gospel in humility in this life, receive their appreciation in the coming Kingdom.

This whole passage appears to be a Christological meditation on Jesus' own teaching that 'the Son of Man came not to be served, but to serve, and to give himself as a ransom for others' (Mark 10:45; Matt. 20:28). Jesus announces this in response to His disciples, who, having just heard again that their Lord is about to suffer death and then be raised to life (Mark 10:33-34), respond by debating which among them would have the seats of honor in His kingdom (10:35-41). Pride of position is causing disunity among His disciples, so Jesus reminds them that the economy of His kingdom does not imitate worldly power politics but that God exalts the humble (10:42-44). He then describes His death in terms of both atonement and example (10:45). His blood is a 'ransom', buying sinners back for God's kingdom, and this ransom is performed as a living example by the Lord, who has stooped down to suffer a shameful death in order to become a servant 'for others'. So we do well to remember that whether or not Paul is overtly referencing this episode in the life of Christ, he is definitely drawing on Jesus' self-understanding of His ministry.

Here, Paul drives home the truth that our Christian lives should imitate the meekness of our Savior as we live humbly in unity with one another.

An Early Christian Hymn?
One significant debate surrounding this passage concerns whether Paul quotes an early Christian hymn. The genre 'hymn' in such academic discussions may imply a worshipful song, but this term has also been understood to include quasi-poetic liturgical texts or highly stylized confessions. The current debate breaks down into at least three key questions: Is Philippians 2:6-11 in the form of an early hymn? If so, did Paul write it himself, or did he borrow it? If he borrowed it, is he intending to affirm all its particulars? The scholarly conversation has been quite complex, so we will discuss some of the most important basic concerns, leaving a bit more for the 'Additional Notes' at the end of the chapter.

Let us begin with the third question: did Paul intend to affirm all the details of this passage? Although this is not an issue that many commentators overtly discuss, it is in reality the most vital issue. On the surface, this appears to be a reasonable query. After all, Paul's main concern (as we have already noted) involves Jesus' humility. Yet 2:5-11 contains much that is not directly connected to Jesus' humility. In particular, some might suggest that the whole discussion of Jesus' deity in 2:6 and His exaltation in 2:9-11 actually appears to redirect the discussion away from His humility (and thus away from what Paul wishes to affirm in his quotation of this hymn). It could even be claimed that such an emphasis on exaltation undermines the assertion that Jesus models humility.

In response, however, we should make several points. First, in certain theological contexts (especially those involving Christology), Paul often ends up moving beyond his central point to the general work and purpose of God through Christ (e.g., Rom. 1:3-6; Col. 2:8-15). At times, it is as if Paul cannot constrain himself to discuss one particular dimension of the gospel without invoking the bigger picture. So, in short, this is consistent with Paul's style elsewhere.

Second, the theology of this great passage is certainly in harmony with the rest of Paul's writings. For example, Paul elsewhere firmly asserts Jesus' deity in a variety of ways. Sometimes, he uses language that directly affirms Jesus as God (Rom. 9:5; Titus 2:13), as do other early Christian authors.[1] He constantly refers to Jesus with titles that Jewish people reserved for God in religious contexts, such as 'Lord' and 'Savior'.[2] Furthermore, Paul employs Trinitarian formulas that set Jesus Christ alongside the Holy Spirit and God the Father.[3] And other passages convey Paul's complex, high Christology (e.g., Col. 1:15-20; 2:9-10). Moreover, Paul rarely discusses Christ's death apart from His resurrection.[4] And Paul strongly affirms the exaltation of Jesus, the Messiah, whom ultimately all of creation and humanity (whether willingly or grudgingly) will acknowledge as Lord.[5]

Third, the early church often closely connected humility and exaltation, following the lead of the Old Testament Scriptures,[6] and Jesus Himself emphasizes the connection when addressing His followers.[7] Those who are humble in this life are promised that God will care for them and exalt them. We have already noted how Jesus taught this, and thus His followers also did so after Him. It is no surprise then that Paul would gladly discuss the exaltation of Jesus, intending for that also to serve as a motivator to Christian humility. As we have died in Christ, so also will we be raised with Him and exalted with Him. Thus, we are motivated all the more in this life to die to ourselves for the sake of others, so that we, and those around us, may be exalted in eternal life with Christ in His glory.

Fourth, the discussion of the deity of Christ in 2:6 serves to highlight all the more the humility of our Lord, who would leave those privileges of deity aside in order to die on a cross. These are vital elements in Paul's thinking and integral to showing just how humble Jesus has been.

---

1 E.g., John 1:1; 20:28; Heb. 1:8; 2 Pet. 1:1.
2 Phil. 1:2; 3:20; cf. Rom. 1:7; 5:1; 10:9; 1 Cor. 1:2-3; 8:6.
3 1 Cor. 12:4-6; 2 Cor. 13:13; Eph. 4:4-6.
4 Phil. 3:10; Rom. 6:5; 14:9; 1 Cor. 15:3ff.
5 1 Cor. 15:23-28; Eph. 1:19-23; 2 Thess. 1:6-10.
6 Prov. 3:34; Ezek. 17:24; 21:26; James 4:6, 10; 1 Pet. 5:5-6; cf. 2 Cor. 11:7.
7 Luke 14:11; 18:14; Matt. 23:12.

Therefore, it seems clear that, whether these verses were Paul's own creation or a hymn he borrowed from the confessional liturgy, Paul theologically affirms the whole of this passage. Even if this were proven to be a pre-Pauline hymn, had he been uncomfortable with any of its theological content, Paul could have easily curtailed the citation. Yet, the theological overlap with his writings is quite profound, with the result that we can be certain that Paul very consciously, and with full intentionality, recorded here in Philippians the entirety of this profound passage. Whether or not it originated from Paul's own hand, this passage clearly affirms Pauline theological truths.

This then raises the question of whether Paul authored these verses himself, or borrowed them from early church hymnody, confession or liturgical prose. In my estimation, this question cannot be answered with full certainty. As just noted, the thoughts of this passage overlap completely with Pauline theology elsewhere, so we cannot distinguish 'pre-Pauline' material based on content. Moreover, there simply is not a large enough sample of words from Paul's writing style to proclaim whether each and every word in this passage matches 'Pauline vocabulary'. Four Greek words are unique to this passage in the Pauline canon (*morphē, harpagmos, huperupsoō, katachthonios* – 'form', 'grasp', 'highly exalted', 'under the earth'), though cognate forms of the first three are well known in Paul. However, such a percentage of unique occurrences of vocabulary appears commonly in various passages in his writings. So Paul could quite plausibly be the original author. Still, there is also nothing to preclude that someone else wrote this passage (possibly someone among Paul's own circle), and that Paul valued his or her work enough to include it in his letter. Both remain plausible alternatives.

One major reason scholars are so focused on the authorship of these few verses involves the academic concern to trace pre-Pauline theology. There are certainly places where Paul appears to cite creeds or hymns that he is 'passing down'.[8] Some scholars believe that by isolating these pre-Pauline creeds/hymns and studying them, we can arrive at an even

---

8 E.g., 1 Cor. 15:3ff.; cf. 1 Tim. 1:15; 3:1; 2 Tim. 2:11-13.

earlier stage in Christian thought – a stage that preceded Paul, instructed him, and was later passed on by him. In this regard, a passage representing pre-Pauline 'high Christology' (i.e., a passage that exalts Jesus as God) would be a plum prize. Yet this text does not possess, as some do, the clear assertion by Paul that he is passing down previous tradition (contrast with 1 Corinthians 15:3 and 2 Timothy 2:11). For that reason, it seems any claim that Philippians 2:5-11 is a pre-Pauline hymn must be made with some modesty.

The last question to address then is the most fundamental. Is this truly a 'hymn'? Was it a passage that was originally penned for liturgical or confessional use? Certainly, it contains 'elevated prose'. It possesses a fine rhythm, an artistry of expression, and an immense confessional content in a little package. It has served throughout subsequent church history in liturgical settings, and is indeed well suited to that purpose. For these reasons, it can be called a hymn. However, if we go on to postulate how it would have been used in the earliest church (for example, whether it was sung or recited) we quickly find ourselves asking questions we cannot answer with any high degree of confidence.

If one agrees that this passage has strong liturgical elements, then it becomes natural to attempt to delineate various poetic lines or strophes. Here is where scholars most disagree, with many conflicting attempts at reconstructing the number of poetic lines. Proposals can range anywhere from two to six or more strophic divisions in 2:6-11. The fact that there is such a wide array of possibilities should caution us about the tentative nature of any conclusions here. As we ponder this question, these are some helpful principles:

(1) It is likely that the structure of the hymn revolves around the basic division between the two halves of the passage (2:6-8 and 2:9-11), with this division being signaled by the contrasting content (humility and exaltation), by the shift in subject of the verbs, and by the discourse transition marker 'therefore' (*dio* in 2:9) that connects these two portions.

(2) Structural proposals should be considered highly suspect if they rely on deleting certain words or clauses from the current text in order to reconstruct a hypothetical pre-Pauline 'hymn' (these proposals typically consider those

deleted clauses Paul's own later insertions, which disrupt the supposedly original poetic shape). Rather, in determining poetic lines, we should work as much as possible with the text as it has been passed down in Paul's own Greek in Philippians.

(3) The contents of the hymn are more determinative as to its meaning than its structure. I am thus most persuaded by viewing the passage as consisting of two parts (2:6-8 and 2:9-11), with each part consisting of nine (or possibly ten) short lines. However, the meaning of this great passage should not rest substantially on this (or any other) structural proposal.

In sum, it is worthwhile considering whether this is a hymn or not, and whether it is Paul's own work or a previous composition. However, we must be careful to note the limitations of our knowledge. Degrees of plausibility are the best we can hope for. Nonetheless, we can strongly affirm Paul's endorsement of the particulars of this passage. It certainly states theology with which he concurred, and it definitely furthers the purposes to which he applies it here in Philippians.

Have this mind among yourselves, which was also in Christ Jesus (2:5).
Paul now directly links the call he has made to Christian unity and humility to the example of Christ. For reasons that soon will be clear, the translation cited here follows the ESV footnote rather than the ESV main text.

There are three translational issues in rendering Paul's Greek into good English, each of which can affect the interpretation.

The first issue concerns the Greek pronoun 'you', which is plural (rendered above as 'yourselves'). Whereas English often does not have distinct plural and singular forms of the pronoun 'you', Greek clearly distinguishes them. Some English translations obscure the Greek plural here, rendering it 'Let this mind be *in you*' (KJV) or '*Your* attitude should be the same as that of Christ Jesus' (NIV). Thus in studying these translations, a reader could mistakenly assume that Paul's command is an admonition to individual Christians. However, both the Greek verb and the pronoun 'you' are plural, reminding us that Paul is still addressing the church as a whole. Paul is inviting church members to act together in imitating Christ's humility as individuals in community with one another. Each is to look out for the interests of all the others (2:4), and collectively we are to approach a unity of mind and purpose as a result (2:2).

The second issue concerns the relative clause ('which was also in Christ Jesus'). This translation from the ESV notes (similarly found in the KJV, NASB, etc.) provides a good literal rendering of the Greek. However, the RSV (and subsequently the main text of the ESV) obscures the Greek, rendering it: 'Have this mind among yourselves, which *is yours* in Christ Jesus.' Paul's original does not include 'is yours', though it does contain 'also' (see 'Additional Note' below for the technicalities). Thus the better translation ('which was also in Christ Jesus') brings out the Pauline truth that the church is to follow the same humble mindset that Christ Himself modeled.

The third issue concerns the main verb in the first clause (above translated as '*have* this mind…'). The Greek can most literally be translated by '*Think this thing* among yourselves….', but this would be awkward in English. Some translations, therefore, shift into the realm of 'attitude'. The NASB, for example, translates '*Have this attitude* in yourselves' (as does the NIV, quoted earlier). Other translations rightly attempt to retain the mental imagery exhibited in the verb, as does the ESV with '*Have this mind* among yourselves' (also the KJV cited above). Preserving the mental imagery is a definite improvement. However, all these major translations obscure a very important feature: the parallel Greek wording in 2:5 and 2:2 (and later in 4:2; cf. Rom. 15:5).

The verb 'think' here is the same verb employed in verse 2, where Paul instructs the church (twice!) to 'think the same thing'. By using the same verb in these two neighboring verses, Paul intentionally connects the call to think like Christ to the call to collective Christian unity of thought in 2:2. Let us recall that the earlier commentary on 2:2 suggested that that verse should be outlined like this:

> Complete my joy
> > in order that you *think the same thing*
> > > having the same love
> > > [being] fellow-souled
> > > *thinking the one thing*

To this let us add an outline of 2:5:

> *Think this thing* among you
>> which [thing] also was in Christ Jesus

And let us anticipate our literal rendering of verse 4:2:

> I entreat Euodia and I entreat Syntyche
>> *to think the same thing* in the Lord

When we observe the parallel Greek wording of these verses, it becomes all the more clear that Paul is connecting the model of humility found in Christ Jesus (2:5) to his call to unity in the Philippian church (2:2), and especially to his command that the present divisions between Euodia and Syntyche be abandoned for the sake of church unity (4:2).

In sum, Paul here is linking his appeal to Christian unity in 1:27–2:4 to the humility of Christ found in 2:6-8 (along with His eventual exaltation in 2:9-11). The mindset of the Christian should be identical in purpose to Christ's mindset. Jesus the Messiah was willing to give up the privileges of Lordship in order to suffer in our place on the cross. So we too must focus on the interests of others and direct our attentions to the unity of the church.

who, though he was in the form of God, did not count equality with God a thing to be grasped (2:6).
Jesus possessed the position of ultimate privilege, but He stripped Himself of His authority as God in order to humbly represent humanity through His salvific death.

This verse begins a long description of the Messiah Jesus ('Christ Jesus' in 2:5) in the structure of an extended relative clause (through at least 2:8 in the Greek). One can compare this with other confessional Christological passages in the New Testament that begin with a relative pronoun (Col. 1:15; 1 Tim 3:16; cf. Heb. 1:3).

This verse reminds the reader of Jesus' pre-existence as the second member of the Trinity. When we speak of 'pre-existence', we actually mean His eternal existence prior to His incarnation in human flesh (cf. John 3:13; 6:62; 17:5). Clearly this verse presupposes not only that Jesus existed before He was Mary's child, but also that He was fully sovereign, especially over His decision to remain 'equal with God' or to become 'born in the likeness of men' (2:7).

At the outset it is important to observe the contrast between Jesus' pre-existent state in verse 6 and His human state in verses 7-8. The contrast, signaled by 'but' (*alla*) at the beginning of verse 7, consists of two 'forms' – the 'form of God' (v. 6) and the 'form of a servant' (v. 7). The Greek word for 'form' (*morphē*) can refer to outward appearance or shape (Judg. 8:18; Isa. 44:13; Dan. 3:19; Mark 16:12); and that typical meaning might perhaps be thought to fit verse 7, though it appears incompatible with verse 6. However, even in considering verse 7, we must acknowledge that Jesus did not traverse this world in the actual physical appearance of a slave (i.e., in the garb of a slave). More likely, these two contrasting 'forms' can be understood as the 'expression of servility' and the 'expression of God'.

We might think that the 'form of God' is similar to the 'image of God' found in Genesis 1:26-28 (cf. Eph. 4:24; Col. 3:10), which humanity possessed in the Garden (and still reflects in a distorted fashion post-Fall). However, that does not do justice to the contrast between 'form of God' and 'form of a servant'. Since 'the form of a servant' is clearly defined in 2:7-8 as being the form of humanity, the 'form of God' must be something substantially more than mere humanity, and, for that matter, more than the 'image of God' which resides in all humanity. Indeed, Jesus lowered Himself immensely by taking on human form. In fact, He lowered Himself from the rights that He had as one in the 'form of God' – that is, as one who had claim to 'equality with God'. In short, He relinquished the privileges of deity itself.

When Paul speaks of 'equality with God' we should recognize that this truly establishes an equivalence relationship between Jesus (in the 'form of God') and God the Father. Intriguingly, this was, according to the Gospels, exactly what Jesus' opponents accused Him of doing in His earthly ministry: They charged Jesus with 'making himself equal with God' (John 5:18) when He called God His Father, when He healed the invalid on the Sabbath, and then when He further claimed that He worked as the Father worked, did as the Father does, judges as the Father judges, gives life as the Father gives life, raises the dead, grants eternal life for those who believe in Him, was the One testified by Moses and Scripture, and was God's uniquely honored and beloved Son.[9] In reality, Jesus' opponents were correct to comprehend that He was equating Himself with God, just as they were when they recognized that no one can forgive sin except God alone (Mark 2:1-12), or that Jesus' claim to be the Son of Man, whom they will see 'sitting at the right hand of Power and coming on clouds of heaven' (Mark 14:62), was nothing short of blasphemy (unless it is true!). Indeed, according to the Gospels, Jesus Himself asserted His claim to deity – both by direct reference or allusion to Himself as God, and by taking on Himself the rights that belong to God alone (e.g., Matt. 22:41-46; John 8:58-59).

Paul says that Jesus did not regard His pre-existence as deity 'something to be grasped'. The Greek word for 'grasp' (*harpagmos*) can bear the notion of robbery or booty, but this does not fit the context here. The next verse shows that the pre-existent Jesus gave up the form of God in order to become the form of a servant; in other words, He already possessed something that He Himself determined not to hold onto. We witness here a willing relinquishment of His own divine prerogatives.

Paul clearly believes in this 'high Christology' – that Jesus is indeed God incarnate, uniquely worthy of the title 'Lord'. Yet, we should acknowledge that the fully developed Chalcedonian Trinitarian technical language of the fourth and fifth centuries did not exist at this stage of Christian history. Though Paul does directly call Jesus 'God' elsewhere (Rom. 9:5; Titus 2:13), here he reserves the title 'God' for God the Father. Paul commonly does this in his Trinitarian expressions, where he speaks of the mutual work of God [the Father], the Lord Jesus Christ, and the Holy Spirit (e.g., 1 Cor. 12:4-6; 2 Cor. 13:13; Eph. 4:4-6). God the Father is the creator of the world who has worked throughout the Old Testament to bring salvation to His people. He is the One True God. It is to that One God that Jesus is equal. Though distinct in His personhood, Jesus fully embraces in His pre-existence the same full form and essence of deity as does God the Father

---

9 John 5:1-47; cf. Matt. 11:25-30; 17:5; John 8:25-59; 14:8ff.; 17:5.

(cf. Col. 1:15-20; 2:9-10). Later in our passage (Phil. 2:9-11) it is to that exalted state that Jesus returns.

Some have marveled that such a high Christology was present so early in Pauline thought, and they have wondered how such a view could have developed among early monotheistic Jewish believers in Jesus. Should its origins be traced back to strands of intertestamental Jewish thought concerning the exaltation of angels, the incarnation of Wisdom, or the elevation of Moses? Or is this some Jewish-Roman hybrid that incorporates pagan tendencies to deify heroes and emperors? In reality, none of these can fully explain the origins of Paul's thought, steeped as he was in the repeated daily saying of the Shema.[10] Rather, the origins of the early church's Christology is best traced back to Jesus' own self-concept of being God incarnate (mentioned just above in our brief survey of the Gospels) and to the radical epistemic demands of Paul's acknowledging Jesus as his resurrected Lord (e.g., Rom. 1:4; Eph. 1:20-23).

but made himself nothing, taking the form of a servant, being born in the likeness of men (2:7).
In stark contrast to the glorious position of Jesus depicted in verse 6, here He is described as having voluntarily relinquished the authority and glory He had in order to become fully human. As mentioned above, the contrast with verse 6 is signaled both by the word 'but' (*alla*) and by the phrase 'form of a servant', which is starkly divergent from 'form of God' in verse 6.

The verb translated 'made himself nothing' literally means 'emptied himself'. One major Greek lexicon (BDAG) paraphrases this as 'divested himself of his prestige or privileges'; that well captures what is being said. The other occurrences of this verb in the New Testament[11] all speak of someone else (or some*thing* else) causing the 'emptying' or nullification of another. Here, however, it is clearly Jesus who divests 'himself'. He, as the subject of the verb, took the active role in such humble divestiture, actively taking on the form of

---
10 'Hear, O Israel: The Lord our God, *the Lord* is one' in Deut 6:4; cf. Rom. 3:30; 1 Cor. 8:6; 1 Tim. 2:5.
11 Rom. 4:14; 1 Cor. 1:17; 9:15; 2 Cor. 9:3.

a servant. For our sakes, He makes Himself poor (2 Cor. 8:9). Even in this act, Jesus acts sovereignly to humble Himself. There has been some debate about the verb 'empty' (*kenoō*). In the early twentieth century, the 'kenosis theory' argued that Jesus had emptied Himself even beyond his privileges and prestige, so that He actually reduced His deific essence. This theory contended that, in becoming man, Jesus left behind his attributes of deity (such as His omniscience, omnipotence, etc.). However, this verse alone certainly does not argue for such a reduction in Jesus' deity. Moreover, systematic theologians rightly caution us about claiming that Jesus 'emptied' Himself of all the central attributes and essence of deity. Early Christianity (as witnessed in the Gospels) clearly represented Jesus as still possessing the self-awareness of deity (see above), and as actively engaging in miraculous works that testify to His omniscience[12] and omnipotence.[13] Though the Gospel authors recognized the role of the Holy Spirit in Jesus' life, they nevertheless attributed these miracles to Jesus' own exercise of his innate authority as God incarnate. Paul recognizes this when he states that Jesus sustains the entire world around us (Col. 1:17). Jesus' 'emptying himself' involved a change in His role and status, rather than in His essential nature or in His attributes.

Rather, orthodox theologians suggest that Jesus engaged in the voluntary limitation of the exercise of His divine attributes in submission to God the Father, following the lead of the Holy Spirit, and in keeping with His commitment to suffer within His humanity (cf. John 10:17-18). The church has historically codified this in acknowledging that the Son of God became incarnate. From the moment of His human conception, the one person of Christ possessed two distinct natures – human and divine – which always worked in harmony and yet were never confused, changed, divided, or separated. In the words of the Chalcedonian Creed (A.D. 451), the 'property of each nature being preserved, and concurring in one Person and one Subsistence, not parted or divided into two persons, but one and the same Son.' Though this goes beyond the limited discussion of the verse at hand, this Chalcedonian Christology

---

12 E.g., Mark 2:8; John 6:64; 16:30.
13 E.g., Matt. 8:26-27; 14:19; John 2:1-11.

is certainly consistent with the dual nature of Christ as fully God and fully man found so evidently in Paul's writings. Just as the 'form of God' does not mean that Jesus was a mere imitation of deity, so also 'form of servant' does not mean that Jesus merely imitated such servanthood. Rather, He fully embodied this servanthood, becoming truly and fully human. We discussed the Greek word for servant (*doulos*) in the very first verse of Philippians (when Paul and Timothy call themselves *douloi*). There we observed that this word in antiquity was applied to slaves, so it conveys the lowly social status of someone in the enslaved service of another. At the same time, this word was often used in the Greek translation of the Old Testament to represent the great 'servants of God' – Moses, Joshua, David, Solomon, etc. Therefore, in these contexts this word carries both the sense of lowliness of position and yet also the privilege of serving one of immense greatness (i.e., God Himself). Paul does not state to whom Jesus acts as servant/slave, and we could speculate on whether He is the servant of God or the servant of men. If we had to choose, there is precedence in the book of Philippians for a servant of God the Father (1:1), though likely Jesus effectively acts as a servant of all. He thus diminished Himself to the lowliest status of a slave, but in having done so, His greatness is now humbly manifest through His relationship to the One whom He faithfully serves on behalf of all.

The nature of Jesus' 'emptying' is specifically identified as 'being born in the likeness of men', which more fully unwraps what it means for Him to have taken the form of a servant. 'Being born' actually renders the Greek word 'becoming' (*genomenos*), which stresses here the beginning of Jesus taking on human likeness and can be contrasted with how He eternally 'existed' (*huparchōn*) in the form of God (in 2:6).

The word 'likeness' certainly conveys similarity,[14] though it would also have been more straightforward simply to say 'born as a man'. Why does Paul speak so indirectly? Notably, Paul elsewhere talks of Jesus being sent by the Father 'in the *likeness* of sinful flesh' (Rom. 8:3). This may be a clue for us, since Jesus can identify with our human body, but does not

---

14 See also Rom. 1:23; 5:14; 6:5; Rev. 9:7.

know our sin. There is no question that Paul believes Jesus to fully partake our humanity.[15] Yet, Jesus also remains without the sin that so characterizes humanity since the Fall.[16] So Jesus is man as man was supposed to be, even if that is discontinuous with fallen humanity in the sense that Jesus does not possess 'sinful flesh'.

Though He takes on the human fleshly form (and all that entails being human), He is not enslaved to our sinful nature. One might protest that this over-theologizes Paul's simple statement, but I would respond that this helps us understand the word 'likeness' in both Philippians 2:7 and Romans 8:3. Thus Jesus has the 'likeness' of men, and the 'outward form' of humanity (see Phil. 2:8). He is fully human, but not entangled in our sinful nature. It is only by becoming fully human that His death in the body can destroy the power of sin for all those who are in Christ (Col. 1:22; Eph. 2:14; cf. Heb. 2:17).

And being found in human form, he humbled himself by becoming obedient to the point of death, even death on a cross. (2:8)

The participial phrase, 'and being found in human form,' re-emphasizes this crucial point: Jesus diminished Himself to the point of taking on a fully human nature. Actually this brief phrase is part of verse 7 in the Greek New Testament, but it belongs better with the material in this verse (and thus English translations typically include it in verse 8). The two preceding participial phrases in verse 7 ('taking the form of a servant' and 'being born in the likeness of men') modify the main verb in verse 7 ('emptied himself') and thus explain what that 'emptying' involved – namely, a divestiture of the privileges of deity in order to become fully human, and a voluntary limitation of the exercise of His attributes of authority. Here this participial phrase, which begins with 'and', is structured in such a way that it modifies the verb that follows it in verse 8 – 'he humbled himself'.

---

15 E.g., Col. 1:22; Rom. 1:3; Gal. 4:4-5; cf. Luke 2:40, 52; Heb. 2:14-18; 4:15; 5:8.

16 Rom. 5:18-19; 2 Cor. 5:21; cf. John 8:29; 15:10; 1 Pet. 2:22-25; Heb. 4:15; 7:26.

The import of this observation is to say that there are (in a sense) two stages pictured here in Jesus' humiliation. It involved a substantial divestiture of His rights as deity simply in order to become human. But to this Jesus added the humility of becoming obedient unto death. Having already been found in human form (see Additional Notes), Jesus proceeds to head to the cross. Again, note that Jesus remains the one who voluntarily (even sovereignly) engages in actively humbling Himself. He remains the subject of the active verb. He acts of His own volition.

'Humbled' here involves a diminishing of oneself for the sake of others. Jesus Himself endorses such humility (Matt. 18:4; 23:12; Luke 14:11; 18:14) and calls Himself humble (Matt. 11:29). Humility stands as a key Christian virtue among Jesus' followers (James 4:10; 1 Pet. 3:8; 5:5-6). Paul himself models humility to his congregations (2 Cor. 11:7; cf. Acts 20:19) and admonishes all Christians to be humble (Rom. 12:16; Eph. 4:2; Col. 3:12). In the Graeco-Roman world, humility was often not regarded as virtuous, and thus this word group, even in the New Testament, can take on overtures of humiliation and debasement (e.g., 2 Cor. 12:21; Acts 8:33). Indeed, in a Roman environment, where strength, pride, and boasting could be considered great virtues, there was something strikingly countercultural about championing humility as the goal of Christian community life.

Of course, Paul has just admonished his own audience to 'in *humility* count others more significant than yourselves' (2:3) and to 'let each of you look not only to his own interests, but also to the interests of others.' By returning to the same word-family (*tapeinophrosunē* in 2:3 and *tapeinoō* in 2:8), Paul is reminding his audience of his main point: Jesus serves as the model of true humility for the Christian church. It is His mindset that we are to follow (2:5).

Jesus has not only voluntarily given up the prerogatives of His deity, He has willingly embraced the redemptive purposes of the Trinitarian God by submitting to the authority of God the Father, even unto death. This is depicted here as 'obedience'. Although the context leading up to 2:8 has especially been emphasizing Jesus' humility as a model for Christian humility (esp. 2:4), Jesus' obedience also serves as an example of the kind of obedience to God that Christians are to engage in as well (2:12). So in His great work of humility, Jesus also models obedience.

One cannot help but reflect on the portrait of Jesus in the Garden of Gethsemane, tearfully willing to submit to the Father's will as He prepares to march to the cross.[17] The prophecies had been there all along, informing Jesus of His fate (Ps. 22:1-18; Isa. 53:1-12). Moreover, Jesus proves Himself to be well aware throughout His ministry of the crucifixion to come.[18] Though Jesus knew victory awaited Him on the other side of the cross,[19] He also fully experienced the real pain of that death (Mark 15:34-37).

Intriguingly, the Greek word translated above as 'to the point of' (*mechri*) actually involves more of the sense of 'until', 'up to', or even 'up to and including'. This likely implies that Paul believes that Jesus' obedience, though it culminates in His death, actually was present all along throughout His human life 'until death'. Still, Jesus' death culminates His years of obedient service to His Father.

Jesus' humility called not only for Him to be obedient until death, but obedient until death on a cross. Substantial study has been done in the past few decades on crucifixion and on how it was perceived in antiquity (for suggested reading on crucifixion, see Additional Notes). Certainly, crucifixion was an immensely painful way to die: wasting away for hours or even days while penned to a cross, naked in public view. Moreover, it was a form of punishment reserved for the lowest ranks of society (the upper Roman classes being typically exempt), especially for violent thieves, rebels, and slaves. It is no wonder then that the Epistle to the Hebrews speaks of the shame of the cross (Heb. 12:2). Crucifixion was also such a common enough punishment that most everyone in the Roman Empire would readily recognize the kind of death Jesus had endured. Though one might sympathize with the plight of victims of the cross (especially those who had been treated unfairly), no one would voluntarily head to such a death.

---

17 Matt. 26:39; Mark 14:36; Luke 22:42; cf. John 12:27; 14:31; 18:1.
18 E.g., Mark 8:31; 9:12, 31; 10:33-34, 45; 14:8, 21, 27.
19 E.g., Mark 10:34; 14:28; John 12:32; cf. Isa. 53:11; Ps. 22:19-31; Heb. 12:2.

A couple of selected ancient texts might better illuminate how people felt about the cross in antiquity. In opposition to a governor who had crucified Roman citizens, Cicero said, 'To bind a Roman citizen is a crime, to flog him is an abomination, to slay him is almost an act of murder: to crucify him is—what? There is no fitting word that can possibly describe so horrible a deed' (*Against Verres* II.v.66). In order to show that there are times when suicide is to be preferred to a brief extension of life, Seneca depicts the plight of the crucified: 'Can anyone be found who would prefer wasting away in pain, dying limb by limb, or letting out his life drop by drop, rather than expiring once for all? Can any man be found willing to be fastened to the accursed tree, long sickly, already deformed, swelling with ugly tumours on chest and shoulders, and draw the breath of life amid long-drawn-out agony? I think he would have many excuses for dying even before mounting the cross!' (*Epistles* 101).

There is strong evidence that, among Jewish people, the crucified person would have been considered 'cursed by God' in keeping with Deuteronomy 21:22-23.[20] No wonder then that Paul describes the gospel of the crucified Christ as foolishness to Gentiles and a stumbling block to Jews (1 Cor. 1:23), even if Jesus' cross actually demonstrates the power of God unto salvation (1 Cor. 1:24-25). The gospel of a crucified Savior, who voluntarily relinquished His authority to prevent His own death (e.g., Matt. 26:53-56), was a shocking revelation that chafed against the Roman ideal of power as virtue; and such a message surprisingly undermined the Jewish expectation of a conquering messiah who would immediately lead them to victory.

Therefore, when Paul speaks of Jesus' humility as culminating in His crucifixion, this would have been all the more striking to the believers in first-century Philippi. Divesting Himself of the privileges of deity and becoming human, Jesus willingly proceeds to associate Himself with the lowliest and most painful death, in order that we may benefit from His sacrificial act. That is true humility. And it is that example that

---

20 E.g., Philo, *De Specialibus Legibus* iii.151-2; 11QTemple 64:6-13; Tosefta, Sanhedrin ix.7; contrast Sifre Deut. 221 and see especially Gal. 3:13.

we are called to follow, alongside one another in the church of Christ.

Therefore God has highly exalted him and bestowed on him the name that is above every name (2:9).
Suddenly the context shifts from Jesus' humility to His exaltation. One intriguing aspect of this shift stems from the important word 'therefore' (*dio*). Paul establishes a logical connection between Jesus' humility and exaltation. This logical connection can certainly be tied to Jesus' 'obedience' in verse 8, but there appears an even broader movement that connects Jesus' 'emptying himself' and 'humbling himself' to God the Father 'highly exalting him'.

As mentioned earlier, key Old Testament passages establish the principle that 'God opposes the proud but gives grace to the humble' (Prov. 3:34; cf. Ezek. 17:24; 21:26). Jesus repeatedly proclaims that in God's kingdom, the humble will be exalted[21] and the 'last will be first'.[22] This also forms a theme in early Christian thought (James 4:6, 10; 1 Pet. 5:5-6), and that theme clearly lies behind Paul's thought here (also cf. Heb. 2:9). It is due to Jesus' humility that He is exalted. God the Father exalts God the Son because He divested Himself of the privileges of deity, fully partook of humanity, and willingly died on the cross for the sins of the world.

Yet, Paul strains at the Greek language in order to express the heights of Jesus' exaltation. He cannot bring himself merely to say that God 'exalted' (*hupsoō*) Jesus, but that He 'highly exalted' (*hyperupsoō*) Jesus. This is the same word used by the Greek Old Testament to render Psalm 96:9 (LXX 97:9): 'For you, O Lord, are most high over all the earth; you are exceedingly *highly exalted* above all gods.' Elsewhere in intertestamental Jewish literature, this word is used repeatedly of God Almighty in the 'Song of the Three Young Men' (in the so-called Additions to Daniel). So, at the least we can say that Paul is proclaiming Jesus to have been exalted to the very highest point imaginable. Moreover, Paul may very well already be alluding to Jesus' position and privileges being again equivalent to that of deity.

---

21 Luke 14:11; 18:14; Matt. 23:12.
22 Matt. 19:30; 20:16; Mark 9:35; 10:31; Luke 13:30.

Early Christian theology emphasized that Jesus, subsequent to His death, was exalted in His resurrection,[23] and then further went to the place of 'session',[24] and will soon return again to establish His kingdom.[25] Paul does not provide specifics as to the timing of Jesus' rule mentioned in 2:9-11. However, it is certainly consistent with Paul's eschatological expectations – both that Jesus will return in glory and judgment, and that Jesus' kingdom has already been inaugurated in the present age, with Him reigning in anticipation of the culmination of His kingdom after His return.

The exaltation of Jesus is accompanied by God the Father granting a 'name' to Jesus. This reminds us of the frequent events of 'naming' in the Old Testament. Beginning in the Garden, God creates and names (and grants to Adam the right to 'name' as well). The patriarchs often received new names from God in order to designate their role in God's plan (e.g., Abraham in Gen. 17:5; Israel in Gen. 32:28). In a Semitic context, the name is more than a mere designation; it personifies the essence of a person's being and/or function in God's economy. A person's name can convey reputation (Songs 1:3; cf. 1 Macc. 3:26), and is to be valued more than riches (Prov. 22:1; Eccles. 7:1). Conversely, the cessation of a person's name is the termination of his or her remembrance (Nahum 1:14). God promises to give an 'everlasting name' to those who hold fast His covenant (Isa. 56:5). God's own name stands for God Himself,[26] and His Old Testament people frequently 'call upon the name of the Lord'.[27] Indeed, God Himself has a special name – YHWH (Exod. 3:13-15; 6:2-3).

We cannot be absolutely certain about what 'name' Paul intends to convey here that God the Father has given to Jesus, although it could well be the deific designation of 'Lord' (*kurios*) that is central to verse 11. What is clear is that this name is 'above every name' (also Eph. 1:21; cf. Heb. 1:4). In 1 Kings 1:47, one blessing that the king's servants make

---

23 E.g., Rom. 6:9-10; 1 Cor. 15:1-23; 2 Tim. 2:8; cf. Matt. 28:18; Acts 13:30-37.
24 Sitting and reigning at the right hand of the Father: Rom. 8:34; Eph. 1:20-23; 4:8-10; Col. 3:1; cf. Acts 2:33; 5:31; 7:55-56; Heb. 1:3-4, 13; 8:1; 10:12; 12:2; 1 Pet. 3:22; Rev. 5:6-14.
25 E.g., 1 Cor. 15:24-28; 1 Thess. 4:13-18.
26 E.g., Pss. 7:17; 79:9; 115:1; 1 Chron. 16:29.
27 Gen. 4:26; 12:8; 13:4; 16:13; etc.

to David is that Solomon would have a name that is above David's own name and a throne greater than David's own throne. This expression then is a way of asserting that the greatness and authority of Jesus has been made superior to all others. Moreover, this reminds us of the authority of the name of God Almighty, since, 'nations will fear the name of the Lord, and all the kings of the earth will fear your glory' (Ps. 102:15). Of God Almighty, we hear, 'Let them praise the name of the Lord, for his name alone is exalted; his majesty is above earth and heaven' (Ps. 148:13).

Thus when Jesus receives the 'name that is above every name', we again witness His returning to the position of honor and glory He possessed as one who was 'equal with God' (2:6), for truly God alone possesses such a 'name.'

so that at the name of Jesus every knee should bow, in heaven and on earth and under the earth (2:10).
All of creation will pay homage to Jesus. When Paul says 'every knee should bow' in verse 10 and 'every tongue shall confess' in verse 11, there is a clear allusion to Isaiah 45:22-23, which reads:

> Turn to me and be saved,
> > all the ends of the earth!
> > For I am God, and there is no other.
> By myself I have sworn;
> > from my mouth has gone out in righteousness
> > a word that shall not return:
> *'To me every knee shall bow,*
> > *every tongue shall swear allegiance.*

Paul quotes this passage in Romans 14:11, which, in context, shows his clear awareness that God Himself is the One before whom every knee shall bow. Therefore, by applying this passage to Christ, Paul again indicates that the exalted Jesus possesses all the same authority and prerogatives as the Almighty God of the universe. Jesus deserves and will receive the worship that belongs to God Almighty alone. This can only be so if Jesus is indeed God the Son.

It is in honor of the name of Jesus that this worship occurs. Note that the concept of name was discussed in 2:9. The worshipful confession in 2:11 is that 'Jesus Christ is Lord', and this context would indicate that here in 2:10 'at the name of Jesus' (or better 'in the name of Jesus') refers to worship being performed by those who glorify God by worshipping the exalted Jesus.

Paul depicts all rational beings throughout the whole of creation worshipping Jesus. The fact that 'every knee' and 'every tongue' is involved in this creation-wide worship indicates that the apostle is speaking about rational beings (i.e., every *person*, and not every *thing*, that is found in heaven, on earth, and beneath). Yet the places in which those rational beings are found encompass the whole of created space. Frequently in Scripture, 'heaven and earth' are paired together to indicate all of creation (Exod. 20:11; 31:17). God is the 'possessor of heaven and earth' and the 'God of heaven and earth' (e.g., Gen. 14:19, 22; 24:3; Deut. 10:14). When it comes to the tripartite grouping Paul uses here (heaven, earth, under the earth), we observe in the Ten Commandments, a person is commanded not to make an idol out of the image of 'anything that is in heaven above, or that is in the earth beneath, or that is in the water under the earth' (Exod. 20:4). Some have pressed this to argue that the ancient cosmology was tri-fold (with earth situated between heaven and the depths), but Paul is not putting forth a scientific theory of the cosmos. Even in the twenty-first century, we too might speak of heaven as 'above' or hell as 'beneath' without making an actual spatial claim as to their geographic locale. Paul is simply employing common nomenclature for all that exists. Yet, his reference to 'under the earth' reminds us that the 'abyss' was the place frequently associated with the place of the dead and, often, the place of demons. Paul is thus assuming that there is a time in which even the dead and the demons will be forced to acknowledge the lordship of Christ.

What time frame is intended here? In short, does Paul speak of the present rule of Christ, or of a future time subsequent to Jesus' glorious return? The tense of the Greek verbs is not determinative here, and the context can allow both present and future references. Yet, due to the mention of 'under the earth', and thus the submission of the dead and the demonic to Christ, it appears the reference is ultimately future (since the enemies of Christ certainly have not yet bowed the knee to Him). However, like so many eschatological truths in Paul, there is a sense of 'already and not yet'. The reign of Christ has been inaugurated, and all creation rightly owes Him its worship and allegiance now. However, Jesus' rule will be fully consummated upon His return. And, at His return, all creation (even those who are Christ's enemies) must acknowledge His lordship and submit to Him.

and every tongue confess that Jesus Christ is Lord, to the glory of God the Father (2:11).
The result of Jesus' exaltation is that He has returned to His position as glorious Lord of the universe, and this magnifies God the Father, alongside God the Son.

The phrase 'every tongue confess' is, like 'every knee should bow', taken from Isaiah 45:23, with Paul's Greek conforming precisely to the Old Greek (Septuagint) translation of Isaiah. We have already noted the Christological implications concerning Christ's deity that stem from connecting this passage (from Isaiah about God Almighty) to Jesus.

Even more striking is the use of the name 'Lord' (*kurios*) applied here to Jesus. Although, the word *kurios* can refer to an earthly master (especially in relationships of slavery), in this context it reminds us of God's claim to the name 'Lord' in the Old Testament (see notes on Philippians 1:2). The Greek Old Testament that the Pauline churches read would have had hundreds of mentions of God Almighty as *kurios* ('Lord'). Starting with Genesis, it was the Lord God who planted the Garden of Eden, placed man in it, and created woman (Gen. 2:8, 15, 18, 22). The Lord God encounters them after the Fall (Gen. 3:8, 9, 13, 14, 21, 23). We can jump ahead to the Exodus, where is it the *Kurios* who calls Moses, grants him knowledge of the divine name, and ultimately acts to lead his people out of Egypt (Exod. 3:4, 7, 15-16). We could go on to show throughout the Old Testament how 'Lord' is a title that especially refers to God Himself.

Therefore, we see, not only from Paul's citation of Isaiah 45, but also from the designation 'Lord', that Paul recognizes Jesus as fully divine. All others who might claim the title of *kurios*, even including Caesar, are themselves to submit – to bow the knee and profess the name of Jesus as the Lord over all. This must inform all the other times Jesus is called *kurios* throughout Paul's writings, especially in Philippians.[28] Of course, Paul elsewhere indicates it is the special mark of the Christian that he or she proclaims Jesus as Lord (Rom. 10:9; 12:3). And indeed, although one could hypothetically translate the Greek as 'and confess the Lord Jesus Christ', it is better to recognize that this profession is an attribution of deific lordship to the Messiah Jesus (i.e., translated better as 'confess that Jesus Christ *is* Lord'; cf. 2 Cor. 4:5; Rom. 10:9; Col. 2:6). Here, those who have confessed Jesus as Lord in this life, and thus are His people saved by His power, are joined by all creation in acknowledging Jesus' lordship. This does *not* mean that all creation (including all people and demons) are saved in the end (cf. James 2:19); that would be inconsistent with Paul's theology elsewhere (2 Thess. 1:6-9; cf. Phil. 3:18). It does mean, though, that Jesus commands all creation, and that everyone will submit to His lordship (even if His enemies are only grudgingly subjected under His feet; 1 Cor. 15:25).

All this is to the 'glory of God the Father'. We again find ourselves plunging into the unfathomable depths of knowledge of the Trinity. The Father is glorified by the Son. Indeed, it is through the Father's glory that Jesus is raised unto exaltation (Rom. 6:4). And thus the exaltation of the Son to His rightful place of deific rule alongside the Father brings glory to them both. Beyond that, we can comprehend here a more general principle: that the exaltation of any humble follower of Christ ultimately brings glory to the God who saves us.

There is insufficient space here to speak of Paul's theology of the glory of God. We shall merely note that Paul, drawing on the immense Old Testament imagery that speaks of God's glory, often returns to this theme. It is the Christian's earnest desire that God would be glorified, even in our own lives. Humanity, however, has fallen from the worship of the glorious God (Rom. 1:23; 3:23). Yet due to the glorious salvation we have in Christ (2 Cor. 3:7-11; 4:17), we can now truly rejoice in God's glory (Rom. 5:2) and seek to magnify Him as His children.[29] And we anticipate the day when we might more fully apprehend His glory and participate in the

---

28 Phil. 1:2, 14; 2:19, 24, 29; 3:1, 8, 20; 4:1, 2, 4, 5, 10, 23.
29 1 Cor. 10:31; Rom. 15:6-7; 2 Cor. 1:20; 4:15; 8:23; Eph. 1:12; Phil. 1:11.

overflow of that glory upon us,[30] even as we taste that glory now (1 Cor. 2:7). Ultimately, it is the eternal glory of God that we seek, as is repeatedly acknowledged in the benedictions of the church.[31]

Summary
Jesus models true humility for His followers. Christ stooped further than we can even imagine. From the heights of equality with God, He left behind His privileges and esteem, and chose to become human. Beyond that, Jesus willingly suffered death, even the shameful and horrendous death of being pinned to a cross. All of this was done for our sake. Christ enslaved Himself that we might be redeemed. When we consider our role in the Christian community, we must remember this pattern (1:27–2:4), for if such humility was the hallmark of our churches, then a deep and abiding unity would envelop our congregations as everyone seeks the good of the other.

Such humility ultimately results in exaltation. As the 'last are made first', so the humble will be exalted. It is only fitting then that Jesus, who humbled Himself beyond human comprehension, should then be exalted beyond all earthly imagining. The Son of God condescends to embrace a human nature and its death, and now as the God-man, He has returned to being exalted alongside God the Father.

The Christological implications of this passage are truly astounding. Centuries before the Nicene and Chalcedonian creeds sought to unify the theological language of Christendom, Paul strained at the Greek language to state two deep truths: Jesus is fully God, and Jesus became fully human. Jesus embraced human form and likeness, with all its suffering and death. Yet He existed before His human birth, and in His pre-existence He was in the form of God, even equal to God the Father. His exaltation returns Jesus to the place of exaltation as God the Son alongside God the Father. The Old Testament proclaims God's name to be exalted, God's worship ultimately to be practiced through the bowing of every knee and the confessing of every individual tongue, and God's position

---
30 Rom. 8:17-18, 21; 1 Thess. 2:12; 2 Thess. 2:14.
31 Rom. 11:36; 16:27; Gal. 1:5; Eph. 3:21; Phil. 4:20; 1 Tim. 1:17; 2 Tim. 4:18.

to be that of *Kurios* ('Lord'). So now, Jesus possesses the name above every name, the worship of every knee and tongue, and the great title *Kurios*. And all this culminates in glory to God the Father through the exaltation of God the Son. This is the Lord whom we serve. May He be glorified in our humble service to Him and to one another.

Questions for Personal Reflection:

1. Briefly summarize what we learn from this passage about Jesus. What most strikes you as you read these words?

2. Have you ever encountered any non-orthodox teachings about Jesus? (For example: teachings that emphasize His humanity to the diminishment of His deity, or ones that emphasize His deity to the expense of His humanity.) Describe that sub-Christian view. How would these verses serve to correct such heterodox understandings of Christology?

3. How does the portrait of the exalted Jesus in 2:9-11 affect your desire to worship Him? How does it influence your view of our present earthly lives?

4. How does the portrait of the humble Jesus in 2:5-8 affect your desire to worship Him? What element in these verses most brings home to you the depth of Jesus' humility?

5. How does our Lord's humility motivate you to become a better servant of others? How does His example motivate us to Christian unity? In your own struggle with pride, in what ways do these verses provide encouragement, challenge, and strength to you?

STUDY QUESTIONS:

1. Read Philippians 2:5-11. As always, it is important to note how this passage fits within its context. Name some of the many ways that 2:5-11 coheres with what precedes it in the letter.

2. Though in these verses Paul does not directly call Jesus 'God', what are some of the marks of Jesus' deity that are evident in this passage? (Hint: Also be sure to compare Philippians 2:10-11 with Isaiah 45:23.) How does this cohere with Paul's theology elsewhere (e.g., Rom. 1:4; 9:5; Col. 1:15-20; 2:9-10; Titus 2:13; etc.)? Name some other places in Scripture that discuss the deity of Christ.

3. This passage can be divided into the humility of the Messiah and the exaltation of the Messiah. What examples does Paul provide of Christ's humility? Of His exaltation?

4. Note the places where Jesus acts in this passage (i.e., where He is the subject of a verb). According to these verses, were the steps in His humility acts of Jesus' own volition? Also note the places where God the Father acts in this passage. How does all this contribute to Paul's overall argument in Philippians 1-11?

5. Study closely 2:6-8. What can we learn about Christ's humility from this section? For example, you might discuss how Jesus' crucifixion serves as a special example of His humility.

6. Read Mark 10:42-45 and note how Paul's teaching here in Philippians overlaps with Jesus' own self-understanding of His ministry. What was the significance of Mark 10:42-45 in its context in the Gospel of Mark? Name some ways that this teaching is applicable to us today.

7. How does the portrait of Jesus' humility in 2:5-8 affect your desire to worship Him? What element in these verses most brings home to you the depth of His humility?

8. Study closely 2:9-11. What evidence is there currently of Jesus' exaltation? How does Jesus' exaltation continue into the future?

9. How does the portrait of the exalted Jesus in 2:9-11 affect your desire to worship Him? How does it influence your view of our present earthly lives?

10. Why do you think Paul appends the words 'to the glory of God the Father' to the end of this section? What does it look like for us to live our lives to God's glory?

11. How can Jesus' own life and ministry motivate us to humility? How does His example stimulate us to Christian unity? What practically should such humility look like in our lives and in our churches? In your own struggle with pride, in what ways do these verses provide encouragement, challenge, and strength to you?

Additional Notes:
2:5-11 The commentary above discusses the issue of the possible liturgical nature of this passage. Further information on the many proposals for strophic divisions in this 'hymn' can be found in the commentaries by Hawthorne or O'Brien (among others). I must admit that I personally resonate with Fee's NICNT commentary (p. 192n.) when he notes that the profusion of discussion and debate on this passage '…has sometimes tended to obscure rather than enlighten, and, even worse, to bog down in debate a passage that should cause the reader to soar. It seems tragic that such a marvelous moment should get inundated by so much talk….'

Another academic issue that could be considered concerns the origins of this 'hymn'. Are there antecedent concepts in the first century that could explain both the pre-existence motif and the humility/exaltation motif in this passage? Once again scholarly suggestions have been many, ranging from Gnostic redeemer myths, to Jewish elevated concepts of wisdom, of martyrdom, or of Adam. Old Testament texts have also been adduced (especially Isaiah 53). However, most of these possibilities fail to account in this passage for all dimensions of either the pre-existence motif or the humility/exaltation motif. Moreover, the proposed Gnostic option clearly retrojects sectarian, second-century, esoteric (even heretical) teaching into the worship of the orthodox early-first-century church (when it is more likely that Gnostic redeemer concepts represent a corruption of earlier orthodox teaching). Concerning some of the possible Jewish antecedents, there are reasons in the New Testament to ponder whether Christological reflection in the early church was performed with an awareness of the exaltation in contemporary Judaism of wisdom, of angels, of Moses, of the Danielic Son of Man, and of other aspects of Messianic belief. Some of those concepts, now transformed in light of Christ's superiority to these figures, could indeed be alluded to at places in this 'hymn'. However, the early church's Christology was most marked by the memories of the life, teaching, death, resurrection and ascension of Jesus.

It is in those historical memories of Jesus Himself that we shall find the core source material for this passage. For example, throughout His own life Jesus intentionally taught and modeled the concept of humility preceding exaltation (e.g., Matt. 18:4; 23:12; Mark 10:43-45; Luke 14:11; John 13:3-17). And evidence for belief in His pre-existence can also be found elsewhere in early Christianity, where it is tied to Jesus' own self-concept as the Messiah sent from His original heavenly abode (e.g., John 1:1; 17:5, 24).

2:5 There are a few technical translation matters in this verse that affect our understanding of the passage (at least at the most detailed level). They involve two issues in the manuscript tradition, and one issue of how to translate a Greek 'verbless clause'.

Many Greek textual witnesses (including some quite early manuscripts) specifically link verse 5 to the preceding context by means of the word 'for' (*gar*), or less commonly by 'therefore' (*oun*). This would serve to explicitly state a *logical* connection between 2:5 and its context. Other early manuscripts, however, do not contain such a connecting particle, and it is more difficult to understand the omission of such a word by ancient copyists than its inclusion. Therefore, the main printed edition of the Greek text today omits such a particle. In any case, the *conceptual* connection is clear enough between 2:5 and the preceding material in 1:27–2:4.

Similarly, following the widespread early manuscript tradition, it is likely that the Greek word underlying 'have this mind' is a second-person active imperative ('you, have this mind' or more literally 'think this!'). The alternative (found in many later manuscripts) is a third-person passive imperative ('let *this mind* be'). But the second-person imperative has the better earlier manuscript support, and it should be preferred.

Concerning the relative clause in 2:5, the translation in the notes of the ESV (*English Standard Version*) is preferable to the ESV text. In short, it is better to translate this clause as 'which *was also* in Christ Jesus' rather than as 'which *is yours* in Christ Jesus'. The difference in interpretive nuance is that in the former translation, Christians follow Jesus' model of humble Christian thought and purpose, whereas in the latter translation, Christians are not so much following Christ's model as they are living out the attitude which they should possess as the result of being found in union with Christ. Theologically, of course, both are possible, but the question here concerns which is the better translation of Paul's Greek.

The debate arises because the Greek literally reads 'which also in Christ Jesus' *without a verb*. Verbless clauses are very common in Greek (it being a major feature of the language not to have to include a verb where it is deemed unnecessary). In such cases, there are two main possibilities in terms of the implied verbal concept: (1) supply the linking verb 'to be' (in the form of 'is' or 'was' depending on context); (2) reiterate the previous verb.

Most English translations (rightly in my estimation) follow the first route. They supply the linking verb 'was' in order to read: 'which also *was* in Christ Jesus.'

The origin of the RSV translation (which the ESV text follows) likely stems from the second approach to filling in the implied verbal concept in a verbless clause. The RSV translation team must be assuming that the verse can be paraphrased as 'Have this mind among yourselves, which *mind you* [also] *have* in Christ Jesus.' Or, to use the most literal Greek translation possible: '*Think* this thing among you, which *you* also *think* in Christ Jesus.' This appears to me the much less probable translation. For one, it assumes that the imperative verb ('think!') in the first clause can then be drawn upon as an indicative verb (a statement of fact *rather than* command) in the relative clause ('which you think'). It also is simply more common to fill in such verbless clauses with a linking verb ('was') unless the context constrains you otherwise. Moreover, the next few verses make the most sense as representing Jesus as a model of humility, whom the Philippians are called to emulate (just as is expressed in the translation 'which also *was* in Christ Jesus'). This theme of Jesus as exemplar of moral behavior appears elsewhere in Paul (1 Cor. 11:1; 1 Thess. 1:6) and can be traced back to Jesus' self-presentation as the humble Messiah whose humility serves as a model for His followers (e.g., Mark 10:45, as noted above).

The omission of the word 'also' (*kai* in the postpositive position) in the relative clause is particularly unfortunate in the RSV translation (and the ESV main text), since that word is clearly found in the Greek text.

2:6 The first phrase in this verse says, in Greek, of Jesus: 'who, being in the form of God.' The participle 'being' (*huparchōn*) begins an adverbial participial phrase. The relationship of this adverbial phrase to the rest of the sentence must be determined based on context. This particular phrase has been understood by commentators as either concessive (*'though* he was in the form of God') or causal (*'because* he was in the form of God'). The former would convey that, although Jesus already possessed the full glory of God, He did not hold onto it; this idea is found in the ESV translation used above. The latter would indicate that Jesus' divine nature led Him to engage in the ultimate act of humility (because God's character is self-giving and humble). Both alternatives are possible grammatically, contextually and theologically. The King James (Authorized) translation refuses to decide (simply translating the phrase 'being in the form of God'), and there is wisdom in this.

2:8 The Greek word for human 'form' (*schēma*) in verse 7 differs from the Greek word underlying the two preceding mentions of 'form' in the ESV translation of verses 6 and 7 (both *morphē*). There is probably little distinction in meaning intended between *schēma* and *morphē,* and both can refer to the 'form' or 'shape' of something. As mentioned above, the two uses of *morphē* ('form') in verses 6 and 7 clearly contrast with one another ('form of God' and 'form of a servant'), and so the shift to *schēma* in verse 8 is likely a stylistic variation intended to prevent its confusion with the contrast evident in the two preceding uses of *morphē*. Also note that a literal rendering of the participial phrase would be, 'and having been found in form as a man'. The ESV puts this into good idiomatic English when it translates it as 'and being found in human form'.

For more on crucifixion, see my *Ancient Jewish and Christian Perceptions of Crucifixion* (Tübingen: Mohr Siebeck, 2008; reprint, Grand Rapids, Mich.: Baker Academic, 2010) or Martin Hengel's excellent short book entitled *Crucifixion in the Ancient World and the Folly of the Message of the Cross* (London & Philadelphia: SCM Press & Fortress Press, 1977).

8

Living as Children of God
(Philippians 2:12-18)

¹²Therefore, my beloved, as you have always obeyed, so now, not only as in my presence but much more in my absence, work out your own salvation with fear and trembling, ¹³for it is God who works in you, both to will and to work for his good pleasure. ¹⁴Do all things without grumbling or questioning, ¹⁵that you may be blameless and innocent, children of God without blemish in the midst of a crooked and twisted generation, among whom you shine as lights in the world, ¹⁶holding fast to the word of life, so that in the day of Christ I may be proud that I did not run in vain or labor in vain. ¹⁷Even if I am to be poured out as a drink offering upon the sacrificial offering of your faith, I am glad and rejoice with you all. ¹⁸Likewise you also should be glad and rejoice with me.

Imagine walking into this church: Some members appear little concerned with how the gospel affects their day-to-day life, while others are proud of their own ability to 'live a good life.' In private conversations, you hear the church members grumbling against one another, and feel the atmosphere of disunity that pervades even the simplest church gathering. Such a church likely appears very much like the pagan world around it.

We all recognize that Christians face challenges in this life. If you personally were to list some of the various potential pitfalls we can encounter in living the Christian life, what would come to mind? Here are some of Paul's concerns: dissension in the church arising from individual selfish pride (see 1:27–2:4), disobedience while presuming on God's grace (2:12) or the opposite danger of generating obedience based on our own strength (2:13), grumbling in the community of God (2:14), and capitulating to a culture mired in sin (2:15-16). With such dangers threatening the church, Paul calls the Philippians to live out the gospel in obedience and communal harmony.

Paul has just briefly, but beautifully, encapsulated the humility and exaltation of Christ, reminding his readers of Jesus' incarnation, death, resurrection, and heavenly exaltation (2:5-11). In light of that gospel reality, Paul returns to his discussion of Christian living that he began in 1:27. Previously, he had called Christians to be good citizens of the gospel, striving side by side for the Christian faith (1:27). Such unity requires humility from each and every believer (2:1-4) – a humility that seeks to imitate our Lord's humble self-giving (2:5ff.).

Now Paul returns to the concerns of Christian citizenship (introduced in 1:27). First, he will focus on the obedient submission that God Himself works into our lives. This obedience also helps to sustain church unity, through calling us to put off all grumbling and complaining. Even in a fallen and twisted world, the church can stand together without blemish, shining the light of Christ into the darkness. Then Paul, like a proud father, motivates his beloved Philippian church by using the image of his joyfully showing off his spiritual children at the return of Christ.

Therefore, my beloved, as you have always obeyed, so now, not only as in my presence but much more in my absence, work out your own salvation with fear and trembling (2:12). Here Paul addresses the obedience that properly flows out from our Christian lives. Christ has died and risen again (Phil. 2:5-11), saving us from our sin. How ought we to respond? Paul pronounces his confidence in the Philippians, and yet he still presses them to excel in their Christian service through the strength that God provides.

Philippians 2:12-18

The opening word 'therefore' (*hōste*) provides some connection with the preceding material. Yet that connection is not immediately clear, and some have suggested that it merely serves as kind of rhetorical transition to a new topic. However, two observations suggest a real link to Paul's earlier discussion.

First, Paul has already broached the topic of Christian living, since that transition occurred back in 1:27. Note that Paul also spoke there about his 'presence' with and 'absence' from the church at Philippi. He followed his initial discussion about Christian community life (focusing in 1:27–2:4 on church unity and the humility that brings it about) with a brief, intervening Christological passage (2:5-11) that illustrated the kind of humility God exalts. That Christological passage furthered Paul's call for humble obedience. So now, Paul is transitioning back to direct exhortation.

Second, the focus of the Christological section (2:5-11) on the death, resurrection, and exaltation of Jesus has reminded Paul's readers of the heart of his gospel. That gospel involves the proclamation of salvation for all who have faith in the crucified and risen Christ. Having just rehearsed those gospel truths, Paul can now address the good works that flow out of that salvation life from those whom Christ has redeemed.

As Paul resumes his direct exhortation of the Philippians, he reminds them again of the intimate relationship he has with them (cf. 1:7-8; 4:1). They are his 'beloved'. Paul often speaks this way with his congregations, especially when he is about to call them to renew and further their Christian service (e.g., Rom. 12:19; 1 Cor. 4:14; 10:14; 15:58; 2 Cor. 7:1). In addition, Paul again refers to his sense of being separated from the Philippians, prompting us to recall his deep desire to return to them (1:8, 25-27; 2:24; 4:1).

Paul delivers this exhortation while simultaneously stating his admiration for the church. He reminds the Philippians of the obedience they had exhibited when he was with them and the ongoing submission to God they have shown during his absence from Philippi. He emphasizes their present fidelity, since he appreciates that they have continued to practice obedience despite their no longer being under the watchful eye of their beloved apostle.

Thus Paul situates his renewed call for Christian obedience in the context of his love for the Philippians and his confidence in their current service to Christ. This serves as a model to us as we minister to others: we must let people know that our concern for their Christian obedience springs from our love for them, from our appreciation of their current progress in the gospel, and from our desire for their continued growth in Christ.

Paul elsewhere employs the verb 'obey' (*hupakouō*) to refer to general Christian obedience[1] and to the obedience a child owes to parents or slaves owe to masters.[2] This involves submission to another, with a particular emphasis on doing what has been commanded. Intriguingly, Paul also repeatedly speaks of 'obeying the gospel',[3] which may seem surprising to those of us who think of the gospel as something that merely needs to be believed.

The most challenging issue in this verse concerns what it means to 'work out your own salvation with fear and trembling'. Does this indicate that we must work to achieve salvation? Alternatively, are we working out a salvation that is already ours in Christ? The latter provides the better option by far. The following four points indicate that Christians are called to live out the salvation Christ has already given them.

First, it would be inconsistent for Paul, who fervently upholds salvation by faith alone and not by works of the law,[4] to now suggest that Christians must rely on their own works to gain entrance into salvation.

Second, the key word in this passage is *katergazomai* ('work out'), which receives the object 'salvation' (*sōtēria*). It must be admitted that in some contexts, an object of *katergazomai* concerns what is *produced* by 'working'.[5] But in other places, the object of *katergazomai* is what one *performs* or *uses* in one's work.[6] The difference is slight, and it is difficult to distinguish the proper nuance in some contexts (e.g., 2 Cor. 9:11), but the

---

1 Rom. 6:16-17; 16:19; 2 Cor. 10:5-6; 2 Thess. 3:14.
2 Eph. 6:1-9; Col. 3:20-22.
3 Rom. 10:16; 2 Thess. 1:8; cf. Rom. 15:18.
4 E.g., Rom. 3:21-31; Gal. 2:16–3:14; Eph. 2:1-9.
5 Rom. 4:15; 5:3; 7:8, 13; 2 Cor. 4:17; 7:10, 11; 2 Cor. 2:12; Eph. 6:13.
6 Rom. 2:9; 7:17, 18, 20; 1 Cor. 5:3; cf. in the LXX Exod. 35:33, 38:24 [LXX 39:1]; Ps. 68:28 [67:29]; Ezek. 36:9.

second meaning accords well here with Paul's theology: the Christian is called to perform (or live out) a salvation which already is his or hers. The gift of salvation motivates the Christian to an obedient response.

Third, context here implies that God is the one who ultimately produces even the obedience we offer back to Him. This is stated quite clearly in the next verse (2:13). We can claim no pride in our works, as though we performed them autonomously. Rather, it is God who works in us (cf. Eph. 2:10).

Fourth, Paul frequently transitions in his writings from Christ's salvific work in the life of the believer to discussing the obedience that is the natural outflow of that salvation. Salvation is freely and graciously given to the Christian, and submission to Christ follows as a response to that great gift. We need only think of Ephesians 2:10 ('For we are his workmanship, created in Christ Jesus for good works, which God prepared beforehand, that we should walk in them'), which follows the great proclamation in Ephesians 2:8-9 ('For by grace you have been saved through faith. And this is not your own doing; it is the gift of God, not a result of works, so that no one may boast'). There, salvation is clearly granted graciously by God through faith to those who believe in the Lord Jesus Christ; yet that salvation necessarily issues into the works God Himself has prepared for the Christian to do. Similar sequences can be found in 2 Thessalonians 2:16-17 and Titus 2:14; and more broadly, in the relationship between Romans 3:21–5:21 and Romans 6 (among other places).

Thus Paul frequently establishes a sequence of salvation (predicated on the saving death and resurrection of Christ) overflowing into good works. Admittedly, that sequence appears less overt here in Philippians 2. However, if we acknowledge that the Christological passage of Philippians 2:5-11 (with its focus on the incarnation, death, and resurrection of Christ) serves as an essential encapsulation of the gospel (though admittedly without overt redemptive language), then the sequence from gospel salvation to Christian obedience is the same here as elsewhere in Paul.

Therefore, the Christian is not called to attain his or her own salvation through performing good works but to 'work out' the salvation he or she already possesses by grace through faith. This indeed reminds us that obedience is the expected outcome of salvation. Paul is not at all abashed at saying that Christians should engage in 'good works'.[7] And earlier, we remarked that Paul talks of 'obeying the gospel'.[8] He also refers to the obedience of faith (Rom. 16:26), with obedience evident in a faithful response to the gospel. Indeed, in the very passages that most directly argue for salvation by faith, Paul often goes on to speak of living out that faith in obedience through the doing of good works (again note Ephesians 2:8-10; or the flow of Romans 3–6; or the transition to discussing Christian living in Galatians 5:13ff.).

Many modern Christians are shocked by the words 'fear and trembling' here. Given God's gracious desire to lavish on us His salvation, what in the world does Paul mean when he speaks of working out our salvation with 'fear and trembling'? Does this not portray individuals cowering in fear before a vengeful God, vainly hoping to please Him?

However, 'fear and trembling' is not a concept that is foreign to Paul. Paul couples 'fear' with 'trembling' to explain his own approach to ministering to the Corinthians as he functions as a faithful servant under the power of God (1 Cor. 2:23). He also speaks of 'fear and trembling' as the proper disposition of a slave in obeying his master (Eph. 6:5). Even the Corinthians, in their desire to display their obedience to Christ, received Paul's servant Titus in 'fear and trembling' (2 Cor. 7:15) and are commended for doing so. In all these events, there is a notion that obedience brings with it a reverential awe in submission to another.

Of course, it is a widespread Old Testament theme that one should 'fear God'.[9] Yet many Christians are not cognizant of just how often that theme appears in the New Testament.[10] Still, we might also contrast these occurrences with passages where one is instructed not to be unduly afraid in the presence

---

7 2 Cor. 9:8; Col. 1:10; 2 Thess. 2:17; 2 Tim. 3:17; Titus 2:14.
8 Rom. 10:16; 2 Thess. 1:8; cf. Rom. 15:18.
9 E.g., Gen. 22:12; Lev. 19:14; 25:17; Deut. 4:10; 6:13, 24; Josh. 4:24; Pss. 67:7; 111:10; Prov. 1:7; Eccles. 12:13; Hos. 3:5; and dozens of other times.
10 E.g., Matt. 10:28; Luke 1:50; 12:5; Acts 9:31; 2 Cor. 5:11; 7:1; Heb. 11:7; 1 Pet. 1:17; 2:17; Rev. 11:18; 14:7; 15:4; 19:5.

of the Lord or His agents.[11] We also know that 'perfect love casts out fear'.[12] So how are we to understand the Christian call to 'fear God', or the summons here to work out our salvation 'in fear and trembling'?

Theologians have long correctly delineated at least two categories of fear of God in the Scriptures. The first is often classified as 'reverential awe', and it recognizes proper human response to the attributes and character of God (such as His authority, power, holiness, and omniscience). Such reverential awe rightly acknowledges God as being so far superior to His fallen creatures that we ought gladly to submit to Him and joyfully concede that we are always under His authority and discipline. This kind of fear is universally promoted in the Bible. The second involves a response that fails to acknowledge the Lord's gracious character, and thus is repelled by thoughts of Him and is constantly afraid of Him rather than being brought into closer relationship with him. This second type of fear is what must be cast out by the hope of the gospel. The first kind of fear rightly results in repentance, obedience, worship, and love; the second results in dread.

Both kinds of fear can be seen alongside, and in contrast to, one another in Exodus 20:20: 'Moses said to the people, "Do not *fear*, for God has come to test you, that the *fear* of him may be before you, that you may not sin."' Moses is admonishing the Israelites not to draw back from God's revelation out of shock and dismay but to brace themselves faithfully for the tests that lie ahead. They are to treat God with reverential awe, which leads to an acknowledgment of their sinfulness and a concurrent commitment to repent, to seek His salvific grace, and to imitate His holiness.

It is then with reverential fear that we tremble before God, though simultaneously mindful of His grace and confident of our deliverance from sin through the death and resurrection of Jesus Christ. With an appropriately submissive demeanor, we act to live out in obedience the salvation that is ours in Christ. We might well wonder, however, how we can hope to live obediently in the present, if as fallen human beings we

---

11 Dan. 10:12; Luke 2:10.
12 1 John 4:18; cf. Rom. 8:15; 2 Tim. 1:7.

have proven ourselves so faithless in the past. To answer that question, we turn to the next verse.

...for it is God who works in you, both to will and to work for his good pleasure (2:13).
In life, there exists the grave danger that we may take too much credit for our good works. On the other hand, when we think that the duty of obedience rests entirely on our frail shoulders, we can easily become overwhelmed. How can we escape both from our arrogant reliance on ourselves and from our own sense of personal inadequacy? Paul's solution is to credit God for the strength that enables Christian obedience.

This is, of course, consistent with Paul's approach elsewhere. Whereas the vileness of the flesh brings forth an evil harvest, the Spirit works holy fruit into the lives of Christ's followers. Thus, we who 'live by the Spirit' must 'keep in step with the Spirit' (Gal. 5:16-26). The Christian is no longer enslaved to sin, but has become Christ's servant (Rom. 6:15-23). All those who have called Christ 'Lord' now have the Spirit of God dwelling within and are led by the Spirit of God to live obedient lives (Rom. 8:9-17). We are 'in Christ', and thus we are dead to the things of the world and made alive by his resurrection power. The Christian has entered into this great Trinitarian relationship. We are in Christ and led by the Spirit, and God Himself works in us to accomplish His good pleasure.

This 'working' vocabulary overlaps well with 'working' out your salvation (2:12). God 'works in' that we might 'work out'. He wills His own purposes and energizes us to perform good works. This will result in His good pleasure (cf. in the Greek, 2 Thess. 1:11; also Eph. 1:5, 9; Phil. 1:15). This 'good pleasure' (which God 'wills' and 'works') testifies both to God's sovereign motives (it is *God's* pleasure that is accomplished through His strength and will) and to our own heart's desire as His people (which is to do that which pleases God).

Do you feel defeated, caught in sins that seem too overwhelming for you to overcome on your own? Then remember that the power of God resides in you, and that the Spirit leads you to an obedient response to the salvation that you already have in Christ. Do you at times catch yourself secretly thinking that you are doing OK on your own, or even asserting that God is lucky to have such a faithful follower like you? Well, then, remember that any strength you and I have to obey comes from outside ourselves. It is God who works in us.

We Christians ought to respond to our salvation and to the tremendous holiness of our God by relying on God's strength to empower us to do works that please Him.

Do all things without grumbling or questioning (2:14).
I have personally witnessed many grave setbacks in various Christian communities that have been initiated by a few people who like to complain. Gradually dissension grows, people become more and more irritated with one another, and fractures develop in a community that once stood in Christian harmony. Granted, we live in a fallen world, working alongside fellow church members who (like us) live in constant temptation to revert back to the flesh rather than to being led by the Spirit. And so there is probably much to complain about. However, a few grumbling comments or ill-phrased questions can sow dissension and disunity into a congregation. Paul's mandate here: 'Stop it!'

We have already observed how the theme of church unity is very significant in this epistle.[13] Paul recognizes, as did Jesus Himself, that our tongues can be dangerous weapons.[14] And the skirmishes (or outright wars) such a weapon foments can endanger the unity of the church.

'Grumbling' (*gongusmos*) refers to the kind of low-tone-of-voice, behind-the-scenes talk in which someone secretly derides another, expressing discontent, muttering, and complaining.[15] 'Questioning' (*dialogismos*) signifies a tendency to debate and to take sides, often in the form of more open bickering.[16] Together these represent airing our grievances, in secret or in public, with the result that divisions arise in the community.

This is not to put a lid on all truly constructive feedback and interaction within a congregation. And this verse should

---

13 Cf. 1:27-30; 2:1-4; cf. 4:1-2.
14 Matt. 12:36-37; 15:11; cf. Prov. 16:23-29; James 3:1-12.
15 Cf. John 7:12; Acts 6:1; 1 Pet. 4:9.
16 Rom. 14:1; 1 Cor. 3:20; 1 Tim. 2:8.

certainly not serve as a pretense for church leaders to refuse to give ear to the real needs and desires of others in the congregation. Indeed, the apostles themselves modeled the kind of gracious Christian leadership that listens even to 'grumbling' and that responds by meeting the needs of the grumblers (see Acts 6:1ff.). However, we must agree that in the Christian church everyone plays on the same team and works toward the same goals. Thus, our speech should be used to edify and not to destroy. We should always give a gracious word, said at the timely moment, for the sake of building up the church. If we have no such word to say, then we must put a bridle on our tongue and control our speech. We do well to remember Paul's comment in Ephesians 4:29: 'Let no corrupting talk come out of your mouths, but only such as is good for building up, as fits the occasion, that it may give grace to those who hear' (see also Eph. 4:30-32).

...that you may be blameless and innocent, children of God without blemish in the midst of a crooked and twisted generation, among whom you shine as lights in the world (2:15). The purpose of keeping a tight rein on our speech (2:14) is that we might live blamelessly as God's children. At first glance, this appears to be an overstatement (if not just a complete *non sequitur*), especially since the opening 'that' in Greek is actually better translated 'in order that' (*hina*). Does what we merely mutter really matter that much? How can Paul truly maintain such a strong connection between what we say and Christian holiness?

We do well here to remember the statement in the epistle of James, 'If anyone does not stumble in what he says, he is a perfect man, able also to bridle his whole body' (James 3:2). James here is drawing on the extensive Old Testament wisdom tradition about the tongue – a tradition that Paul also knew very well.[17] Jesus notes that 'it is not what goes into the mouth that defiles a person, but what comes out of the mouth; this defiles a person' (Matt. 15:11). The things we say tell a good deal about our hearts. Indeed, speech is the heart revealed in words, and it often anticipates the further physical actions

---

17 E.g., Prov. 18:21; 21:23; see further Prov. 10:20, 31; 12:18-19; 15:2, 4; 17:4, 20; 21:6; 25:15, 23; 26:28; 28:23; 31:26.

that we perform (whether for good or for ill). Thus, the ability to control our speech is a vital concern in Christian obedience.

This point deserves to be emphasized a bit more. We often downplay the words we speak as if they were unimportant. 'It was just talk; I didn't mean anything by it,' we might say. Meanwhile, we have injured people by what we have just said. However, for those who truly wish to be obedient in Christian holiness, the tongue becomes a monitor of the heart itself.

Moreover, mischief and destruction in the church can be blamed more often on harsh words than on brutal actions. Churches occasionally divide over actions, but more frequently it is words that are the cause of dissensions that lead to factions. For example, one church leader repeatedly demeans another, and this quickly spirals into divisions within the community. Or the local church gossip spreads news about the goings-on among various cliques, and this hardens the opposition of these groups toward one another. Paul reminds us that if we want to be blameless, we must watch our tongues.

In this verse, Paul piles on the imagery of Christian purity. 'Blameless' means there is nothing worthy of censure. God, in a central Old Testament text, calls for Abraham to be 'blameless' (Gen. 17:1); and Job, though he overrates his own virtue, is repeatedly praised for his blamelessness (Job 1:1, 8; 2:3). 'Innocence' refers to a lack of experiential knowledge of evil (cf. Rom. 16:19; Matt. 10:16). Such is the goal of the Christian church, that she both collectively and individually be 'without blemish' before her Lord.[18] 'Without blemish' draws on the concept of purity, such as the purity expected from any sacrificial offering made to the Lord (e.g., Exod. 29:1; Lev. 1:3). In short, all of these terms portray the moral purity of the church. For that deep holiness and purity to pervade our churches, we must be obedient through the Lord's strength, especially in our speech to one another.

This purity of the church is set in stark relief against the darkness of a crooked and twisted world. With the Fall, humans entered into a state of sin, and thus the sin that pervades individuals infiltrates society as a whole. Paul compounds two words to imply that what should be metaphorically

---

18 Cf. Eph. 1:4; 5:27; Col. 1:22; cf. 1 Thess. 3:13; Jude 24.

'straight' has been 'twisted' and made 'crooked'. Elsewhere the present world is presented as a 'generation' that is evil,[19] 'crooked',[20] and 'twisted'.[21] Paul alludes to how Christians live among a world of people who are like the rebellious Israelites described in Deuteronomy 32:5: 'They have dealt corruptly with him; they are no longer his children because they are blemished; they are a crooked and twisted generation.' Unlike those faithless Israelites who are 'no longer his children' and 'are blemished', the Christian church ought to stand in the tradition of the remnant of true Israel, as God's adopted children, pure in the way they reflect His good pleasure.

We do well to remember that the church must persevere among a fallen world that is enslaved to sin. Therefore, the church must live out Christian fellowship in the midst of such opposition. Rather than retreat and hide, the church is called to shine its light in this fallen world. The world is to perceive a different and better way – a way that leads to salvation and obedience to the Lord. Paul likely has in mind here Jesus' own teaching (which was well remembered in the early church) that His followers are to be 'lights' to the world around us.[22] This 'light' consists not only of representing the gospel in words, but in purity of Christian obedience.

...holding fast to the word of life, so that in the day of Christ I may be proud that I did not run in vain or labor in vain (2:16).
It is by 'holding fast to the word of life' that Christians shine as lights in this world. What is the 'word of life'? Is it the Scriptures or is it the gospel message? This very question betrays a false dichotomy. Certainly in the New Testament, the 'words of life' can refer to the gospel (Acts 5:20), especially as announced and embodied by the Lord Himself (John 6:63, 68; 1 John 1:1). Such usage likely draws on Deuteronomy's reference to God's message as the 'word' which is 'your very life' (32:47). Moreover, Paul elsewhere speaks of '*holding on* to the teaching' (1 Tim. 4:16). But this reminds us that the gospel, and all Christian instruction, was deeply tied to the revealed word of Scripture as Paul taught

---

19 Matt. 11:16; 12:39; 16:4; 17:17.
20 Acts 2:40; cf. Deut. 32:5; Ps. 77:8.
21 Acts 13:10; cf. Matt. 17:17; Luke 9:41; Acts 20:30.
22 Matt. 5:14-16; Mark 4:21; Luke 8:16; 11:33; cf. Isa. 49:6; 60:3; 1 Thess. 5:5.

it. Thus, the Christian is here called actively to pursue at all times the gospel and its Scriptural witness, for these bring true life to the faithful hearer and doer. Such Christian obedience to the word of life shines in this dark world.

There is a strong note of perseverance in this verse. Christians are to 'hold fast' (*epechō*) to the word of life – to maintain their grasp on the gospel and its Scriptural witness. In the midst of a 'crooked and twisted generation' (2:15), the opposition to our faith can dissuade us from fidelity to Christ. Therefore, even amid such opposition, we must 'hold fast' with the strength that God supplies, and we should look forward to the day when Christ returns and every knee bows to Him.

Paul anticipates the return of Christ. That moment when Christ returns represents the culmination of eschatological expectation. In other words, while we have a foretaste of Christ's rule in the present age, we still look forward to a future age when Christ returns to establish His everlasting rule over all creation. That is the 'day of Christ'. We noted earlier in examining Philippians 1:6 and 1:10 that the 'day of Christ' is the 'day of the Messiah', which Paul uses interchangeably with the important Old Testament theme of the 'Day of the Lord'.

On that day, Paul will be proud. Really, Paul, 'proud'? Has Paul not just argued stridently for the need for humility in the Christian life (Phil. 2:1-5)? How can he claim to boast now? However, there is indeed a sense in which Paul is happy to boast in the faithfulness of others in Christ. Paul rightly rejoices with what the Lord has done through him, as Christ has brought many people from the nations into His kingdom.

I think we must envisage this in the same way that a father will say to his child, 'I am proud of you!' The Philippians, Paul's children in Christ, would have been glad to hear that their spiritual 'father' was proud of them. Indeed, Paul elsewhere speaks of the pride he has in the congregations among whom he has ministered.[23] Their perseverance in the gospel in this present age will result in great blessing at the return of Christ, and that will make their spiritual father (Paul) proud. Moreover, Paul hopes that these Christians will be motivated by this image to persevere in their present lives.

---

23 E.g., 2 Cor. 7:4, 14; 8:24; 9:2; 1 Thess. 2:19.

Paul frequently employs the Greek for 'pride' or 'boast' (*kauchēma* and its cognates) in a negative sense.[24] Yet there are times when such pride can have positive overtones, such as when Paul 'boasts' in his weakness,[25] or when he endorses others to boast in the same (2 Cor. 5:12). Paul boasts in 'the testimony of our conscience that we behaved in the world with simplicity and godly sincerity, not by earthly wisdom but by the grace of God' (2 Cor. 1:12). Paul frequently 'boasts' about the Christian faith of other believers (2 Cor. 9:3). And elsewhere (as he does here) he speaks of the kind of boasting Christians can experience at the return of Christ as they rejoice at being welcomed into Christ's kingdom (see 2 Corinthians 1:14: '…on the day of our Lord Jesus you will boast of us as we will boast of you'). In fact, earlier in this letter, Paul told the Philippians, 'in me your boast may abound in Christ Jesus' (Phil. 1:26 – see our previous comments on this verse).

Ultimately Paul boasts in the gospel (Gal. 6:14) and in God the Father and His Son, through whom we have redemption (see Romans 5:2, 11 – where 'boast' [*kauchaomai*] is often translated 'rejoice'). However, it is clear, even when Paul boasts of his accomplishments on behalf of the gospel (Rom. 15:17), that they have not been done under his own strength but through 'what Christ has accomplished through me to bring the Gentiles to obedience' (Rom. 15:18) and through 'the power of the Spirit of God' (Rom. 15:19).

Paul thus lives out his own creed: 'Let the one who boasts, boast in the Lord.'[26] Such Christian boasting rejoices both in the Lord's salvation of us and in the work He has accomplished through us. It is not wrong to take joy in the work of our hands as long as we continually remember that all we receive and all that we do has been accomplished by God graciously working in us.

Concerning the word 'run', Paul likes to use athletic metaphors to depict how hard he works,[27] even speaking elsewhere of the danger of 'running in vain' (Gal. 2:2). Similarly, the word 'labor' (*kopiaō*) is a frequent descriptor of

---

24 Rom. 2:23; 3:27; 4:2; 1 Cor. 1:29; 4:7; 5:6; 2 Cor. 11:12; Gal. 6:13; Eph. 2:9.
25 2 Cor. 11:16–12:10; cf. 1 Cor. 9:15-16; Rom. 5:3.
26 1 Cor. 1:31; 2 Cor. 10:17; cf. 1 Cor. 1:28-31; 2 Cor. 10:12-17; and see Jer. 9:24.
27 Phil. 3:12-14; also 1 Cor. 9:24-27; 2 Tim. 2:5; 4:7-8.

Paul's ministry[28] and of the service of his co-workers in the gospel mission.[29] 'Labor' is a word that evokes committed and diligent work. Christian ministry requires great toil as we pour our lives into others for the sake of the gospel, even in the midst of a 'crooked and twisted generation' (2:15).

Paul often conveys his own awareness of how hard he has labored for the sake of the gospel (cf. 2 Cor. 11:16–12:10). It has cost him much, including having been imprisoned. It was difficult work that had its frustrations as people repudiated Christ, and as churches fractured and fell prey to dissensions and heresies. In such harrowing times, there was the danger that Paul's work might come up 'empty' or 'in vain' (*kenos*; cf. 1 Thess. 3:5). Paul's awareness of this danger causes him repeatedly to rest on the assurance he has in Christ that it will indeed all be worthwhile.[30] Nevertheless, this work is also what his Lord has called him to do, and it results in the joy of seeing others come to Christ.

Still, in the midst of his personal struggles and toil in spreading the gospel, Paul can take confidence that he will be proud of the Philippians when Christ returns. Paul hopes the Philippians, for their part, find encouragement in this. They will be motivated to Christian obedience – to being lights in a dark world – in part because they know it makes their beloved 'father' in the faith proud of them, and will continue to make him proud, especially at the return of Christ.

Even if I am to be poured out as a drink offering upon the sacrificial offering of your faith, I am glad and rejoice with you all (2:17). Evoking the depth of toil he expends in his ministry, Paul compares his unremitting service to an Old Testament sacrifice. Nevertheless, his work is connected to his relationship with the churches he helped found, so his sacrificial service is poured out on their own ministry of faith. And, though such labors are draining, still they can rejoice together in the fruit of this service.

The verb translated as 'poured out as a drink offering' (*spendomai*) referred in pagan antiquity to the common action of pouring out wine in honor of a god or goddess. In the Septuagint

---
28 1 Cor. 4:12; 15:10; Gal. 4:1; Col. 1:29; 1 Tim. 4:10.
29 Rom. 16:6, 12; 1 Cor. 16:16; 1 Thess. 5:12; 1 Tim. 5:17; 2 Tim. 2:6.
30 1 Thess. 2:1; 3:5-10; cf. Isa. 49:4; 65:23; 1 Cor. 15:58.

translation of the Old Testament, this verb can be used to depict those who poured out drink offerings to idols (Jer. 39:29; 51:17), but in the Old Testament it especially refers to the Jewish offering of pouring out wine to God (Num. 4:7; 28:7), which was often combined with animal sacrifice. In Paul's metaphorical usage, he connects this sense of a sacrificial offering to God with the idea of the personal toll exacted by such sacrificial labor. It is as though Paul is being drained of himself for the sake of others. He is being expended and poured out in the act of worship. Paul also touches on this metaphor again toward the end of his life: 'For I am already being poured out as a drink offering, and the time of my departure has come' (2 Tim. 4:6).

This verse can be most literally rendered into English: '*But*, even if I am poured out as a libation onto the sacrifice *and service* of your faith, I rejoice and I *rejoice with* you all.' Such a translation highlights three minor items that could be missed in the ESV translation above. First, the verse in Greek begins with a strong contrast to the preceding verse ('but') – whereas those who run and labor can expect a reward for their work, those who are 'poured out' see no immediate benefit for their service. Even if Paul were to be spent up in sacrificial service without immediate hope of reward for himself, he will rejoice because his ministry has led to the benefit of those who come to faith in Christ.

Second, where the ESV translates 'the sacrificial offering of your faith' the Greek literally reads 'the sacrifice *and service* of your faith' (e.g., KJV, NASB, NIV translations). The word 'service' (*leitourgia*) is a term for the actions of those who provide cultic service in worship (especially priests). Since such worship principally involves offering sacrifices, it is possible that the combination of 'sacrifice and service' forms a so-called hendiadys (two items connected by 'and' that really only convey one meaning), and thus the combination intends the idea of a 'sacrificial service' or 'sacrificial offering'. In any case, the image appears to depict a drink offering being poured onto some other worshipful offering. Metaphorically, the drink offering is Paul's labor, but the 'sacrificial offering' comes from the faith of the church as a whole (cf. Rom. 12:1).

Third, the combination of 'I rejoice' (*chairō*) and 'I rejoice with' (*sunchairō*) emphasizes that not only does Paul experience joy individually, but he also experiences it in community with the

Philippians. Paul's ministerial service, despite its cost, still brings him joy, and that joy is something he shares with the Philippian church.

Likewise you also should be glad and rejoice with me (2:18). This short verse re-emphasizes the mutuality of joy Paul speaks about in verse 17. It repeats the exact same Greek words he uses there but with a different grammatical subject (the Philippians rather than himself). Paul clearly encourages the Philippians to rejoice with him in his sacrificial service and also in the resulting outcome in their own faith and sacrifice. See Additional Note.

Throughout the book of Philippians we have observed how often Paul speaks of 'joy'.[31] This concept receives special emphasis here in verses 17-18, with four verbs in two verses all intoning the refrain of rejoicing. As elsewhere (1:18), the most striking feature of Paul's appeal to joy here is that it comes despite his difficult circumstances and in the midst of his strenuous toil in Christian service. Paul clearly found his joy not in the ephemerals of everyday life, but in fulfilling the purpose of his calling to minister Christ to others. And he invites the church of Christ to embrace that same joy.

Summary
Paul has just sung of the humility and exaltation of Jesus (2:5-11) – most exemplified in Christ's incarnation, sacrificial death, resurrection, and session at the right hand of God. That passage reminds us of Paul's gospel, and it exemplifies a proper humble Christian disposition toward others. Having emphasized those gospel truths, Paul returns to his overarching call to Christian citizenship (1:27ff.). As those who have been given salvation in Christ, Christians are to work out that salvation through obedience (2:12). This is performed in the context of a reverential awe of God Almighty. Yet, such obedience cannot be self-generated, rather God Himself is the one who works within us so that we may do good works in a way that pleases Him (2:13).

Returning to the disposition of the Christian community, Paul then calls Christians to be careful about how they speak – grumbling and complaining are to be set aside (2:14). What we say matters, so much so that Paul considers the putting

---

31 Phil. 1:4, 18, 25; 2:2, 17-18, 28-29; 3:1; 4:1, 4, 10.

off of such grumbling necessary in order to achieve Christian purity (2:15). We must be careful lest our speech undermine the harmony of the church.

In the midst of a world that opposes God, and is thus 'crooked and twisted', the purity of the Christian life should serve as a beacon of light. And, in order to shine that light, Christians must grasp onto the Good News found in Scripture, with the goal of persevering until Christ returns (2:16).

As Paul reflects on such matters, he is also well aware that he can motivate these dear fellow believers to perseverance in some measure by appealing to his status as the spiritual 'father' of the Philippian church (2:16). They can make him proud by their perseverance. Nevertheless, though Paul is eager for their gospel light to shine, he is content in his ministerial service, even rejoicing that he is being spent up and poured out like a drink offering (2:17-18). Finally, he invites the Philippians to share in his joy.

In these few verses, we learn much about Christian life and ministry. The Christian life flows out of God's own empowering work within us. Nevertheless we are not passive in this endeavor, but we must always submit in reverent awe and actively work out the salvation that is already ours. We ought to perform the good works that are in keeping with the gospel reality that has been graciously granted us. Even the seemingly unimportant issue of what we say with our tongues provides a window into our souls. Christian purity requires that we be careful about how we treat others – especially in what we say. The peace and purity of the church requires that we keep a tight rein on our words. The Christian also must persevere and do so while looking forward to the time when Christ will return and establish his reign over the whole world. In the meantime, opposition is to be expected in a world mired in sin. In the midst of this world, we, as ministers of the gospel (and truly that is all of us who hold on to the 'word of life'), rejoice to pour ourselves out in sacrificial service to others on behalf of our Lord. May we indeed live out this calling!

Questions for Personal Reflection:
1. Some people may be concerned about the phrase 'work out your own salvation with fear and trembling' (2:12). How would you interact with their concerns?

What is meant by 'fear and trembling'? How can we best teach that salvation is by faith and that obedience to the law does not grant a righteous status before God (cf. 3:9) without also diminishing the need to respond to God's gift of salvation with thankful obedience? How does 2:12-13 help us with these questions?

2. Explain how we can find encouragement to persevere in obedience when we know that 'God works in you, both to will and to work for his good pleasure' (2:13)? How does this phrase speak to issues concerning the sovereignty of God and the willing actions of a Christian?

3. On what occasions in life are you especially tempted to participate in 'grumbling and questioning'? How can such activity imperil a Christian community? Name some ways you and others can seek to avoid this temptation.

4. Give some examples you have witnessed of Christians who have shone as lights in this world (2:15), or who have held fast to the word of life (2:16) in the midst of a crooked and twisted generation (2:15). What are some ways that we can encourage each other to live as faithful disciples of Christ in this generation?

5. Reflect on how 2:16-18 would have sounded to Paul's original audience. If you were in their midst, how would you have responded to Paul's words?

Study Questions:

1. Read through 2:12-18. In what ways do you see these verses connecting with the rest of Philippians?

2. What does it mean to 'work out your own salvation with fear and trembling' (2:12)? Does this imply that our good works accomplishes salvation? How do grace, faith, works, and salvation relate together elsewhere in Paul (e.g., Eph. 2:8-10; Titus 3:5-8)? Are those relationships any different in this passage? You may want to compare this with Philippians 3:9-10.

3. In what ways can you find encouragement from 'it is God who works in you, both to will and to work for

his good pleasure' (2:13)? How do you understand this passage? What does this say about God's sovereignty? What does it say about our ability to persevere and to perform good works as Christians?

4. Why do you think Paul puts such an emphasis on 'Do all things without grumbling or questioning' (2:14)? What does he mean by 'grumbling' and by 'questioning'?

5. On what occasions in life are you especially tempted to participate in 'grumbling and questioning'? How can such activity imperil a Christian community? Name some ways you and others can seek to avoid this temptation.

6. What does verse 2:15 say about the proper relationship between the Christian and the world?

7. What does it look like to 'hold fast to the word of life'? Name some of the resources that we as Christians can draw on as we persevere to this end.

8. How would 2:16–18 serve as an encouragement to perseverance for those who knew Paul as a close friend and as a father in the faith?

9. Give some examples you have witnessed of Christians who have shone as lights in this world (2:15), or who have held fast to the word of life (2:16) in the midst of a crooked and twisted generation (2:15). What are some ways that we can encourage each other to live as faithful disciples of Christ in our own generation?

Additional Notes:

2:18 The verbs 'be glad' (i.e., 'rejoice') and 'rejoice with' here in verse 18 can be either indicatives that describe the Philippians' current state or imperatives that command them to rejoice (both indicative and imperative forms would be the same here in Greek). In other words, this could be translated either 'you rejoice and rejoice with me' or 'you *should* rejoice and rejoice with me.' Most modern English translations assume they are imperatives, though the King James does not. The use of this verb as an imperative in 3:1 and 4:4 would favor this interpretation here as well. Yet the difference is a minor one, since Paul is clearly in context seeking to encourage the Philippians to rejoice with him.

9

Two Exemplars of Faithful Service
(Philippians 2:19-30)

[19]I hope in the Lord Jesus to send Timothy to you soon, so that I too may be cheered by news of you. [20]For I have no one like him, who will be genuinely concerned for your welfare. [21]They all seek their own interests, not those of Jesus Christ. [22]But you know Timothy's proven worth, how as a son with a father he has served with me in the gospel. [23]I hope therefore to send him just as soon as I see how it will go with me, [24]and I trust in the Lord that shortly I myself will come also.

[25]I have thought it necessary to send to you Epaphroditus my brother and fellow worker and fellow soldier, and your messenger and minister to my need, [26]for he has been longing for you all and has been distressed because you heard that he was ill. [27]Indeed he was ill, near to death. But God had mercy on him, and not only on him but on me also, lest I should have sorrow upon sorrow. [28]I am the more eager to send him, therefore, that you may rejoice at seeing him again, and that I may be less anxious. [29]So receive him in the Lord with all joy, and honor such men, [30]for he nearly died for the work of Christ, risking his life to complete what was lacking in your service to me.

Paul conducted ministry in relationship to others, and he was not the solitary apostle that we can sometimes imagine. Rather, as is repeatedly emphasized in the book of Acts,[1] Paul relied heavily on those traveling with him as well

---

1 E.g., Acts 13:2; 15:40; 16:3, 25; 19:22; 20:4-6.

as on his local hosts. And Paul is not abashed to speak with great fondness of these men and women (cf. Romans 16). Moreover, Paul knew the value to the churches of good exemplars of Christian service, and some excellent examples were to be found among his own traveling retinue. Thus these few verses provide a brief glimpse into Paul's relational ministry, and these two servants of Christ provide patterns for us to emulate.

I hope in the Lord Jesus to send Timothy to you soon, so that I too may be cheered by news of you (2:19).
This verse appears on the face of things to introduce a rather abrupt change of topics. However, the Greek actually contains a loose connecting particle (*de* – variously translated 'and' or 'but', cf. KJV), which provides a moderate connection with the preceding verses. Although such a connection could be in place merely to keep the rhetorical flow of the epistle going, the reader is not wholly unprepared for this transition. At the end of the previous paragraph in chapter two, Paul has spoken in more personal terms about his relationship to the Philippians (for whom Paul labors, over whom he wants to be proud, and with whom he rejoices). There is also the conceptual connection between the 'rejoicing' mentioned repeatedly in 2:17-18 and the desire to be 'cheered' in this verse. Moreover, Paul's separation from immediate contact with them means that he wants to hear more news of them. He remains their spiritual father who longs not only to be proud of them in the future (2:16), but also to rejoice in their Christian growth in the present. Thus the reader can appreciate why Paul now discusses his plans to send Timothy and Epaphroditus to Philippi.

Timothy is mentioned in the opening salutation of this epistle (1:1). The present reader may wish to return to our comments on Philippians 1:1 in order to learn more about Timothy. That verse portrays Paul and Timothy as co-authors of this letter. However, as we noted earlier, Paul often speaks in this letter in the first person singular ('I' or 'me' or 'my'; see e.g., 1:3, 7, 8, 9, 12, 16, 18, 19). And here, Paul as author mentions his plans to send Timothy to the Philippians. Paul is clearly the main author of the epistle, as this verse indirectly emphasizes.

Nevertheless, Paul is preparing the way for Timothy to travel on his behalf to Philippi. He wants the church there to receive Timothy as the apostle's own delegate. Thus he emphasizes, even before Timothy leaves for Philippi, that Timothy's visit will be at Paul's behest (2:19). Paul further anticipates this visit by rallying respect for Timothy, predicated on his own admiration of his spiritual son and ministerial colleague (2:20-22). It may be that the 'co-authoring' of this epistle was itself designed to increase the esteem the Philippian church had for Timothy (1:1).

Yet, Timothy was not unknown to the Philippians, since Acts implies his presence in Philippi at the beginning of Paul's ministry there.[2] Certainly this passage before us assumes that the Philippians remember Timothy (Phil. 2:22). Paul is thus connecting relationally with the Philippians through Timothy, but also he is reminding them of who Timothy is – a trusted delegate and companion of Paul who, like Paul, is concerned for the Philippians.

Paul's plan to send Timothy has not yet been put into action, but he 'hopes' (cf. 2:23) to do so 'in the Lord Jesus'. Elsewhere, when Paul announces such travel plans, he frequently mentions the word 'hope'.[3] Though hope is an important theological term for Paul,[4] we need not read all of that theology into this occurrence, except perhaps to suggest that Paul recognized his plans were always dependent on the Lord's will. We have previously studied the theological importance of Paul calling Jesus 'Lord' (cf. comments on Phil. 1:2; 2:11). While Paul often employs the fuller expression 'the Lord Jesus Christ', in many other places he refers simply (as he does here) to the 'Lord Jesus'.[5]

Paul is the one who will 'send' Timothy, reminding us that in the midst of the deep collegial relationship between Paul and Timothy, Paul remained the apostle and Timothy his spiritual son. Yet, as one 'sent' by an apostle to a church, Timothy will serve there as an apostolic delegate, with the apostle

---

2 Cf. Acts 16:1-3 as it flows into Acts 16:11ff.; cf. further Acts 19:22 and possibly 20:3-5.
3 Rom. 15:24; 1 Cor. 16:7; 1 Tim. 3:14; Philem. 22.
4 Cf. e.g., Rom. 5:4-5:5; 8:24-25; 1 Cor. 13:13; Titus 2:13.
5 E.g., Rom. 10:9; 14:14; 1 Cor. 11:23; 12:3; 16:23; 2 Cor. 4:14; 11:31; Eph. 1:15; Col. 3:17; 1 Thess. 4:1-2; 2 Thess. 1:7; Philem. 1:5.

himself directing the church to heed Timothy's preaching and ministry. Though Paul is non-committal about when his plans to send Timothy will come to fruition, he nevertheless hopes to do so 'soon'. Elsewhere, Paul anticipates a similar immediacy of action (1 Cor. 4:19; 2 Tim. 4:9). Even in this passage, Paul himself wants to come 'soon' to the Philippians (see comments on 2:24).

By sending Timothy, Paul purposes to learn more about the situation in Philippi. He also anticipates that he will 'be cheered by news of you'. This simultaneously conveys optimism over the state of the church, and calls the church to live up to the enthusiasm of their beloved apostle. The Greek word translated 'cheered' (*eupsucheō*) is found only here in the New Testament; it means to 'hearten' someone – to encourage them and make them glad. The English 'news of you' translates the more idiomatic Greek 'knowing the things concerning you.'

Thus in this short verse, Paul announces his plans to send Timothy as his apostolic delegate, and he further motivates the Philippians to Christian obedience on the basis of their desire that Paul will receive from Timothy an encouraging report.

For I have no one like him, who will be genuinely concerned for your welfare. They all seek their own interests, not those of Jesus Christ (2:20-21).
On the face of things in these verses, Paul explains why he has selected Timothy as his delegate to the church in Philippi. Yet, there are at least two undercurrents here. First, Paul continues to build their respect for Timothy because he desires them to receive Timothy well. Second, Paul is building up Timothy and Epaphroditus as models of Christian ministry to be imitated and honored by the church (cf. 2:29).

Paul provides two rationales for selecting Timothy for this job. The first reason he plans to send Timothy concerns the unique kindred spirit he and Timothy share. Where the ESV translates 'I have no one like him', the Greek reads 'I have no one like-minded' or better 'I have no one like-souled'. The Greek 'like-souled' (*isopsuchos*) conveys the idea that Paul and Timothy partake of what we might call a 'kindred spirit' (see Additional Note).

This leads into the second rationale Paul offers for selecting Timothy for this assignment: he, like Paul, is truly concerned for the Philippians' well-being. The relative clause (beginning with 'who') indicates one important way that Paul and Timothy are 'like-souled' (i.e., both Paul and Timothy are united in their concern for the Philippians). Yet, this clause also indicates that Timothy's care for the Philippians makes him well suited to the task.

This relative clause could literally be rendered 'who truly will be concerned about the things concerning you'. The word here for 'concern' (*merimnaō*) can bear both positive connotations (as here; cf. 1 Cor. 7:34; 12:25) as well as negative ones (as in Phil. 4:6). In the latter instance, care turns to anxiety. However, there remains a proper place for an appropriate care and concern for others, and Paul is convinced Timothy shares his compassionate devotion to the Philippian church.

Paul, then, in order to support his claim that he has 'no one like' Timothy, contrasts in verse 21 Timothy's concern for the church with others who are self-absorbed. The most striking feature of this verse stems from the little word 'all'. How can it be that they 'all' seek their own interest? Surely, Paul knows other Christians who are not so selfish. The apostle must be employing hyperbolic language. Just a few verses later, Paul has some very complimentary things to say of Epaphroditus (2:25-30), who is called a 'fellow worker and a fellow soldier' (2:25), who is to be 'honored' (2:29), and who not only 'risked his life' for Paul's sake (2:30) but also longed for his fellow Philippians (2:26). If we were to take Paul's hyperbolic language in 2:21 to indicate that everyone other than Timothy and Paul was selfish, then the kind words about Epaphroditus, which immediately follow this passage, make little sense.

Therefore, Paul exaggerates a bit out of his passionate feeling that so many people fall far short of fully giving themselves to the concerns of Christ and His church. We could even speculate that his attention has flipped back briefly to those he mentioned in 1:15 – people who 'preach Christ from envy and rivalry'. Certainly Paul has experienced first-hand the selfishness that can rear its ugly head within the church. By contrast, these experiences have made Paul all the more appreciative of Timothy's genuine concern and proven worth.

Yet, there may be another nuance here. The last time he spoke of 'their own interests' was back in 2:4. There, in the midst of his call to Christian unity, he instructs each member in the church to 'look not only to his own interests, but also to the interests of others' (2:4). This requires that they '[d]o nothing from rivalry or conceit, but in humility count others more significant than yourselves' (2:3). In essence then, Timothy models the very kind of Christian behavior Paul calls forth from the Philippians. Conversely, the others who 'seek their own interests' (2:21) serve as the antitype of the behavior the apostle endorses. So, this brief verse serves not merely as an embittered complaint about selfishness in the church, but as an instructive aside to the Philippian church to align themselves with the kind of considerate people whom Paul applauds – people like Timothy.

But you know Timothy's proven worth, how as a son with a father he has served with me in the gospel (2:22).
The Philippians do indeed know Timothy, as we remarked earlier. Yet they know, in particular, that he is a man of excellent character. The Greek word translated 'proven worth' (*dokimē*) stems from a family of words that refer to being 'tested' (cf. 2 Cor. 8:2; 13:3). In this context, what has been 'tested' is Timothy's character (cf. 2 Cor. 2:9; 9:13). Paul has said elsewhere, 'We rejoice in our sufferings, knowing that suffering produces endurance, and endurance produces character [*dokimē*], and character [*dokimē*] produces hope' (Rom. 5:3-4). Timothy is a man whose character has been tested and approved.

Paul highlights one particular aspect of Timothy's character – his service alongside Paul as a son would assist his father. In much of the Western world today, it is difficult to recognize the original impact of these words, since family values do not presently achieve the same standard as they do in other parts of the world or as they did in antiquity. The family was the basic social unit in Judaism, and indeed in much of the ancient Mediterranean world. And in a society that modeled itself on an agrarian economy and ethos, family farming was the prototype of how such a social unit functioned. Father and son tilled the field together. Even in urban life, the son was expected to labor in the family enterprise and inherit the family business. Moreover, fathers were the ones in charge of the whole household, and the most basic response expected of children was obedience to the father. Therefore, in the ethic of the day, sons were to be diligent co-laborers with their fathers, submissive to them in all respects (cf. Col. 3:20; Eph. 6:1-4). One of the best things you could say about the character of any son in antiquity was that he was attentive to his duties to (and alongside) his father. This was so fundamental to both Jewish and Graeco-Roman ethics that Paul's words would have resonated as a deep endorsement of Timothy's character.

Beyond that, in such first-century contexts, the son served as the ultimate representative of the father. The authority of the son rested on the respect accorded to the family, of whom the ultimate representative was the father. After the son reached maturity, he could be granted the right to represent the interests of the family. Thus in this verse, Paul also reminds the Philippians that when Timothy comes, he bears the commission and authority beyond that of a mere ambassador of Paul, but that of Paul's own son in the faith.

Nevertheless, we should also recognize that this testifies to a dear relationship between Paul and Timothy. When Paul was at Lystra, the young disciple Timothy had earned a good reputation among the churches in that part of Asia Minor; and Paul specifically wanted Timothy to accompany him on his second missionary journey (Acts 16:1-4). From that time on, it appears that Timothy was a trusted traveling companion. Moreover, Paul must have taken a special interest in the discipleship of young Timothy, raising him in the faith as a father would a son. Thus Paul addresses Timothy as 'my beloved and faithful child in the Lord', as 'my true child in the faith' (1 Tim. 1:2; also used of Titus in Titus 1:4), and as 'my beloved child' (2 Tim. 1:2). Paul elsewhere employs such language to whole churches, who are his spiritual children.[6] All such contexts exhibit a strong notion of compassion and concern. Thus, Paul's fatherly love for Timothy also shines through this verse.

---

6 Gal. 4:19; 1 Cor. 4:14-15; 1 Thess. 2:11-12; cf. Philem. 10.

Timothy served with Paul in the gospel. The verb for 'serve' here (*douleuō*) is related to the typical word for 'slave' (*doulos*), and such servitude is sometimes explicitly connected to slavery in the New Testament.[7] However, the worship of God Almighty is also often depicted in Scripture in terms of such submissive service.[8] This reminds us that Paul (and Timothy) readily adopt the title *doulos* ('slave' or 'servant') to describe their position of service before God (see notes on Phil. 1:1). Certainly, Paul conveys that he and Timothy participate faithfully in the kind of service that gives oneself fully and wholly in submission to God.

Paul and Timothy serve in the 'gospel'. Found repeatedly throughout Philippians (1:5, 7, 12, 16, 27; 4:3, 15 – see notes on these verses as well), this is the 'good news' of salvation found in Christ though His redemptive work in His incarnate life, death, and resurrection. This remarkable good news comes with the hope of Christ's return, and with the awareness that Christ reigns even now, empowering His servants to be His agents in this world (cf. Phil. 2:5-11). This message calls the Christian to faith, and it impacts the whole of one's life under God. By ministering this gospel message, Paul and Timothy are privileged to be submissive servants of the Triune God.

I hope therefore to send him just as soon as I see how it will go with me, and I trust in the Lord that shortly I myself will come also (2:23-24).
Paul again states his 'hope' to send Timothy to Philippi (see comments on 2:19). Yet there are competing factors: one concerns Paul's desire to send Timothy soon (2:19) in order that Timothy may encourage the Philippians and may return a good report to Paul, but the other concerns Paul's desire to have Timothy by his side as he continues to endure his imprisonment (2:23). So Paul decides to wait for a while in order to better determine what will happen with his trial.

Paul also uses this opportunity to state again his desire to be with the Philippians (cf. 4:1). We can speculate as to Paul's motive in mentioning this: he could be wishing to reassure

---

7 John 8:33; Rom. 6:6; Gal. 4:8, 25; Titus 3:3; cf. Gen. 31:41; Exod. 14:5; 21:2.
8 Cf. Matt. 6:24; Acts 20:19; Rom. 12:11; 14:18; Eph. 6:7; Col. 3:24; 1 Thess. 1:9; cf. Judg. 2:7; Ps. 2:11.

the Philippians of his optimism that he will be released from prison (cf. 1:25; contrast 2:17), or he could desire to motivate them in their Christian service by his potential return (cf. 2:12, 19), or he might want them to know that he did not consider sending Timothy to be a replacement for his own personal visit. Likely a combination of motives would have been present. What is clear here is the source of Paul's confidence that he will return to Philippi – his trust is 'in the Lord'. Imprisoned, and certainly aware of the lack of control he has over his future, Paul entrusts his plans to the Lord. Yet he anticipates that his return will happen 'shortly' or 'quickly' (*tacheōs*).

I have thought it necessary to send to you Epaphroditus my brother and fellow worker and fellow soldier, and your messenger and minister to my need, for he has been longing for you all and has been distressed because you heard that he was ill (2:25-26).
Although Paul plans to send Timothy to Philippi in the future, he has delegated Epaphroditus to accompany this letter now (cf. 2:29). By speaking in such fond terms of Epaphroditus, Paul both eases his return to the Philippians and establishes his character and faithful service as an example to the church. Epaphroditus had apparently accompanied the gifts the Philippians had sent to Paul (4:18), delivered messages from the church (2:25), and then stayed on to minister to Paul's needs in his imprisonment (2:25, 30). At some point, Epaphroditus contracted a life-threatening illness (2:26-27), and Paul's desire for him to return to Philippi stems in part from Paul's wish for the Philippians to know that he is again in good health (2:28).

The name 'Epaphroditus' is found in the New Testament only in Philippians (Phil. 2:25; 4:18). The name itself seems to be connected to that of the goddess Aphrodite, and so it is likely that Epaphroditus was a convert from a pagan family. Under the assumption that he is elsewhere referred to as 'Epaphras' (Col. 1:7; 4:12; Philem. 1:23), some have asserted that he is the same man who is called a 'fellow prisoner' of Paul in Philemon 1:23 (on 'fellow prisoner', cf. Rom. 16:7; Col. 4:10). This cannot be verified, however, and it is significant that Epaphras appears to have been better known to the church at Colossae in Asia Minor than to the churches of Macedonia (where Philippi is located).

Paul gives Epaphroditus five titles of endearment and service – the first three involve his relationship to Paul ('brother, fellow worker, and fellow soldier'), while the last two testify to his service to Paul on behalf of the Philippians. Let us examine these two groups in more detail.

Paul often speaks of the spiritual bond among Christians in the church in terms of familial language, especially in terms of 'brotherhood'.[9] He recognizes a further camaraderie with Epaphroditus when he refers to him as a 'fellow worker' (*sunergos*; see Phil. 4:3). This title in Paul's writings serves as a mark of fellowship in Christian service; it is one he employs to assert his high admiration for others.[10] When he calls Epaphroditus a 'fellow soldier' (*sustratiōtēs*; cf. Philem. 2), Paul evokes the military metaphor he occasionally uses in reference to Christian life and service. Christians wage war against demonic strongholds (2 Cor. 10:3-4), and ministers of the church serve especially on the front lines (1 Tim. 1:18) as those who suffer and who must be intent on serving their King and Commander (2 Tim. 2:3-4).

Together these first three titles indicate Paul's respect for Epaphroditus, and they also imply the relational way Paul worked alongside others for the sake of the gospel. For example, both 'fellow worker' (*sunergos*) and 'fellow soldier' (*sustratiōtēs*) are compounds in Greek formed by prefixing the Greek preposition *sun* ('together with') to an original root word. These terms emphasize Paul's ministerial 'togetherness' and 'with-ness' alongside his ministerial compatriots. In that spirit of mutual fellowship and ministry, Paul addresses Epaphroditus as a 'fellow' and as a 'brother'. Christian leaders today would do well to convey such respect and mutuality in their service alongside others for the sake of the gospel.

Epaphroditus also served as 'your messenger and minister to my need'. The Greek word here for messenger (*apostolos*) most often appears in Paul as a designation for the office/role of 'apostle'; however, the word etymologically merely speaks

---

9 Cf. Phil. 1:14; 3:1, 13, 17; 4:1, 8, 21.
10 Cf. Rom. 16:3, 9, 21; 2 Cor. 8:23; Phil. 2:25; 4:3; Col. 4:11; 1 Thess. 3:2; Philem. 24.

to a person as 'one who is sent out', and thus can indicate a person who serves as a delegate on behalf of others (cf. 2 Cor. 8:23; Heb. 3:1). Since Epaphroditus is 'your' *apostolos* (i.e., the one sent *from you*), rather than being a person designated of apostolic status by the broader church, we should understand this *apostolos* title to refer here to his acting as a 'delegate' or 'messenger' of the church in Philippi. Epaphroditus also labors as 'your minister to my need' – with the word for 'minister' especially indicating one who is employed in worshipful service (*leitourgos*; see Rom. 15:16; Heb. 8:2; cf. Phil. 2:30). Paul's 'need' here was certainly physical and monetary (Phil. 4:16; cf. Rom. 12:13), and Epaphroditus did indeed bring the monetary and physical gifts sent by the Philippians (Phil. 4:14-19). Yet Paul undoubtedly found Epaphroditus' ministry of great spiritual encouragement as well.

The specific reason Paul gives for sending Epaphroditus back to the Philippians concerns Epaphroditus' own desire to return to them, stemming from reports of his illness. Epaphroditus' own 'longing' for the Philippians matches Paul's yearning for them (Phil. 1:8) – in both places Paul uses the verb *epipotheō* ('yearn' or 'long for'; cf. Rom. 1:11; 2 Cor. 9:14; 1 Thess. 3:6; 2 Tim. 1:4). Moreover, Epaphroditus was also 'distressed' or 'troubled' (*adēmoneō*). The reason he was so distressed was because he knew the Philippians had heard reports of his illness. Epaphroditus was concerned that these reports may have been disconcerting, and therefore, after he had recovered, he was eager to return to them. We can easily empathize with such a human moment in this letter, and can imagine Epaphroditus' desire to return home due to his concern for the Philippians and to his desire to be back among his beloved fellow church members after such a dire illness.

Indeed he was ill, near to death. But God had mercy on him, and not only on him but on me also, lest I should have sorrow upon sorrow. I am the more eager to send him, therefore, that you may rejoice at seeing him again, and that I may be less anxious (2:27-28).

Paul does not describe Epaphroditus' illness, but clearly it was life-threatening, since he came 'near to death'. Paul attributes his return to health to God's mercy – a twofold mercy to both Epaphroditus and to Paul.

Paul willingly shares that, had Epaphroditus died, he would have suffered 'sorrow upon sorrow'. This could well refer to Paul's sorrow being compounded – either that on top of the sorrow of Epaphroditus' illness, there would have been the deeper sorrow of his death, or that on top of Paul's present sorrow in his ministry (stemming from his imprisonment and other opposition to the gospel), he would have witnessed a beloved co-laborer die. The word for sorrow here (*lupē*) is used elsewhere in the New Testament to refer to the grief the disciples felt at Jesus' crucifixion (John 16:20-22) and to the grief Paul felt at the lack of Jewish response to his gospel (Rom. 9:2). It thus resonates as a deep emotional response to the loss of something dear.

Epaphroditus' death would have resulted in sorrow and grief for Paul. Paul does indeed have confidence that death in this world is not the end. Rather, the dead in Christ shall be raised (Phil. 3:20-21; 1 Cor. 15:50-57)! And Paul can even welcome death, since his own death will result in his being with the Lord (Phil. 1:21-23). Nevertheless, death remains an enemy (1 Cor. 15:26), and there is an appropriate grief that results from being cut off in this life from those we love. Paul's sorrow is also striking in a letter filled with 'joy' (see notes on 2:17-18). Perhaps we should learn from this that Paul does not have a naïve sense that one must simply pretend to be happy all the time. Rather, joy and sorrow often exist side by side in the Christian life, with our deepest and most joyous hope being the coming cessation of sorrow at the return of Christ.

Since Paul knew of the sorrow that would have come had Epaphroditus died, he could empathize with the Philippians' desire to witness Epaphroditus' return to health. Thus Paul earnestly and eagerly sought to send him to deliver this letter (with *spoudaioterōs* indicating an earnest intent, cf. Luke 7:4; 2 Tim. 1:17; Titus 3:13). He knew it would bring joy to the Philippians to greet Epaphroditus in person (again note that theme of joy), much as Epaphroditus' return to health had been a merciful encouragement to Paul.

Paul also admits that this would make it so that Paul himself 'may be less anxious'. The Greek word here (from *alupos*) can be opposed with the word 'sorrow' (*lupē*) that Paul mentions in verse 27. In addition to bringing joy to the Philippians, the sending of Epaphroditus will also allow Paul to be less concerned, even less sorrowful, as he knows that the Philippians will be rejoicing to see their beloved brother again.

So receive him in the Lord with all joy, and honor such men, for he nearly died for the work of Christ, risking his life to complete what was lacking in your service to me (2:29-30).
Paul concludes this paragraph by directing the church at Philippi as to how they should respond to Epaphroditus' return. They are to rejoice and to honor him. Some have speculated that Paul was concerned that the church might have wondered whether Epaphroditus had returned too early and questioned whether he had completed his job, so Paul is careful to state his esteem for Epaphroditus. This, however, seems too speculative. The overall tenor of the preceding verses indicates that Paul's main desire was to alleviate concern in Philippi for Epaphroditus' health. In these two concluding verses, therefore, Paul is providing the Philippians with their own homegrown model of Christian service to imitate.

In verse 29, which is connected to verse 28 via 'so' (*oun* = 'therefore'), Paul summons the Philippians to rejoice, just as he anticipated they would 'rejoice' earlier in verse 28. Paul sends Epaphroditus back in order to increase the joy in Philippi and to alleviate his own sense of burden (2:28); therefore, he directs the Philippians to fulfill his purpose in returning Epaphroditus by giving him a joyous reception. This marks at least the eleventh appearance of 'joy' or 'rejoice' in this short book[11] – with five left to go.[12] Paul elevates this particular mention of 'joy' by commanding that the Philippians should receive Epaphroditus with 'all' joy. He truly wants Epaphroditus' return to be an occasion filled with celebration in Philippi.

Paul is also careful to remind all parties of their connection in union to Christ and to one another – they are joyfully to receive Epaphroditus *in the Lord*. Moreover, Paul calls for the Philippians to honor such servants of Christ – with the Greek literally reading, 'hold such people with honor.' The word

---

11 See Phil. 1:4; 1:18 [2x]; 1:25; 2:2; 2:17 [2x]; 2:18 [2x]; 2:28.
12 Phil. 3:1; 4:1; 4:4 [2x]; 4:10.

'honor' (*entimos*) conveys the notion of esteeming someone due to some quality he or she possesses. Here Epaphroditus should be honored for his commitment to the 'work of Christ' and to his ministerial service (2:30). That commitment has been particularly evident in how he almost died while engaged in such work. It is likely that Paul refers to the life-threatening danger posed by Epaphroditus' illness depicted in 2:26-27, which occurred when he was away from his own homeland and involved in ministering to Paul. Commentators have rightly noted the striking parallel found in the Greek between Epaphroditus here, who is laboring for Christ and comes near 'until death' (*mechri thanatou* – translated here 'nearly died'), and Christ Himself who humbled Himself by being obedient 'until death' (*mechri thanatou*; 2:8 – there translated 'to the point of death'). Epaphroditus is shown to be following in his Master's footsteps, and thus also serves as a model for the Philippians of imitating Christ through humble self-sacrifice.

The 'work of Christ' is similar to the 'work of the Lord' (1 Cor. 15:58; 16:10) and to the 'fruitful work' in which Paul is engaged (Phil. 1:22). This 'work' is conceptually parallel to the 'service' mentioned in the final clause in 2:30. Such 'service' (*leitourgia*) comes from the same Greek stem as 'minister' (*leitourgos*), which is found earlier in verse 25. Both words indicate the kind of ministerial service in which a temple priest would engage. Also here (as in verse 25) this ministerial service is accomplished for (and to) Paul. Epaphroditus' 'work of Christ' was his religious ministerial duty performed through caring for Paul.

As the delegated 'messenger and minister' (2:25) of the Philippians, Epaphroditus acted in this ministry on behalf of the whole church at Philippi. His ministry on their behalf 'completes what was lacking' in what the Philippians gave to Paul. We must view this as an indirect way of reminding the church at Philippi that they should honor Epaphroditus because he sacrificially served as their ministerial delegate to meet the needs of the apostle Paul during his imprisonment.

It is right for the church to esteem those who sacrificially give of themselves for the sake of others. They are worthy of such honor, given their work. Yet perhaps more importantly, they can serve as models to us all as we seek to live humbly and peaceably in Christian community with one another (1:27ff.).

Summary

As we reflect on these two paragraphs, several themes stand out. First, the apostle exhibits the importance of a relational ministry. Paul well recognized the necessity to labor together for Christ alongside 'brothers, fellow workers, and fellow soldiers'. Despite his privileged position as an apostle, he readily speaks of his 'fellows'. And he also openly references his own need to receive ministry from others, even while he himself is ministering the gospel.

Second, Paul also establishes the ministries of Timothy and Epaphroditus as examples of Christian service. Soon, Paul will overtly call the church to 'imitate' his own Christian walk (3:17), and here he puts forth other models of those who have given their lives to Christ's work. Among the traits these two servants possessed, Paul particularly cherished their capacities to be concerned for the welfare of others (2:20), to engage in service alongside him as a son to a father (2:22), and to pour out their lives in self-giving sacrifice (esp. 2:30). Such exemplars of Christian commitment are to be honored and to serve as role models for us all.

Third, Paul's personal concern for the Philippians continues to be evident in this passage. He plans to send his trusted Timothy to them, even though that will be costly to Paul, with the purpose of strengthening contact with this church. Meanwhile, though Epaphroditus has been ministering to his needs, Paul recognizes that the time has come for him to return to Philippi. And for both of these men, Paul does not shy away from establishing their Christian credentials (measured in commitment and service) in order to encourage the Philippians to heed such representatives of the gospel.

In light of Paul's words, we might well reflect on whether we sufficiently value the importance of relationships in our Christian ministry. Do we truly engage in ministry as a team, or are we overly reliant on our own abilities? Do we openly champion the labors of others? Who among us serves as a good model of Christian living? Do we imitate the good ways that they serve others in Christ? Are we willing to value the needs of others over our own? Do we therefore encourage those around us to serve others who are in need?

Questions for Personal Reflection:

1. Name some people whose Christian walks you admire. Why do you admire them? How would you describe them to others? How can such examples properly motivate us in our own Christian lives? Are there ways that looking to such examples can be detrimental?
2. When you engage in ministry, do you like to work together with others or by yourself? What are some advantages of laboring alongside others? What are some challenges?
3. Do you find it challenging to receive ministry from other people? If so, why?

STUDY QUESTIONS:

1. Name some people whose Christian walks you admire. Why do you admire them? How would you describe them to others? How can such examples properly motivate us in our own Christian lives? Are there ways that looking to such examples can be detrimental?
2. Read Philippians 2:19–30. In the context of this epistle, what are some of the reasons why Paul singles out these two exemplars of Christian life and ministry?
3. What does Paul admire about Timothy (2:19–24)? In what ways does Timothy's example serve as a model for the Philippians? What can we learn from Timothy's example?
4. Why is Paul planning on sending Timothy to the Philippians? Why is he delaying? And why do you think Paul is telling them all of this ahead of time?
5. How does Paul describe Epaphroditus? Which descriptors speak to his relationship to Paul, and which ones refer to Epaphroditus' relationship to the Philippians?

6. What might be some reasons why Paul mentions Epaphroditus' illness here?

7. In what ways does Paul portray Epaphroditus as an example for the Philippians to follow? How can we learn from Epaphroditus?

8. Do you find it challenging to receive ministry help from other people? If so, why?

9. Overall, how does this passage depict Paul's relationships with his fellow workers in the gospel? Why do you think the great apostle Paul felt the need to surround himself with other fellow workers? What could the Philippian's learn from this? And what can we learn as well?

10. When you engage in ministry, do you like to work together with others or by yourself? What are some advantages of laboring alongside others? What are some challenges?

Additional Note:
2:20 Paul's use of *isopsuchos* can rightly be understood as an intentional employment of a cognate word from *psuchē* (i.e., English 'soul'). Thus we can observe in *iso* + *psuchos* something akin to 'equal-souled' or 'kindred-souled'. While it can often be inappropriate to break down compound words into their component parts (an error known as the etymological fallacy), here it appears proper to do so. Paul elsewhere uses *psuchē* compounds with apparent awareness of the *psuchē* root (especially *sumpsuchos* in Phil. 2:2 and *eupsucheō* in Phil. 2:19). The meaning 'kindred-souled' also overlaps with the one known instance of this word in the Greek Old Testament (Ps. 54:14 LXX = Ps. 55:13 in English). Paul and Timothy are the ones in this context who are said to be 'fellow-souled' (rather than Timothy and the Philippians), as is clear from the following relative clause in 2:20 (Paul and Timothy both share a concern in the Philippians' welfare) and from the father-son comparison in verse 2:22 (Paul and Timothy share an almost kindred bond).

10

We Who Glory in Christ Jesus
(Philippians 3:1-11)

¹Finally, my brothers, rejoice in the Lord. To write the same things to you is no trouble to me and is safe for you.

²Look out for the dogs, look out for the evildoers, look out for those who mutilate the flesh. ³For we are the real circumcision, who worship by the Spirit of God and glory in Christ Jesus and put no confidence in the flesh— ⁴though I myself have reason for confidence in the flesh also. If anyone else thinks he has reason for confidence in the flesh, I have more: ⁵circumcised on the eighth day, of the people of Israel, of the tribe of Benjamin, a Hebrew of Hebrews; as to the law, a Pharisee; ⁶as to zeal, a persecutor of the church; as to righteousness, under the law blameless. ⁷But whatever gain I had, I counted as loss for the sake of Christ. ⁸Indeed, I count everything as loss because of the surpassing worth of knowing Christ Jesus my Lord. For his sake I have suffered the loss of all things and count them as rubbish, in order that I may gain Christ ⁹and be found in him, not having a righteousness of my own that comes from the law, but that which comes through faith in Christ, the righteousness from God that depends on faith—¹⁰that I may know him and the power of his resurrection, and may share his sufferings, becoming like him in his death, ¹¹that by any means possible I may attain the resurrection from the dead.

It is a very human compulsion to define ourselves, and thus to develop a self-identity, based on what we do or founded on our family heritage. That self-presentation in some societies can be so important that, very early in meeting someone, we get to the crux of the matter. We ask, 'What do you do?' or, 'Where is your family from?' or, 'Are you related to this family or that one – this tribe or that tribe?' Sometimes such questions are merely part of getting to know someone, but often they can betray a deeper desire for identification.

Such a compulsion was evident in the first century as well. A person's name related them to their family group and/or geographical home. Their occupation could be codified into guilds and trade associations. Most fundamental of all, their family might identify with the worship of a particular deity or set of gods/goddesses. Self-identity was based in large measure on these sets of relationships.

Another way that we can achieve our self-identity is based on our success (or failure) in pursuing our goals and commitments. Then it is not merely about what we do, but how well we do it – about our performance. Or it is not merely about belonging to a particular family, tribe, or group, but about how well we are respected within that social setting. Or it is not merely about belonging to a particular religious organization, but about being esteemed in our service to that organization.

These very modern forms of achieving self-identity were also well-recognized in the first century. Paul, formerly the promising young rabbi Saul, could well have sought his identity in his fine family heritage, in his esteemed religious circle, and in his zealous devotion to the religion of his youth. All of that shattered, however, when Paul encountered Christ on the Damascus road. In his new life in Christ, Paul's identity was wrapped up in Christ and in his service to the Lord. All else became of no value to him.

In many ways, the core of this section can be found in the juxtaposition of those who 'put confidence in the flesh' with we who 'glory in Christ Jesus' (3:3). Christian identity sets aside worldly measures of personal identity and worth, considering it 'loss because of the surpassing worth of knowing Christ Jesus my Lord' (3:8). The gospel speaks instead of the righteousness from God that comes by faith in the atoning death and the powerful resurrection of Christ (3:8-11). In that identity, Paul is secure.

Thus Paul shares his transformed Christian identity as a model of how the Philippians too should focus their lives on Christ. In following this model, these believers will be protected from those who would insinuate themselves into the church in order to win people back to a religion based on externals (3:2).

Finally, my brothers, rejoice in the Lord. To write the same things to you is no trouble to me and is safe for you (3:1).
The English reader may find it surprising that we are barely just over halfway through the letter, with two chapters still left to go, when Paul says 'finally.' However, Paul employs similar expressions elsewhere (2 Cor. 13:11; cf. Gal. 6:17; Eph. 6:10), even in the middle of other epistles (1 Thess. 4:1; 2 Thess. 3:1). In these circumstances, Paul's Greek idiom here (*to loipon*), which he will repeat in Philippians 4:8, principally works as a transition to some new material, likely with some special emphasis on the instructions to follow. Having recounted his plans to send Epaphroditus and (ultimately) Timothy to Philippi, Paul now returns to address the Philippian church directly. The import of this transition is further emphasized by Paul's renewed appeal to the Philippians as 'brothers' in the family of Christ.

Nevertheless, though we are clearly transitioning to a new set of instructions, there remains a strong connection to the immediately preceding material through the concept (yet again!) of 'joy'. The Philippians were to receive Epaphroditus with 'all joy' (2:28-29). Moreover, previous to that section on Timothy and Epaphroditus, Paul had invited the church to rejoice with him. Thus once again, Paul emphasizes the call to 'rejoice'.[1]

Here Paul clearly commands the church to 'rejoice in the Lord' (cf. Phil. 4:4). The verb 'rejoice' is an imperative, and the context is highly directive. We sometimes think of 'joy' as an emotion that can only be achieved spontaneously, and thus ought not to be compelled. However, here Paul clearly assumes that 'joy' can be a chosen response. We can choose to live in the joy of the Lord. Paul demands that the church members voluntarily embrace joy. How they are to do so is best determined by surveying the passage as a whole.

In this context, Paul's insistence that Christ's followers rejoice in the Lord contrasts with the heretical teachings he mentions in the next verse. Those who rejoice in the Lord are people whose identity remains fixed on the Lord and on the Good News of

---

1 See Phil. 1:4, 18, 25; 2:2, 17, 18, 28, 29; 4:1, 4, 10.

salvation and righteousness through faith in Him. Therefore, those whose joy is found in Christ will not put their confidence in the flesh. So a key dimension of finding joy in the Lord comes from focusing on the gospel of Christ's sacrificial suffering and death and on the joyous hope of His resurrection and return. It is a choice to contemplate these truths – to captivate our minds to these realities. Then, we re-format our life goals around imitating Christ in this life – and thus sharing in His sufferings, death and resurrection. Those who glory in Christ and in His work find deep-seated joy even in the midst of the ups and downs – the victories and the sufferings – of this life. In short, joy is a choice. It is a commitment to rejoice *in our relationship to Christ and our identity in Him*.

This concept, it appears, is not new to the Philippians. Indeed, they have heard it from Paul before. Paul writes the 'same things' again. When the translation above says that it is no 'trouble' for Paul to repeat himself, this indicates that he is not reluctant or hesitant to repeat himself (*oknēros*). Rather, he knows that this is 'safe' (*asphalēs*) for the church. It will make them spiritually more secure and stable in their faith if they rejoice in the Lord and watch out for the joy-stealers that come in the form of heretics, who insist on external physical proof of conversion.

Look out for the dogs, look out for the evildoers, look out for those who mutilate the flesh (3:2).
Paul has repeatedly encountered in his ministry various heresies that can broadly fall under the label of 'Judaizers', and here he strongly cautions the Philippians against such a danger. Strikingly, 'those who mutilate the flesh' is contrasted with 'the [real] circumcision' in verse 3, thus indicating that Paul is concerned about those who promulgate a false circumcision. Though there exists an ongoing academic debate about who the opponents were that Paul warned about here (see Additional Notes), the context of circumcision would indicate that he was cautioning the Philippians about Judaizers.

Early in the history of the church, disputes arose about whether Gentile converts to Christianity must be circumcised (see Acts 15). The question was perhaps natural, given that Gentile converts to *Judaism* were required to undergo circumcision (as well as to keep the law and possibly undergo proselyte baptism), especially according to the traditions of the Pharisees and their rabbinic descendants. Early Christianity was closely connected to its Jewish roots, and thus many Jewish practices were incorporated into the Christian church. It is not surprising, therefore, that some of the Pharisees who had joined the early Christian community were among the first to insist that Gentile converts to this messianic Christian movement also must be circumcised (see Acts 15:5). Paul, as a former Pharisee (Phil. 3:5), was well aware of the theological implications of this.

Paul's response to this issue reaches substantive expression in the book of Galatians, and it is clear that his concern was deeply theological, not merely sociological. It was not simply the case that requiring Gentiles to undergo the painful procedure might discourage some from converting to Christ, or that it might set up a two-tiered hierarchy in which circumcised Christians looked down on their non-circumcised brothers. Rather, Paul considered it to be an abandonment of the gospel itself for anyone to insist that circumcision be required for full admission into the Christian church (Gal. 1:6-9). This is because, following the logic of earlier Pharisaic teaching, male converts to Judaism circumcised themselves alongside making a commitment to keep the whole law (Gal. 5:2-3). Thus to circumcise oneself was the equivalent of putting oneself 'under the law' (Gal. 4:21).

Yet, Paul recognized that no one can keep the law (Gal. 3:10; 6:13). To mandate circumcision is, in effect, to say that salvation comes through obedience to the law – through 'works of the law'. However, Paul insists that salvation comes not through works but through faith in Jesus Christ (Gal. 2:15-16; 3:21-28; 5:4-6), especially a faith rooted in Jesus' sacrificial death and glorious resurrection. Likewise, the Spirit comes not in response to those who keep the law, but is given to those who respond to the gospel in faith (Gal. 3:1-9). Any requirement to circumcise thus contravenes a salvation rooted in the righteousness that 'comes through faith in Christ' (Phil. 3:9).

After writing Galatians, Paul found himself repeatedly encountering others who insisted on circumcision of Gentile Christians and who mandated that Christians follow other aspects of Jewish ritual practices.[2] There appears to have been

---

2 See also Col. 2:8-23; Titus 1:10; cf. Rom. 2:25-29; 14:1ff.; 1 Cor. 7:19.

some regional theological differences between these various heterodox Judaizing movements, as can be evident in close comparison of each of these Pauline writings. However, Paul's response is always the same: physical circumcision is not a necessary component of Christian conversion, and anyone who insists otherwise is cutting at the very root of Christian faith. Whether such a heresy had already been introduced in Philippi is impossible to know with certainty from this verse. Paul does not here admonish the Philippians to remove heretics from their midst, so it would seem that they had not yet succumbed *en masse* to a Judaizing movement. Nevertheless, Paul had experienced how often such heresies attacked his congregations elsewhere. So the menace was real, and the apostle is adamant.

Paul's wording in this verse is harsh, and intentionally so. With great rhetorical force, Paul commands the Philippians three times to 'look out' (*blepete*). These commands are intended to put them on their guard.[3] There is a real danger here, and Paul insists that they be wary.

Paul also employs three extremely derogatory metaphors for these opponents of the gospel. First, they are 'dogs'. Most canines in antiquity were used as watchdogs or lived in feral, roving packs. Thus we should not picture here a cute little terrier or a primped miniature poodle. These are snarling beasts on the hunt. To call someone a 'dog' was often a term of derision.[4] Moreover, the picture of a dog in Judaism could refer to an unclean animal,[5] and thus Gentiles could be likened to 'dogs' (Matt. 7:6). Paul appears to reverse this term back onto those who would require circumcision of Paul's Gentile converts. These Judaizers are despicable hunters, seeking to capture souls by ensnaring them into their spiritually unclean ways.

Second, these Judaizers are 'evildoers' – with two separate Greek words (*kakous ergatas*) here designating 'evil' and 'workers'. Note that 'evil' here clearly labels these Judaizers as malevolently opposed to the righteousness of God. And 'workers' implies that they are laboring to this end. In contrast

---

3 Cf. Col. 2:8; Gal. 5:15; also e.g., Mark 8:15; 12:38; 13:5; Heb. 3:12; 12:25.
4 Cf. 1 Sam. 17:43; 2 Sam. 3:8; 16:9.
5 Consider Exod. 22:30; 1 Kings 20:19; Luke 16:21; 2 Pet. 2:22; Rev. 22:15.

to the workers who serve as evangelists of the true gospel,[6] they are heralds of a wicked anti-gospel (cf. 2 Cor. 11:13).

The echoes of the Old Testament Psalter here might very well signal that Paul is indicting them as evildoers who work lawlessness (e.g., Pss. 5:5; 6:8; 14:4; 36:12). Though the Greek terminology varies slightly, a connection between dogs and those who perform evil is also strikingly found in Psalm 22:16: 'For dogs encompass me; a company of evildoers encircles me.'

Third, they are 'mutilators of the flesh'. Again, this contrasts with the 'real circumcision' in the next verse. In Greek, 'mutilation' is *katatomē*, while 'circumcision' is *peritomē* – with two different prepositional prefixes (*kata* and *peri*) applied to the cognate stem *tomē*. The irony in antiquity would have been striking. Pagan Gentiles were known to deride the Jewish religion for the way it required men to mutilate their bodies through the act of circumcision. Paul, though raised in highly conservative Jewish circles, almost appears to endorse this Gentile critique (cf. Gal. 5:12). We must quickly state that Paul is not abandoning his Old Testament roots, where God Himself had commanded circumcision of His people Israel. Rather, Paul is aware of a deeper circumcision mentioned in the text of the Old Testament – a circumcision of the heart. To that concept, he turns in the next verse.

For we are the real circumcision, who worship by the Spirit of God and glory in Christ Jesus and put no confidence in the flesh (3:3).

The Old Testament repeatedly refers to a deeper spiritual circumcision – a circumcision of the heart.[7] Thus Deuteronomy anticipates a future time when physically circumcised, but wayward, Israel will return to the Lord: 'And the Lord your God will circumcise your heart and the heart of your offspring, so that you will love the Lord your God with all your heart and with all your soul, that you may live' (Deut. 30:6). This is not a physical act, but an inward work in the covenant people to engage in a true covenantal relationship with God, and this spills out into living in light of the righteousness and love for God that is in the inner heart. The fact that this teaching appears in the heart

---

6 1 Tim. 5:18; 2 Tim. 2:15; cf. Matt. 9:37-38.
7 Deut. 10:16; 30:6; Jer. 4:4; 9:25-26; cf. Rom. 2:28-29; Acts 7:51.

of the Torah itself indicates that God's goal all along was not to generate a people who bore the mere outward, physical effects of circumcision, but to create a covenant community with an inner, abiding, covenantal connection to Him.

Physical circumcision was to be a visible sign and seal of the inner covenant reality. However, due to the sinful response from so many members of physical Israel, it became necessary to chasten them by bringing them under oppression and exile[8] with the purpose of producing a future generation who would truly engage in repentance, circumcision of the heart, and a return to the blessing of relationship with the Lord.[9] It is this change in the inner person that is specifically anticipated as the New Covenant reality.[10]

Paul's insight is that we now stand in the New Covenant age – the age of circumcision of the heart. Having been crucified, buried, and raised with Christ, and having had the Spirit of God poured out into our hearts, God has accomplished an inner work of redemption that far surpasses the mere outward sign. Moreover, God had always intended that such redemption reach beyond the physical confines of Israel and involve all nations (cf. Eph. 2:11–3:13; Rom. 3:21-30). Gentiles now enter into the community of the New Covenant as baptized participants who are saved by faith, who truly worship by the Spirit, and who glory in Christ Jesus. The hearts of Gentiles and Jews alike were spiritually circumcised in Christ (cf. Col. 2:11-15, where baptism signifies the spiritual circumcision of being identified with Christ's death and burial). Thus they had no need of receiving a fleshly mark that was only a shadow of the inner reality. Indeed, to accept such a physical circumcision could imperil the person by directing him to put confidence in the fleshly symbol, when the real circumcision and righteousness comes in a true relationship with the crucified and risen Lord (3:7-11).

Examining this verse more closely, Paul clearly asserts the vast superiority of this spiritual circumcision over the physical. The word 'for' explicates the contrast between the 'mutilators of the flesh' (i.e., the Judaizers who mandate physical circumcision) and the 'we' who practice the spiritual circumcision. The

---

8 Deut. 29:16-29; Jer. 3:19-25; 9:12-22.
9 Deut. 30:1-8; Jer. 4:1-4; 9:23-26.
10 Jer. 31:31-34; 32:39-40; Ezek. 11:19; 36:26-27.

translation above states, 'we are the *real* circumcision.' The Greek actually states more boldly and simply, 'we are *the* circumcision' (cf. the Authorized Version). Some modern translators have added the word 'real' (which is not found in the Greek) in order to explain Paul's logic and to make more readily apparent his thought (in addition to the English Standard Version above, one might also compare the NASB, RSV, etc.). Yet, there is something even more definite in Paul's simple statement that, 'we are *the* circumcision.' The Christian is indeed (spiritually) circumcised, whereas those who rely on their physical circumcision really possess no valid circumcision before God at all.

This statement is then followed in Greek by three participial phrases that define who the 'we' are, and thus also indicate why the 'we' are those who are truly 'the circumcision'. This relationship can be diagrammed as follows:

> For we are the circumcision
>> the [ones] who worship by the Spirit of God
>> and who glory in Christ Jesus
>> and who do not put confidence in the flesh

The three Greek participial phrases (above rendered in English as relative clauses with 'who') are all brought together in Greek by a single definite article (equivalent to 'the'). This, along with repetition of 'and' (*kai*), indicates that all three descriptors must be taken as a whole. It is not the case that some Christians worship by the Spirit, while others glory in Christ, while still others do not put confidence in the flesh; rather, the Christian is a person who does all three.

When Paul speaks of those, 'who worship by the Spirit of God', it is appropriate for us to situate this in his broader theology of the Holy Spirit. On the one hand, Paul acknowledges the deity of the Spirit in the midst of the Trinitarian relationship. Note that in this short verse, the Spirit, Christ Jesus, and God are all mentioned, as is frequently the case in Paul.[11] The Spirit, as the third person of the Trinity, is fully divine and also fully possesses the qualities of personhood.

Beyond this, however, we remember that Paul envisions the Spirit indwelling all those believers who have by faith

---

11 E.g., Rom. 15:30; 1 Cor. 6:11; 2 Cor. 13:13; 2 Thess. 2:13.

received the righteousness of God and thereby live in union with Christ in His death and resurrection (Rom. 8:1-11). In short, those who live through salvation by faith in Christ are indwelt by the Spirit; those who do not live by faith remain in the flesh and do not have the Spirit within. In Galatians 3:2-3 he boldly asks, 'Did you receive the Spirit by works of the law or by hearing with faith? Are you so foolish? Having begun by the Spirit, are you now being perfected by the flesh?' In that context, it is clear that Paul juxtaposes those who are redeemed (who have the Spirit) with those who rely on their circumcision and fleshly works. The Philippian believers did indeed 'receive the Spirit' by 'hearing with faith' and not by 'works of the law'. Hence, in this brief phrase in Philippians 3:3, Paul alludes to his broader teaching elsewhere that it is those who have the Spirit indwelling them who are the true worshipers and the true circumcision.

Those who 'worship by the Spirit of God' are redeemed people, who are enabled by God Himself (in the specific agency of the Third Person of the Trinity) to truly worship. Any other worship lacks the agency of the Spirit working in the heart of the worshiper. This Greek word for 'worship' (*latreuō*) invokes the notion of religious service in worship of God (cf. Deut. 6:13; Rom. 12:1). Such 'worship by the Spirit' would not be an appeal to ecstatic experiences, rather it reflects the simple reality that all those who belong to Christ have the Spirit indwelling them and thus worship God from a transformed heart through the agency of the Spirit.

Christians also 'glory in Christ Jesus'. Significantly, the Greek word for 'glory' here (*kauchaomai*) at root refers to 'boasting'. Often this is a negative term – especially when people 'boast' in their own good works and in keeping the law (Rom. 2:23; Eph. 2:9), or boast in their own wisdom (1 Cor. 1:29), or (especially in this context) boast in their circumcision and Jewish heritage (Gal. 6:13). Yet, 'boasting' can be proper if people take pride and glory in the right object of their boast. So, Paul himself can 'boast' in his relationship to his spiritual children[12] or 'boast' in his suffering service to Christ (2 Cor. 11:30ff.; 12:9). More importantly Christians rightly 'boast in the Lord' (Phil. 1:26; 1 Cor. 1:31) and

---

12 Phil. 2:16; cf. Rom. 15:17; 1 Cor. 15:31; 2 Cor. 7:14; 1 Thess. 2:19.

especially boast in His work on the cross (Gal. 6:14). Our pride and joy – our glory – is found in Him. This again reminds us of the juxtaposition in Galatians between the Judaizers who boast in the circumcised flesh, and Paul who boasts in the work of Christ (6:13-14; cf. Rom. 3:27; 4:2). Those who have the true spiritual circumcision in Christ will boast of Christ and His work, and they will not glory in any physical mark of circumcision.

Finally, those of the true circumcision are people who 'put no confidence in the flesh'. The word translated 'confidence' (*pepoithotes*) comes from the verb *peithō*, which in the perfect tense conveys the sense of 'entrusting oneself'. Our trust is not in an external physical sign. Moreover, 'flesh' (*sarx*) in Paul's writings can refer either to the physical realities of the body[13] or to a fallen fleshly nature that opposes God.[14] Here, the physical is certainly emphasized (Christians do not entrust themselves to the physical mark of circumcision), although there may linger a negative connotation as well. This final phrase then provides the launching point for the next few verses.

…though I myself have reason for confidence in the flesh also. If anyone else thinks he has reason for confidence in the flesh, I have more: circumcised on the eighth day, of the people of Israel, of the tribe of Benjamin, a Hebrew of Hebrews; as to the law, a Pharisee; as to zeal, a persecutor of the church; as to righteousness, under the law blameless (3:4-6).

In a deft rhetorical move, Paul drives home his point that Christians must 'put no confidence in the flesh' (3:3) through his own personal example. If anyone had the necessary fleshly credentials to claim a physical right of membership in God's people Israel, it was Paul, as he so aptly demonstrates (3:4-6). From his birth Paul possessed the right religious credentials and the proper genealogical lineage, and he continued to zealously perform his religious duties well into adulthood. However, Paul considers rubbish any such attempt to secure a relationship to God through such boasts (3:7-8). Surely, if Paul is willing to discard any such physical markers of his religious worth, how much more should the Philippians (who have no hope to claim

---

13 Cf. Phil. 1:22, 24; Gal. 1:16; 2:20; Rom. 1:3; 2 Cor. 4:11.
14 Cf. Gal. 3:3; 5:16-21; Rom. 8:4-8; 13:14.

the kind of credentials Paul once had) rely on the work of Christ rather than on circumcision and keeping the law.

The Judaizers whom Paul has in mind had established the essential markers of Jewish religion (circumcision being the foremost) as a test for real inclusion in the people of God. Since it is Jewish identity that counts in their estimation, Paul proves that he outshines all others on that score. Yet, though he has the greatest capacity to put confidence in such fleshly physical externals, he considers such things to be of no account.

The connections to the preceding verse are clear. The transitional word 'though' (*kaiper*) provides one such link. The noun 'confidence' (*pepoithēsis*) in verse 4 is overtly related to the verb 'put confidence' (*pepoithotes*) in verse 3. Also 'in the flesh' occurs in both verses. Paul is briefly going to depart from what he considers true markers of spiritual circumcision (worship by the Spirit, boasting in Christ, not placing confidence in the flesh) in order to show that he himself could have excelled on the external calculations of religion being championed by the Judaizers.

Indeed, Paul is willing effectively to put his external religious qualifications up against those of any other person. The outcome from such a comparison, he insists, would show he possesses better credentials than any of his opponents. The book of Acts indicates Paul's keenness to apply his autobiography in order to evangelize or to encourage the church (Acts 22 and 26). In other epistles, he engages in similar duels of autobiographical comparison.[15] Here, given the context of concern over Judaizers, Paul selects all of the biographical data to exhibit how he excelled by every major first-century Jewish measure. And then he insists, by his example, that at the end of the day, such measures must be discarded by true Christians in favor of the righteousness that comes through faith in Christ.

First, he was circumcised on the eighth day. Ever since this covenant sign was first granted to Abraham, the eighth day is precisely when a Jewish male was expected to be circumcised.[16] In this context, not only is Paul saying that he was given the

---

15 E.g., Gal. 1:13-14; 2 Cor. 11:16–12:10.
16 Gen. 17:12; Lev. 12:3; cf. Luke 1:59; 2:21.

external fleshly circumcision in keeping with the law, but he can also claim that his circumcision (performed as it was at the earliest possible moment and as a sign of his inclusion into God's people Israel) would be superior to any Gentile proselyte procedure (performed much later in their adult years). So Paul demonstrates that he surpassed from the outset anything Gentile converts in Macedon could hope to achieve.

Along these lines, Paul can lay claim to inclusion among the nation of Israel literally from the moment of his conception. The Greek word for 'people' here (*genos*) indicates more than just national heritage; it particularly references Paul's racial descent. Though Gentiles could convert to Judaism and thus be numbered among the people and nation of Israel, no Gentile could ever hope to achieve the status of physical descent from Israel. In fact, the Philippians may have been aware of the rabbinic teachings that did not accord to Gentile proselytes the full breadth of privileges inherited by a native-born Israelite. For example, limitations were placed on who could legally marry Gentile proselytes. Furthermore, for some legal purposes, later rabbinic sources assume that it takes ten generations before the children of a proselyte receive all the rights accorded to a native Israelite. Perhaps more importantly, Paul could claim inclusion from birth in the covenant community of Israel, along with all the privileges that status brought: 'They are Israelites, and to them belong the adoption, the glory, the covenants, the giving of the law, the worship, and the promises. To them belong the patriarchs, and from their race, according to the flesh, is the Christ who is God over all, blessed forever' (Rom. 9:4-5).

Moreover, Paul can trace his own ancestry to the tribe of Benjamin. He elsewhere emphasizes this heritage: 'I myself am an Israelite, a descendant of Abraham, a member of the tribe of Benjamin' (Rom. 11:1). This tribe was the only one of the twelve to remain attached to the tribe of Judah following Solomon's death (1 Kings 12:21) and through the post-exilic era (Ezra 10:9). The holy city of Jerusalem was actually within the tribal borders of Benjamin. And Paul was originally named 'Saul,' a name associated with the first king of Israel, who himself was from the tribe of Benjamin (1 Sam. 9:16, 21; 10:20-21; Acts 13:21).

Paul is a 'Hebrew of Hebrews' (in Greek, this most literally indicates a 'Hebrew *from* Hebrews' – *Hebraios ex Hebraiōn*). Elsewhere, in defending his ministry against opponents in Corinth, he contends: 'Are they Hebrews? So am I. Are they Israelites? So am I. Are they offspring of Abraham? So am I.' (2 Cor. 11:22). When Paul calls himself a 'Hebrew from Hebrews', he speaks emphatically of his Hebrew and Jewish descent. Yet, might we say more? The term *Hebraios* elsewhere refers specifically to a speaker of Hebrew or Aramaic as opposed to Hellenistic Greek-speaking Jews and converts (Acts 6:1); and the cognate term *Hebraisti* refers to that Semitic language, which Paul spoke (Acts 21:40; 22:2; 26:14). Though he was born in Tarsus, Paul's parents sent him to be trained in Jerusalem (Acts 22:3; 26:4-5). So, Paul's upbringing proves that his heritage is equivalent to that of a fully Hebrew person without the possible taint that could come with being a Hellenist.

Paul then follows these markers of his exquisite Jewish lineage with three particular signs of his adult Jewish credentials: 'as to the law', 'as to zeal', and 'as to righteousness under the law' (each structurally parallel in Greek). These three items (law, zeal, and righteousness) mark key values in first-century Judaism, especially in the circle of the Pharisees.

The written Torah, or law, was the set of written instructions from the first five books of the Old Testament that informed all proper Jewish behavior. This written law was combined in Pharisaic religious training alongside the 'oral Torah', which constituted the handed-down oral traditions of rabbinic teachers. These oral traditions, as interpretations of the written law, helped define how people ought to conduct their lives.

In the New Testament, though Jesus penetratingly identified the Pharisees as 'hypocrites' (Matt. 23), as did John the Baptist before him (Matt. 3:7), such an indictment would likely have been most shocking in his day. Evidence from Josephus, a first-century Jewish historian,[17] testifies to the respect accorded to Pharisees in Judea, and we get hints of the popular respect accorded them in Palestine even in the New Testament.[18] They were the ones who 'sat on the seat of Moses'

---

17 E.g., *Jewish War* 2.162; *Antiquities* 18.12-15.
18 Mark 2:18; Acts 5:34; also cf. Matt. 23:38; Luke 11:43.

(Matt. 23:2), and thus they provided the main source for most people for religious interpretation of the Mosaic law. And the Pharisees also appear to have been esteemed because of their own efforts at keeping the law (at least as they understood it). Reflecting on this, when Jesus says to the assembled throngs that their righteousness must exceed that of the scribes and Pharisees (Matt. 5:20), it is likely that most in the crowd would have asked themselves, 'How could I hope to live such a legally pure lifestyle?'

Many overlook the fact that Paul was not the only Pharisee to join the fledgling church (Acts 15:5), although there is also substantive evidence that many Pharisees were among those most opposed to Jesus,[19] for which Scripture repeatedly condemns them.[20]

Paul refers to his Pharisaic training here as the highest possible education in Jewish religion. In the book of Acts, Paul specifically identifies his training as being in accord with the 'strictest party of our religion' (26:5; cf. 22:3) – note that the word 'strict' here (*akribeia*) likely implies the most precise, which to many would have meant the most perfect. He traces his rabbinic discipleship to the famed Pharisaic teacher Gamaliel (Acts 22:3; cf. 5:34). Furthermore, Luke reports that Paul was a 'Pharisee, a son of Pharisees' (Acts 23:6), which would imply that he can trace his upbringing in Judaism to a strong family lineage of rabbinic teachers.

In short, Paul's legal credentials are top-notch. Not only did he have the best training, and therefore the best likelihood of correctly understanding the law, but he also belonged to the party most people considered to be among their most righteous Jewish leaders.

Next, in verse 6 Paul writes, '…as to zeal, a persecutor of the church.' The quality of 'zeal' (*zēlos*) was much admired by many Jewish people. Elsewhere, he comments that he was, 'advancing in Judaism beyond many of my own age among my people, so extremely zealous was I for the traditions of my fathers' (Gal. 1:14). Phinehas served as one of the most renowned Old Testament exemplars of zeal – especially because he had slain an Israelite who went over to Midian and

---

19 E.g., Matt. 9:34; 12:2, 14, 24; 16:1; 19:3; 22:15; 27:62; John 7:32; 9:13-34; 11:57; 12:42.
20 E.g., Matt. 16:6, 12; Luke 7:30; 11:37-54; Matt. 23:1-39.

to the worship of Baal (Num. 25:11). In this, Phinehas served as a model for others who would persecute (even to the point of death) heretics within Judaism. During the Jewish revolt (A.D. 66–73) one whole movement of Jewish people fought violently against pagan oppression suffered under Roman control (and against Jewish supporters of pagan Rome), and they were known by the epithet 'Zealots.'

In such a context, Paul's actions would have been understood as 'zealous' when he persecuted Christians, since the Jewish leaders in Jerusalem would have portrayed these Christians as messianic Jewish heretics.[21] Indeed Luke, in describing Paul's speech before the Jewish leaders (who desired to kill him because of his commitment to Christ), records Paul as saying of his own earlier zeal in persecuting the church that he was '…being zealous for God as all of you are this day' (Acts 22:3). Naturally, Paul, after his encounter with Jesus on the Damascus road,[22] saw matters quite differently. He realized he had actually been persecuting the true Messiah of Israel and maltreating Christ's followers (Acts 9:5). So, it is undoubtedly with a touch of sarcasm that Paul declares, '…as to zeal, a persecutor of the church'. Yet, we might also wonder whether, in a backdoor manner, Paul is warning the Philippian church that, if zeal in Jewish externals is to be the measure of religious fervor, then persecution may well be on the horizon for those true Christians who oppose the Judaizers.

Paul's final evidence for his excellent Jewish record concerns 'righteousness under the law' in which he was 'blameless'. Paul contrasts 'righteousness under the law' (or 'righteousness which is by [performance of] the law') a few verses later with 'righteousness which comes through faith in Christ' (Phil. 3:9). We shall consider both of these phrases further below in verse 9, but it is clear that Paul here is not talking about 'righteousness' in any abstract sense. This is a specific form of righteousness that comes from executing religious directives in keeping with the Pharisaic interpretation of the law. By the measure of his Pharisaic compatriots, Paul not only knew what commandments he had to keep, he followed them to the letter.

---

21 Acts 22:3-5; 26:9-11; cf. Gal. 1:13; Acts 8:1; 9:1-2.
22 Gal. 1:15-16; Acts 9:3ff.; 22:6ff.; 26:12ff.

Of course, Paul is famous for arguing that no one is truly righteous (e.g., Rom. 1:18–3:20), and that no one truly fulfills the law.[23] Rather, the law is a pedagogue, a servant that leads us into an awareness of our sin and directs us to the justification by faith found in Christ alone (Gal. 3:24-25). Any person who seeks to live up to the requirements of the law inevitably falls short – so far short that everyone stands condemned by the law. Only Jesus' sacrificial death and glorious resurrection break the power of the law over others.

So, how can Paul say that he was 'blameless'? The key here is that Paul was projecting his readers back to a time when he had been confident that he was doing all he had to do. Due to his own limited interpretation of the law and his own stunted self-reflection, he once saw himself as doing pretty well. More importantly, there is a strong implication here that, at that same time, other Jewish colleagues looking at Paul's external performance as a zealous Jewish leader would have arrived at much the same conclusion. For all intents and purposes, he appeared outwardly blameless. In other words, he did about as well as anyone could hope to. Yet all of it he has exchanged for a righteousness that far surpasses anything he could have imagined, and thus he counts his previous religious performance as loss and rubbish – this he makes clear in the next few verses.

Before we leave these three verses (3:4-6), we would do well to reflect on our own response. It is quite clear from Paul's rhetoric that he is encouraging his audience to reflect deeply on any points of comparison they might have with him. Clearly Paul's specific application for the Philippians was to caution them that, whatever the Judaizers may have desired to impose as an external measure of their religious success, none of it mattered in comparison to glorying in Christ and His work. We might well inquire whether there are external measures of our own religiosity that we are still secretly holding onto (or worse, that we are applying to others). Paul would call us to leave behind those external measures as we focus instead on knowing Christ Jesus.

---

23 E.g., Rom. 3:20; Gal. 2:16, 21; 3:10-12.

But whatever gain I had, I counted as loss for the sake of Christ. Indeed, I count everything as loss because of the surpassing worth of knowing Christ Jesus my Lord. For his sake I have suffered the loss of all things and count them as rubbish, in order that I may gain Christ and be found in him (3:7-9a).

Paul reflects back on all those external measures of his achievements in Jewish religion, and discards them all. Indeed, he is happy to lose those external markers of success (i.e., his 'confidence in the flesh'). For Paul, such a loss is worthwhile because he has gained so much more in relationship to the Lord Jesus Christ.

The reader is immediately struck by the repeated juxtaposition of 'gain' and 'loss' in these two verses. Whereas previously Paul had attained great success in his religious achievements, that 'gain' is now 'loss'. In the midst of that 'loss', Paul has 'gained Christ' – a gain that makes any loss infinitely worthwhile.

It is important to realize that Paul endured a true 'loss' in order to gain Christ. When he says, 'But whatever gain I had…', we must recognize that there was indeed real 'gain' in his previous position. There were very few people in Paul's day who could claim such quality external credentials as Paul lists in verses 4-6. By all measures that counted, he would have been at the very pinnacle of respect accorded to young Jewish leaders. That was what he had to give up in order to gain Christ.

Yet, in order to gain Christ, he willingly considered these 'gains' as 'loss'. This Greek word for 'loss' (*zēmia*) is employed in the New Testament (and in the main Greek translation of the Old Testament) to refer to a physical loss that brings consequent hardship. For example, in Acts, the 'loss' of all the contents of a ship occurs through a shipwreck (Acts 27:10, 21). Just as Paul had possessed a real 'gain' in his previous external credentials, so too did he experience real physical 'loss'. Although Paul does not expand here on specifically what that loss entailed, it is not difficult to picture the apostle imprisoned, rejected by his Jewish countrymen, and reliant on the gifts of others. We could list again the multitude of sufferings Paul had endured (e.g., 2 Cor. 11:16–12:10), and might easily imagine that none of that would have fallen against him had he simply avoided Christ. He could well instead have been honored and esteemed in Jerusalem at that very moment he was writing his letter.

Then, with a strong emphatic declaration at the beginning of verse 8 (beginning with 'indeed' – or better, an emphatic 'but rather'; *alla menounge*), Paul goes on to state that not only does he consider all those external Jewish measures of his success forfeit, but he also considers 'all things' loss. Add whatever you like to the list of the 'gains' he possessed in verses 4-6, he would still merrily discard them all for the sake of knowing Christ.

The reason Paul can throw it all away is that he now has a much higher purpose. He wants to know Christ Jesus. He describes this privilege of knowing the Messiah as something of great excellence – of 'surpassing worth'. Such knowledge is certainly cognitive, but it is also fundamentally relational. Perhaps that is why Paul speaks of Christ Jesus as '*my* Lord'. As a servant engages in relationship to his master, now Paul longs to find himself in service to his messianic Lord. Paul elsewhere refers to 'knowing Christ',[24] and in a similar manner, he can speak of knowing the 'glory of God' (2 Cor. 4:6; cf. Eph. 1:17) or the 'grace of our Lord Jesus' (2 Cor. 8:9). In colloquial terms, this is both 'head knowledge' and 'heart knowledge'.

In order to emphasize this point further, Paul repeats that it is on Christ's account that he suffered the loss of all things. Then he stresses the depth of his willingness to accept such loss by adding that he considers all other things 'rubbish'. The Greek word here (*skubala*) can refer to garbage, or kitchen scraps, or excrement; however, in the plural, it can be quite a crude term and most likely connotes human feces. That is how thoroughly Paul is willing to discard anything that stands in the way of knowing his Lord.

Paul now states a second set of overlapping purposes in throwing it all away. The first purpose was to know Christ; the second combines 'gaining Christ' with 'being found in him'. All loss pales in comparison to this gain. Paul now is

---

24 E.g., 1 Cor. 2:2; 2 Cor. 2:14; cf. Eph. 4:3; Col. 2:2.

in relation to the Messiah. Moreover, Paul is 'in him'. This reminds us of the frequent Pauline theme that Christians are those who are 'in Christ'. They are found to be in union with Him. What that specifically means in this context is spelled out more in the next verse.

...and be found in him, not having a righteousness of my own that comes from the law, but that which comes through faith in Christ, the righteousness from God that depends on faith (3:9). This represents an unfortunate place to start a new verse. As the punctuation in this translation rightly emphasizes, the phrase 'and be found in him' is really the second part of the purpose clause starting in verse 8 with 'in order that I may gain Christ'. Part of Paul's purpose in rejecting his earlier claims to fame in Judaism (and indeed in anything else that stood in his way of knowing Christ) was that he desired to be found 'in Christ'.

Repeatedly in this epistle, Paul has spoken of being 'in Christ',[25] and this is consistent with his terminology in other letters. Here Paul focuses on the Christian being in union with Christ and the saving benefits that such a union entails. Indeed, the context clarifies one central benefit of being 'in Christ'. The immediately following participial phrase ('not having...but...') indicates that union with Christ issues forth into a righteousness that God Himself grants the person who trusts in Christ.

Righteousness was a concept of great importance both in first-century Judaism and in Christianity. In both, it was assumed that only the righteous pleased God and could receive benefits from Him (including ultimately life in the world to come). While there were various strands in first-century Judaism concerning how one achieved righteousness, there is ample evidence that one significant view considered it requisite to meticulously seek to keep the law in all its aspects. It certainly seems that Paul's Judaizing opponents believed that keeping some (if not all) of the external regulations of the Mosaic law (especially circumcision) were necessary for a Gentile to enter fully into a salvific righteous status with God. As far as Paul is concerned, there are competing views of righteousness at stake.

---

25 E.g., Phil. 1:1, 26; 2:1; 3:14; 4:7, 19, 21 – see notes on 1:1.

Paul is casting off any claim to possessing his own legally generated righteousness. Earlier in life, he may have had cause to boast of his Jewish heritage (3:5) and of his fidelity in keeping the law as he interpreted it through his Pharisaic training (3:6). He could even consider his 'righteousness under the law' to be 'blameless'. Now, however, he rejects any claim to 'righteousness of my own that comes from the law' (3:9). It is worth comparing these two parallel phrases in verses 6 and 9 briefly, since there is much that is similar, but enough that is different in order to add clarity to the meaning of each. Below I render in highly literal English the two Greek phrases:

> 'righteousness which is by/in [the] law' (3:6)
> 'my righteousness which is from [the] law' (3:9)

We immediately note the parallelism of these two phrases, thus it is likely that each can help us interpret the other. One issue that arises concerns the fact that the definite article ('the') before the word 'law' is not actually found in either verse in the Greek text. Some might be inclined to conclude from this that Paul is speaking of 'law' in general (any human law) as opposed to 'the law' (especially the Torah of Moses). However, it is clear in the context of verse 6 that the Mosaic law and consequent Jewish tradition is intended (otherwise, why would Paul include this among his Jewish credentials in 3:4-6). Moreover, the definite article ('the') is often omitted in prepositional phrases in Greek (such as 'in the law' or 'from the law'). More importantly, note that the overall context of verses 4-6 concerns Paul's having excelled in all the main measures of Jewish accomplishment. In verse 5, he says 'according to [the] law, a Pharisee' (the definite article is also not found in the Greek prepositional phrase here). Since the Pharisee would have considered only the written Torah (of Moses) and the oral Torah (of the rabbinic Fathers) to be 'law', there is no question that this occurrence of law refers to Jewish law. That is followed immediately in this overall Jewish context by 'as to righteousness which is in [the] law, blameless' – which speaks to Paul's sense of accomplishment in performing the Jewish law as he understood it. Given the parallelism between verses 6 and 9, we rightly contend that the Jewish law is in view in both verses.

In comparing these phrases in verses 6 and 9, the most striking difference concerns the change in prepositions – verse 6 speaks of 'righteousness *by* [or *in*] the law' and verse 9 of 'righteousness *from* the law'. In reality, this variation serves to clarify the mutual meaning of each phrase.

In verse 6, Paul writes of a righteousness 'by/in the law' (*en nomō*). The preposition (*en*) in context most likely refers to either 'in the sphere of the law' or 'by means of the law'. In reality, both possibilities overlap conceptually: the first would imply a righteousness that comes through living within the confines of the law, whereas the second would imply a righteousness that comes by keeping the law. Both cases define a person's right standing with God by success in following the conduct required by the law.

In verse 9, Paul speaks of righteousness 'from' (*ek*) the law. While the Greek preposition *ek* can occasionally mean 'by', it typically means 'from', and the parallel with 'righteousness from [*ek*] God' later in the verse would indicate that the normal translation of *ek* as 'from' fits best here too. Thus verse 9a speaks of a righteousness thought to flow to people from their conduct in keeping the law. The conceptual overlap between these parallel phrases in verses 6 and 9 lies here: in both cases, the person is expecting to derive a righteous status from the law – from living sufficiently in line with its stipulations as to be considered 'righteous'.

As there were two related phrases in verses 6 and 9 that defined the kind of righteousness Paul has considered 'loss' and of no avail, so there are two related phrases in verse 9 that define what kind of righteousness Paul now seeks. Rendered in an over-literal translation those phrases would be:

> the righteousness which is through faith of Christ
> the righteousness from God on the basis of the faith

Yet again, we observe that the prepositions are key to understanding what Paul is saying. Beginning with the second clause, we have already observed that there is a stark contrast between 'righteousness from God' and the earlier 'righteousness from the law'. While the latter entails a person's seeking to receive the label of 'righteous' from his or her own successful conduct in keeping the law, the phrase 'righteousness from God' indicates that Paul believes instead that God graciously grants him the status of 'righteous'. It is not that Paul was unaware that the law came from God (e.g., Rom. 7:12; 8:7; 1 Tim. 1:8-9), but he is well aware some think that having received the law, they can now earn their own righteous status by law-keeping – this Paul believes to be impossible. Our only hope is for God to intervene and provide some other way for us to be deemed righteous. (See Additional Notes.)

There is an obvious comparison in both of these parallel phrases between 'through faith' (*dia pisteōs*) and 'on the basis of faith' (*epi tē pistei*). The Greek distinction between 'through' (*dia*) and 'on the basis of' (*epi*) is slight – both imply that this righteousness comes predicated on faith. The faith in question is clearly the same in both instances (since in Greek the second mention of 'faith' has what is known as an anaphoric use of the article – it is 'the' faith that was spoken of previously in the verse).

One debated issue concerns Paul's reference to 'faith *of* Christ' (*pistis Christou*) in the phrase: 'the righteousness which is through faith *of* Christ.' Since faith is normally faith in something, one possibility (followed by nearly all English translations) is that this refers to 'faith *in* Christ'. On that accounting, Christian righteousness is predicated on believing in Christ. The other option is to understand 'faith' as 'faithfulness' and to translate 'faith of Christ' as 'Christ's faithfulness'. Following that option, then Christian righteousness is predicated on Christ's faithful work (in His death and resurrection) on our behalf. Both options are possible in Paul's theology.

However, because it is clear in this epistle that Christians possess faith (2:17; cf. 1:25) and are those who 'believe in him' (1:29), the idea of 'faith *in* Christ' is the most probable interpretation here. This is confirmed by the vast number of instances in which Paul speaks of Christians possessing faith *in* Christ and His work.[26] Moreover, in other New

---

26 E.g., Rom. 1:8; 10:17; 1 Cor. 15:14; Eph. 1:15; 3:17; 4:13; Col. 1:4; 2:5; 1 Thess. 1:8; 3:2; 1 Tim. 1:14; 3:13; 2 Tim. 1:13; 3:15; Philem. 6; cf. Acts 20:21; 24:24; 26:18.

Testament-era writings, the words 'faith of' often should best be understood as 'faith in'.[27] Indeed, a good case can be made for 'faith in Christ' as being the most probable rendering of the other instances of 'faith of Christ' (*pistis Christou*) in Paul.[28] Therefore, though cognizant that the preceding was a quick summary of what is a substantive academic debate, I strongly prefer the ESV translation of verse 9. Paul speaks here of the righteousness 'which comes through faith *in* Christ'.

The term 'righteousness' (*dikaiosunē*) is clearly a key to this passage. Whole academic dissertations have been written on this word alone, and it would not be appropriate to bore my readers with the details. However, a general summary is not too difficult. In ancient theological contexts, *dikaiosunē* basically means 'right conduct' before God, but in Paul we also find it associated with 'right standing' before God. To summarize Paul's arguments in Romans and Galatians: God Himself possesses pure righteousness because all His acts are just and morally good. Humanity can attempt to achieve right conduct, but we will inevitably fail in some significant measure at that task when left to our own devices. Even though the law instructs in right conduct, it is powerless to empower the individual to that end, and thus the law becomes a standard against which one's failure can be measured. Thus 'righteousness from the law' is of no avail. Rather, the only hope is to believe in Christ and receive from God the righteousness that comes through faith.

Theologians ask whether 'righteousness' is a present possession of the believer or an expression of a future state of right standing before God. This context here in Philippians actually points in both directions. On the one hand, Paul wishes to be found without a legally predicated righteousness but having one based on faith in Christ. This appears to speak primarily to the present, since he has abandoned his legal righteousness in the present for something better. Yet the context in verses 10-11 goes on to speak of 'attaining the resurrection from the dead'. So, it is evident that Paul is appealing to a righteousness through faith in Christ that presently avails to the believer yet

---

27 Mark 11:22; Acts 3:16; James 2:1; Rev. 14:12.
28 See Rom. 3:22, 26 (cf. 3:25, 28; 4:3, 5); Gal. 2:16; 3:22 (cf. 2:20 and esp. 3:26).

will also be especially evident at the culmination of history as the dead are raised in Christ.

To summarize this rather lengthy discussion of this important verse: Quite simply, Paul has considered as 'loss' and 'rubbish' the righteousness he once sought to achieve by law-keeping. Now his entire goal in life is to be united with Christ and thus to possess a righteousness that comes from God to those who believe in the crucified and risen Jesus as Messiah and Lord. One key application for the Philippians must have been that they must not permit themselves to be misled by any Judaizer who would require them to put themselves under the law as a means to righteousness (3:2). Rather, they must remain faithful to Christ and to the righteousness that comes by faith in Him. Moreover, all Christians are called by this verse to entrust ourselves to Christ and to His saving work. We have no hope of earning our way into God's kingdom; rather, we must receive the righteous status God grants to those who place their faith in Christ.

…that I may know him and the power of his resurrection, and may share his sufferings, becoming like him in his death, that by any means possible I may attain the resurrection from the dead (3:10-11).

Paul brings to a conclusion this long sentence that goes back to at least 3:8 in Greek (and arguably to 3:7 or 3:3). Here Paul states the intended result that comes from 'gaining Christ and being found in him' (3:8-9). That result constitutes a relational knowledge with three components, as is clarified by this literal structural translation of the Greek:

> that I may know… him
> and the power of his resurrection
> and the fellowship of his sufferings

Knowledge here is not a mere intellectual awareness, but a true experiential relationship with Christ and identification with His work. Paul has already expressed his deep desire to know Christ (3:8), which he considers of 'surpassing worth'. Again, this conveys a deep relational connection with his Lord (see comments above on 3:8).

Yet, Paul also goes on to speak of knowing the 'power of his resurrection'. Elsewhere, Paul refers to the authority involved in raising Jesus from the dead (cf. Rom. 1:4; Eph. 1:19-20). That power avails toward believers (Eph. 1:19), and Paul desires to see that strength operative in his own life. He understands his ministry to be a channel of the power of God found in the gospel and mediated through the Holy Spirit.[29] He also anticipates, however, that it is a relational identification with Christ's resurrection power that will allow him (and all believers) to be raised from the dead (3:11, 21).

Moreover, Paul also addresses his desire to know 'the fellowship of his [Christ's] sufferings'. The ESV translation 'may share his sufferings' above, though it breaks the structural parallelism in the original Greek, does a good job of unpacking what such a fellowship entails. Any true relational knowledge of Christ calls forth identification with Him in our daily lives, including fellowship with His sufferings. As the Master suffered, so will His followers. And Paul repeatedly emphasizes this point.[30] One of the great dangers of the so-called 'health and wealth gospel' (so popular in our days) is that its proponents overlook this very vital point. Christ's followers will suffer in this life. Though such suffering should not be sought out, nonetheless when it comes, it is to be embraced as a privilege.

This threefold knowledge – knowledge of Christ, of the power of His resurrection, and especially of the fellowship of His suffering – is the intended result that Paul embraces as the consequence of 'gaining Christ' and being found 'in him' (3:8-9). Through such knowledge, the Christian engages in spiritual unity with Christ. One aspect of that unity involves being made like Christ in His death. The Greek word for 'being like him' (*summorphizō*) speaks to 'sharing the same form'. Suffering on behalf of Christ conforms the Christian to the travails He engaged in on our behalf. Such identification with Christ, made possible through relational knowledge of Him, makes the believer like him. And this identification extends even to identification with Christ's death. To quote another famous Pauline statement, 'I have been crucified with Christ. It is no longer I who live, but Christ who lives in me.

---

29 E.g., Rom. 1:16; 15:19; 1 Cor. 2:4-5; Col. 1:29; 1 Thess. 1:5; cf. 2 Tim. 1:7.
30 E.g., Rom. 8:18; 2 Cor. 1:5-7; Col. 1:24; also Heb. 10:32; 1 Pet. 4:13; 5:9.

And the life I now live in the flesh I live by faith in the Son of God, who loved me and gave himself for me' (Gal. 2:20).

Paul thus desires to be so closely identified with Christ's death that his only hope comes from a further identification with Christ's resurrection – 'that by any means possible I may attain the resurrection from the dead' (3:11). At times, Paul can relate the Christian's union with Christ to a present possession of resurrection power (e.g., Rom. 6:5-11; Col. 2:12). Yet even in those contexts, there is the anticipation of a real future resurrection of the body that leads to eternal life in the world to come (Rom. 6:5, 8; Col. 3:4). Here, Paul looks forward expectantly to the culmination of his identification with Christ in the resurrection to come (Phil. 3:11-12, 21).

The words 'by any means possible' in the translation above (ESV, also see the KJV) may make it seem that Paul is striving under his own volition to accomplish his own resurrection. The Revised Standard Version makes this sound even less certain by translating this as 'if possible'. In reality, the New International Version actually provides the most literal rendering of the Greek: 'becoming like him in his death, and so, *somehow*, to attain to the resurrection from the dead'. What the 'somehow' is doing in this verse is showing the magnitude of what Paul is expectantly hoping to receive: Paul is not yearning for a mere shadowy existence in the Elysian Fields, or for a few extra minutes added to his earthly life, or for a commendation of service. What he anticipates somehow to achieve is the greatest possible future existence for any human being – an eternity of resurrection life in the presence of his Lord. Such a 'somehow' existence is ultimately beyond his reach if Paul were left to his own devices, but it is surely graciously offered to all those who have been united to Christ through faith in Him.

Paul is not expressing his own ability to accomplish his resurrection, nor is he alluding somehow to his doubts about the outcome of his faith in Christ. Rather, we can witness Paul's confidence in 3:20-21: 'But our citizenship is in heaven, and from it we await a Savior, the Lord Jesus Christ, who will transform our lowly body to be like his glorious body, by the power that enables him even to subject all things to himself.'

Summary
In this passage Paul has emphatically introduced (via 'finally') a very important command: 'rejoice in the Lord' (3:1). When we fully exult in our privilege of being in relationship with Christ, all other pursuits will pale in comparison. Such joy in the genuine gospel of the true Christ serves then to stave off those false leaders who would steal into the Philippian church and rob them of the gospel by requiring Gentiles to keep the circumcision stipulations of the Jewish law. Instead, Paul points out that true circumcision is a circumcision of the heart, evidenced by genuine worship of the Triune God flowing from the Holy Spirit.

Paul certainly possessed the credentials for worldly success as rated by the external measures available in the Judaism of his day. However, all of it he counted as human rubbish as he passionately gave himself over to a relational encounter with the resurrected Messiah. Paul no longer hoped to achieve righteousness by external law-keeping, but abandoned such endeavors so that he might rely through faith on the righteousness that comes by faith in the Lord Christ. Paul has chosen to lose all else so that he may gain Christ and may be found in relationship to Him. That choice issues forth in a relational knowledge of his Saviour and in identification with Christ in His sufferings and in the power of His resurrection.

How ought we to apply Paul's words? There are many important points here, but we shall touch on just a few. Certainly, it is worth abandoning any earthly gain for the sake of being counted as Christ's disciple. Some have achieved great social standing in this life, and they stand to lose it should they follow Christ. Some have family members who would dissociate with them should their profession of Christ be made public. Some simply are caught in the fleeting pleasures this world has to offer. These things must be deemed worthless should they stand in the way of a wholehearted commitment to Christ.

Yet such self-abandonment is not in itself salvific, nor does it add to the salvation that Christ Himself has earned on our behalf. The gospel calls us to get rid of any of our attempts to merit salvation and a right standing before God. We simply cannot be good enough, and thus there is no real hope to be found in our own performance. Rather, we must cast off such attempts and instead entrust ourselves to Christ. United with Him, we receive the startling benefits of union with His death and resurrection, with the consequent, confident hope in the unimaginable glory of resurrection life with Him.

Nonetheless, Christians in this life face great trials, and at times suffer mightily. In those moments, we again have the opportunity to display our unity with our crucified Savior. As He suffered, so His followers can expect to suffer. We need not seek out such travails, but neither should we flee them when faithfulness calls us to endure.

Overall, we as Christians are called to rejoice! We rejoice in our Savior and Lord. His work on the cross has paid for our sin. His resurrection has vouchsafed our glorious hope in Him. And He Himself is worthy of our joyful exaltation. When we meditate on these truths then, regardless of the hardships and the ups and downs in this life, we truly experience the joy of the Lord. Such joy enables us to endure – to endure both the external pressures of this world and the internal dangers of false teaching. Moreover, such joy brings glory to the Triune God, who alone is worthy of exaltation.

Questions for Personal Reflection:

1. How do you personally react when you read Paul's command to 'rejoice in the Lord'? What would such joy look like in your life?

2. Name some of the heretical teachings that are around today. What ways can we best respond to those who follow such teachings? Name some other points of view in the Christian church that you think may be incorrect but are not heretical. How should we respond to those points of view?

3. What are some of your accomplishments (and your social positions of heritage, status or wealth) in which you might put fleshly confidence? What steps can you take to enable you to say truly, 'I count everything as loss because of the surpassing worth of knowing Christ Jesus my Lord'?

4. Do you at all times believe that your righteous status before God is solely based on the work of Christ? Where in your life are you tempted to achieve your own righteousness before God based on your own works?

5. What impact does Christ's resurrection have on the way you live your life?

STUDY QUESTIONS:

1. How do you see Philippians 3:1 relating to its context? What does it look like to 'rejoice in the Lord' throughout all of life?

2. Who is Paul warning against in Philippians 3:2–3? Where else in Paul's writings has he encountered similar 'evildoers' who have crept into the church? Why do you think he is so passionate about the church 'watching out' for such individuals?

3. Contrast Paul's choice of words in Philippians 3:2 with those in 1:15–18. Why do you think there is a difference in tone between these two passages? What does this say to us as we deal with self-seeking ministers, or with church divisions, or with heresies? How should our attitudes vary depending on the situation at hand?

4. Name some of the heretical teachings that are around today. What ways can we best respond to those who follow such teachings? Name some other points of view in the Christian church that you think may be incorrect but are not heretical. How should we respond to advocates of those points of view?

5. Contemplate Paul's statement: 'we are the real circumcision, who worship by the Spirit of God and glory in Christ Jesus and put no confidence in the flesh' (3:3). Work clause-by-clause through this statement and ask: What does all of this mean? What Old Testament ideas come to mind in this short verse? Why does he say this here?

Philippians 3:1-11

6. Paul gives a short, but punchy, list of his 'reasons for confidence in the flesh' (3:4-6). How do you think this list would have sounded in the context of first-century Judaism? Why might Paul have wanted to cling to these things? How do you think he found the strength to discard them all for sake of Christ? *impressive*

7. Why does Paul in 3:7-8 count as 'loss' the items listed in 3:4-6? What are some of the ways this applies to us today? What areas of your life (e.g., accomplishments, family connections, social standing, etc.) might you be tempted to cling to even in your Christian life? How is God calling you to relinquish those past identity markers? *no eternal value and would be prayers to knowledge of Christ.*

8. What does it mean to 'know Christ', to 'gain Christ', and to 'be found in Him' (3:8-9)? *live in power of H.S. goal union in the scripture?*

9. How does Philippians 3:9-11 summarize the gospel? And how does Paul employ the word 'righteousness' in these verses?

10. Do you at all times believe that your righteous status before God is solely based on the work of Christ? Where in your life are you tempted to achieve your own righteousness before God based on your own works? *nope*

11. In what ways do you see Paul talking about his present status before God in 3:9-11, and where do you see him referring to his future hope? *resurrection*

12. How might a greater focus on our resurrection hope assist us in living our lives in Christ today?

Additional Notes:

3:2 This verse provides some key information about the potential adversaries of the Philippian church. As was mentioned in the introduction to this commentary, scholars debate the nature of Paul's opponents in this epistle. This brief additional note addresses this matter in somewhat greater detail.

One issue involves how many different groups of opponents are mentioned in the letter. Are the 'dogs' and 'mutilators' in 3:2 the same as the enemies of the cross condemned in 3:18-19? Are these the same as those individuals referenced in 1:15-17 or in 1:27-28? Some might also add 2:14-16 and 3:15 into the discussion.

However, the people who 'preach Christ from envy and rivalry' in 1:15-17 are evidently preaching in some proximity to Paul in Rome (see the context in 1:12-17) rather than working in Philippi. This would caution us that they may not be the same individuals as the potential adversaries of the Philippians mentioned in 3:2. Moreover, though Paul critiques the motives of the individuals mentioned in 1:15 and 1:17, he appears satisfied that their work is nevertheless leading to the spread of the gospel (1:18). In contrast, Paul expresses deep concern in 3:2 about the dangerous theological nature of the preaching of the 'mutilators of the flesh'. He strongly warns the Philippians to 'look out' for them and their teaching in a way that is much harsher than any language in 1:15-17. Therefore, the people in 1:15-17 are likely different than those in 3:2.

Similarly, the 'crooked and twisted generation' mentioned in 2:15 appears to be a broad reference to the whole world that opposes Christ and His church (see commentary on this verse), rather than being limited to the heretical opponents in 3:2. Those who 'think otherwise' in 3:15 are clearly acceptable members of the congregation, and Paul confidently believes that they will come to concur with him in the foreseeable future. In contrast the 'mutilators' in 3:2 are strongly indicted by Paul and are not to be accepted in the congregation. Thus we should separate the issues in 2:15-17 and in 3:15 from the dire concern Paul articulates in 3:2.

On the other hand, 3:18-19 appears sufficiently proximate to the context of 3:2 for there to be some possible overlap between the 'mutilators of the flesh' (3:2) and those whose 'end is destruction, their god is their belly, and they glory in their shame, with minds set on earthly things' (3:19). Though there are no certain textual features connecting 3:2 and 3:18-19, there are also no markers that Paul is discussing a separate group in 3:18-19 than the one he began to speak about earlier in 3:2.

This mention of 'destruction' in 3:19 could potentially be connected with the 'destruction' that awaits the Philippians' opponents in 1:28, opening up the possibility that 1:28 and 3:19 refer to the same group. However, since Paul had not explicitly mentioned heretics in the epistle prior to 1:28, and since the initial opposition that the Philippians faced likely came from pagan Gentile quarters (see Acts 16:19-24), I take 1:28 to refer broadly to any that oppose the Christian church in Philippi, and not to be limited just to the concerns mentioned in 3:2 or 3:18-19 (see commentary on 1:28). All the 'opponents' of the church will meet destruction (unless they repent), and the foes mentioned in 3:19 are a specific subset of those whose destruction is assured.

Therefore, of the many texts that could provide more information on the specific opponents that Paul cautions about in 3:2, the only other verses that might afford some additional evidence are 3:18-19.

The most discussed options concerning the opponents in 3:2 and/or 3:18-19 include: Judaizing heretical branches of Christianity (who teach Gentiles must be circumcised), Jewish missionaries (who seek to capture the church back into the Jewish religion), Gnostics (who believe special spiritual knowledge is necessary to be lifted out of the material plane of existence), and libertine heretics (who assert that Christians are free to abandon traditional moral constraints). Scholars have also connected these options in various combinations.

As the commentary on 3:2 remarked above, some connection to Jewish practices must lie behind the contrast between 'those who mutilate the flesh' (3:2) and those of 'the real circumcision' (3:3). A Judaizing influence among the opponents in 3:2 would further explain why Paul emphasizes his own Jewish credentials in 3:4-6, as well as why he makes wordplays on 'dogs' and 'evildoers' in 3:2 (where he is likely subverting terms that Jewish people could use to denigrate Gentiles).

However, we need to ask whether these could be 'Jewish missionaries' from outside the church. In this regard, note that Paul appears urgent in 3:2 (evidenced in part by the threefold repetition of 'look out'), and this would imply that these teachings have swayed other Christians under Paul's care. Yet when we examine Paul's other epistles, we do not discover any mention of Jewish missionaries who have successfully lured Christians out of the church, but we do witness Paul's frequent encounters with Judaizing heretical sects of Christianity. It is the danger from heretics within the church that has so often preoccupied Paul. In particular, such Judaizers have sought to mandate that Gentiles be circumcised in order to be fully accepted into the Christian church (see commentary on 3:2 above).

The next question then is whether this Judaizing tendency had been mingled with a nascent Gnosticism, and/or whether it had been combined with a licentious approach to life. Frankly, Paul's discussion here is too limited to pronounce definitively on the details of the Judaizers' teaching (aside from their insistence on circumcision), and any deductions on the specific doctrines of these Judaizers rests on combining 3:2 with 3:18-19 (when that connection is not certain). The principal evidence for Gnostic or libertine teachings is found in 'their god is their belly, and they glory in their shame, with minds set on earthly things' (3:19). This certainly implies a tendency toward fleshly indulgence. Yet the phrase 'their god is their belly' may well be an indictment of how they sell their teachings for profit (compare this with Romans 16:18). And the other phrases in 3:19 may simply indicate that these foes did not sufficiently appraise the spiritual/heavenly realities of Jesus' death and resurrection and the ethical implications of the gospel. Similarly, Paul's insistence that they walk as 'enemies of the cross of Christ' (in 3:18) need not be thought to imply that they taught (like some Gnostics) that Jesus did not die on the cross. Rather, this is best understood to refer to their opposition to Paul's gospel of the crucified Jesus, as evidenced in how they did not recognize the radical implications of the atonement and the consequent call to obedience that springs from thankfulness to Christ.

So, where do we stand? Certainly we can affirm that these opponents could be classed among the 'Judaizers.' Greater specificity would be based on slender testimony. Perhaps the best summary would be to say that they represent Judaizing itinerant heretics, who oppose Paul's gospel of the crucified Christ, who insist on circumcision, and who are greedily seeking earthly recompense for their teaching.

3:7 Many early Greek and Latin manuscripts omit the word 'but' (*alla*) in the opening '*But* whatever gain I had…' Nonetheless, it is clear from verses 7-8 that Paul intends a rhetorical contrast with verses 4-6 regardless of whether the 'but' is originally from his hand or not.

3:9 One ongoing debate in Christian academia concerns whether the 'righteousness of God' (*dikaiosunē theou*) in Paul's letters refers to 'righteousness from God' or 'God's own righteousness' (cf. Rom. 1:17; 3:5, 21, 22, 26; 10:3; 2 Cor. 5:21). That is to say, the words 'of God' (i.e., 'God' in the Greek genitive case) in 'righteousness of God' can be understood either as designating a source of righteousness for Christians (righteousness 'from God') or as indicating that the righteousness in question is actually the righteous activity that God Himself possesses and/or performs ('God's righteousness'). The debate is especially acute in Romans 3 and elsewhere. Without going into great detail about this debate, it is at least significant that here in Philippians 3:9 when Paul speaks of a 'righteousness' (*dikaiosunē*) 'from God' (*ek theou*), he includes the preposition *ek* ('from'). This clarifies that (in Philippians at least) Paul envisions righteousness flowing out from God to the believer. This strongly increases the theological possibility that Paul intends to speak of righteousness flowing out from God to believers in at least some of the occurrences of 'righteousness of God' (*dikaiosunē theou*) in his other letters.

11

Pressing on Toward Our Heavenly Citizenship
(Philippians 3:12-21)

[12]Not that I have already obtained this or am already perfect, but I press on to make it my own, because Christ Jesus has made me his own. [13]Brothers, I do not consider that I have made it my own. But one thing I do: forgetting what lies behind and straining forward to what lies ahead, [14]I press on toward the goal for the prize of the upward call of God in Christ Jesus. [15]Let those of us who are mature think this way, and if in anything you think otherwise, God will reveal that also to you. [16]Only let us hold true to what we have attained.

[17]Brothers, join in imitating me, and keep your eyes on those who walk according to the example you have in us. [18]For many, of whom I have often told you and now tell you even with tears, walk as enemies of the cross of Christ. [19]Their end is destruction, their god is their belly, and they glory in their shame, with minds set on earthly things. [20]But our citizenship is in heaven, and from it we await a Savior, the Lord Jesus Christ, [21]who will transform our lowly body to be like his glorious body, by the power that enables him even to subject all things to himself.

If you are running a race, it is important to know why you are running it and what you hope to win. If you are climbing a mountain, it is vital to know where the peak is and why it is worth the effort. So too in the Christian life, it is crucial that we keep our eyes on the prize at the end of the race.

In these verses, Paul speaks both to the process of living the Christian life today, and to the eternal hope that motivates us until the end. The prize is a resurrection body and eternity with our Lord and Savior. The process involves pressing forward toward maturity in Christ. Paul's own personal testimony serves as a model for Christian believers everywhere to imitate him in his passionate pursuit through the process of striving in this life toward the maturity and resurrection life that are fully given to us in the age to come.

Not that I have already obtained this or am already perfect, but I press on to make it my own, because Christ Jesus has made me his own (3:12).
Though it is common in English translations to initiate a new section with this verse, it is fairly certain that the opening words of this passage refer back to the preceding discussion. When the ESV translation says 'not that I have already obtained *this*,' we should acknowledge that 'this' is not actually in the Greek, although it is clearly implied. The question is to what does the 'this' refer? While the 'this' could look forward to the 'prize' in verse 14, it more likely looks back to (and here it becomes difficult to choose): 'knowing Christ' (3:8), 'gaining Christ and being found in him' (3:8-9), 'the righteousness of God that depends on faith' (3:9), the 'resurrection from the dead' (3:11), or even the trilogy in verse 10 ('knowing him, and the power of his resurrection, and the fellowship of his sufferings'). Arguments can be advanced to favor some of these options over others, but in reality, it is worth remembering that all these items are so closely intertwined in Paul's future expectation that it is unwise to unravel them.

Paul looks forward to a fuller knowledge of Christ that culminates in a righteous status before God, in an intimacy of relationship with Christ, and in a participation in the resurrection life of the Messiah. Paul remains in process in this life. He knows Christ, but longs to know Him more. He is justified freely by faith in Christ, but that righteous status before God will most fully be declared true at the judgment day yet to come. And though Paul presently experiences the new life and resurrection power that enables him to live as Christ's servant, he looks expectantly to the resurrection life to come, when he will be granted a resurrection body in the presence of his Savior. Thus Paul has not yet fully 'received' or 'obtained' any of this. Indeed, he has not yet been 'perfected' (3:12). So these verses continue the sense of what life is like in the present, while Paul (and all believers) gaze into the future and long for the culmination of Christ's kingdom.

When Paul says that he is not 'already perfect', it is important to realize that he is using a Greek passive construction – 'not that I have already been made perfect'. We associate 'perfection' with personal achievement through good works. For Paul, the achievement of 'perfection' comes from God working in us in order to fully conform us to what God Himself desires in all aspects of our being. The will of God is that which is 'good, acceptable, and *perfect*' (Rom. 12:2). We strive through God's power as His redeemed people to this end. Often English translations render cognate perfection vocabulary in Paul's writings with the notion of 'maturity' (e.g., 1 Cor. 2:6; 14:20; Col. 4:12). There are many indications (such as here) that Paul anticipates the mature perfection of believers will only truly be attained in the eschatological future (Eph. 4:13; cf. 1 Cor. 13:10). Indeed one of Paul's key purposes in his ministry is that at the end he 'may present everyone mature in Christ' (Col. 1:28).

Though Paul recognizes how far he has to go in order fully to obtain this resurrection life in the knowledge of Christ, and though he is keenly conscious that he has not yet been made perfect, he still strives toward that eschatological day when Christ returns and perfects His people. The Greek word for 'press on' (*diōkō*) means to 'pursue'; and Paul, through God's empowerment, is earnestly pursuing the goal of obtaining that which he so desires.

There is an interesting wordplay in the Greek that is less apparent in the English. Three times in this verse, Paul employs the Greek verb *lambanō* ('receive/obtain') and its cognate *katalambanō* ('receive/attain/seize'). We could crudely translate: 'Not that I have obtained…but I pursue that I also may obtain, because I also was obtained by Christ.' See Additional Note. Thus Paul connects Christ's call ('Christ Jesus has made me his own') to his own desire to lay hold of Christ and all His gracious benefits.

Brothers, I do not consider that I have made it my own. But one thing I do: forgetting what lies behind and straining forward to what lies ahead, I press on toward the goal for the prize of the upward call of God in Christ Jesus (3:13-14). Paul now first reiterates that he is still in process toward his goal, and then employs a marvelous athletic metaphor to depict that process. Addressing his readers again as his dear 'brothers' and family members in the faith (cf. 1:12, 14; 2:25; 3:1, 17; 4:1, 8, 21), Paul makes sure they know he is running this race (imperfect as he is) right alongside them. When Paul reflects on his current position, he acknowledges again that he has not yet attained the perfection and the relationship with Christ that he is pursuing in 3:12. As in 3:12, where the Greek verbs *lambanō* and *katalambanō*, make for an interesting wordplay, Paul applies that wordplay one last time with *katalambanō* – 'I do not consider that I have obtained.'

When we are in process toward a goal, it is often easy to become dissatisfied with our lack of progress and to want to give up. Paul here reminds his readers that the Christian life is a pursuit of a goal, and that this goal is so worthy of our affection that we simply must keep in the race. In the midst of Paul's acknowledgment that he has far left to go (he has not yet attained to his goal), he nevertheless gives us a sense of his single-minded intent: 'But one thing I do...'

Paul enjoys drawing on athletic metaphors in his epistles, especially those that come from foot races.[1] Many ancient Roman cities possessed gymnasia and athletic fields, and some sponsored their own version of the Olympic games, so this imagery would have been as familiar to his readers as football (or soccer) would be to moderns. Anyone who has ever raced, even in school gym class, knows that the successful athlete must possess determination, an ability to set aside other distractions, and a commitment to reach for the finish line.

Paul commits himself to laying aside past distractions. He 'forgets what lies behind'. In context, this could easily refer to all those matters that could lead to boasting and 'confidence in the flesh' (3:4-6). These are the very identity markers he

---

1 1 Cor. 9:24-27; 1 Tim. 6:12; 2 Tim. 4:7; outside Paul cf. Heb. 12:1.

has 'counted as loss' (3:7-8). This again serves as a model to a congregation in Philippi that may well face heretical attempts to drag them back into external markers of religious achievement (3:2). Similarly, we today are not to seek to establish a righteousness of our own that comes through performance of the law (3:9); rather, we are to rest in the confidence of Christ's righteousness that comes to us by faith, and on that basis, be encouraged in the race set before us.

Like a good racer, especially as he nears the finish line, Paul extends himself forward – he 'strains forward to what lies ahead'. That which 'lies ahead' is the 'goal' and 'prize' that Paul 'presses on toward' or 'pursues' (the Greek *diōkō* as in 3:12). The words for 'goal' (or 'target'; in Greek *skopos*) and 'prize' (*brabeion*; cf. 1 Cor. 9:24) expressly indicate that Paul is thinking about an athletic venue, particularly a race in which one 'strains forward'. It is not enough for a racer to leave behind distractions, he or she must have a goal to aim at. The prized goal itself establishes the whole reason for the race.

In this case, Paul names his goal and prize: 'the upward call of God in Christ Jesus' (3:14). Paul frequently mentions the 'calling' of the Christian. Sometimes it refers to the specific earthly life situations into which God has called particular Christians to be His agent (1 Cor. 1:26; 7:20). Yet more often (as here), it refers to the salvation that Christians receive through God's election, and thus it signifies the eternal inheritance that lies before them.[2] Often the very privileges of that salvific 'calling' necessitates a response of living before God in a way that brings glory to the one who has called us (Eph. 4:1; 2 Thess. 1:11). In this context in Philippians, this calling is certainly one God has initiated ('upward call *of God*') and has brought about through relational union with Christ ('in Christ'). The results of that calling have already been introduced throughout this epistle – especially most recently in verses 8-11 (e.g., knowing, gaining, and being found in Christ, as well as participating with him in His sufferings, death and resurrection) and soon in verses 20-21 (possessing a heavenly citizenship and being transformed into a glorious

---

2 Eph. 1:18; 4:1; 2 Thess. 1:11; cf. 2 Tim. 1:9.

resurrection body). This calling and this prize make it worth enduring the travails of the race.

Let those of us who are mature think this way, and if in anything you think otherwise, God will reveal that also to you. Only let us hold true to what we have attained (3:15-16). Paul now makes his official appeal for Christians to model their goals in this life on the example he has set (see also 3:17). He has not been describing the way he thinks simply for the sake of a human-interest biography or for reasons of self-congratulation. Rather, he desires that his example motivates believers to follow him in this pursuit.

What Paul just shared (3:7-14) is how 'mature' (*teleios*) believers are to think. And while he has just said that he has not been perfected (3:12, using the verb *teleioō*), here he is calling some believers *teleios*. Although this adjective *teleios* could be translated 'perfect', it is clear from Paul's earlier statement (3:12) that utter perfection cannot be obtained in this life. Believers continue on the road to seeking holiness and maturity in this life in response to the gracious gift of salvation and through the work of the Holy Spirit in their lives. The 'mature' are always maturing, having never arrived and yet always (like Paul) straining forward to achieve Christian maturity in this life.

The mature are to 'think' as Paul has just modeled. The goal of their lives ought to be focused on living out the upward call of Christ (3:14; cf. Col. 3:2). The word for 'think' (*phroneō*) is the same word Paul used when he was encouraging the church to 'think one thing'[3]. Indeed, it could be this very goal upon which he wants them to meditate continuously together. By contrast, the enemies of Christ 'think' about earthly things (3:19; cf. Rom. 8:5).

Certainly, most in Paul's audience would want to be placed in the 'mature' category. Nevertheless, he allows that not everyone in Philippi will fully comprehend the urgency of seeing the Christian life as a race. Paul addresses those Christians in a rather blunt rhetorical move, letting them know that 'God will reveal' the truth of what Paul has been saying.

---

3 See notes on Phil. 2:2; 2:5; and 4:2; cf. Rom. 12:16; 15:5; 2 Cor. 13:11.

Surely, this conveys a confidence in God, who through His Spirit, works to bring Christians to maturity. However, it also expresses Paul's confidence in his message and his assurance that 'mature' Christians will ultimately concur with him. In other words, since they eventually will agree with him, they should ponder Paul's words carefully without delay and embrace his appeal to seek the prize of God's call.

At a minimum, Paul calls the Philippians not to forsake the gospel truths they already possess. Rather they are to 'walk in,' or 'hold true to,' the gospel message they have already accepted. This word for 'hold true to' (*stoicheō*) is the same that Paul uses in Galatians 5:25, when he says 'let us walk by the Spirit'.[4] In short, it refers to conduct of life. All Christians in Philippi are charged to live in accord with the gospel, while at the same time, they are informed that the path to maturity involves focusing their lives on the goal of pursuing the Christian race.

Brothers, join in imitating me, and keep your eyes on those who walk according to the example you have in us (3:17).
Even more explicitly than he does in verse 15, Paul calls the Christian recipients of his letter to imitate his apostolic example (also see 4:9). This provides an important key to understanding the many autobiographical references in this great letter.[5] Paul frequently provides the church glimpses of his life in order to instruct by example in Christian thought and conduct. Yet he recognizes he is not the only model that believers have before them, and so he also encourages the believers at Philippi to look around for other exemplars of the manner of Christian living the apostle endorses (cf. 1 Thess. 2:14).

Paul again addresses fellow Christians as beloved 'brothers' (see above on 3:13). He commands them to 'be imitators of me,' with the Greek *summimētēs* indicating that they are to follow the pattern he has established. In this context, his directive has special reference to the 'Christian race' metaphor, and beckons them to emulate his 'pressing on' toward the future reward that awaits believers in Christ (3:13-16, 20-21). Yet

---

4 Cf. Gal. 6:16; also Acts 21:24; Rom. 4:12.
5 Esp. 1:12-26; 2:17-18; 3:3-16; 3:20-21; 4:11-13.

this command likely also applies to imitating Paul's apostolic example of Christian living in its broadest scope.

The parallel imperative in this verse directs the Philippian Christians to closely observe (*skopeō*, translated 'keep your eyes on') others. The ones they are to observe are those 'who walk according to the example you have in us.' Paul's apostolic pattern should remind the Philippians of others in their Christian community who likewise have given themselves over to the passionate pursuit of maturity in Christ. And their example (*tupos*) becomes another model of how to walk. Paul frequently employs the metaphor of 'walking' to depict the Christian life.[6] 'Walking' is an apt metaphor since it speaks to daily continuous activity in life. While the Christian life is a 'race' in terms of running for a goal/prize (3:13-14), it also is a 'walk' in terms of a step-by-step progress through life, with the objective that each step be made to God's glory.

The concept of imitation is so common in Paul's letters that many scholars now speak of the *imitatio* theme in his ethical instruction,[7] and Paul is not alone in asserting this idea within the early church (Heb. 6:12; 13:7). His most simple, yet profound, statement can be found in 1 Corinthians 11:1: 'Be imitators of me, as I am of Christ.' We have already seen that Paul was not unaware of his shortcomings and his imperfection in achieving maturity (Phil. 3:12). Yet he also knows the practical benefits of real-life exemplars. Consequently, he lives his life in imitation of Christ for the benefit of others, and he openly discusses his own life and internal motivations for the sake of bringing others to maturity. Moreover, the fact that he encourages others to likewise serve as models (Phil. 3:17; 1 Thess. 2:14) reminds us that human illustrations of Christian living, imperfect as they may be, can be part of how the Holy Spirit trains us up in godliness. Therefore, we also can look around for contemporary instances of Christian biography that motivate us to maturity. And Christian leaders must view part of their duty in this life is to open their lives

---

6 Rom. 6:4; 8:4; 13:13; 1 Cor. 7:17; 2 Cor. 5:7; Gal. 5:16; Eph. 2:10; 4:1, 17; 5:2, 8, 15; Col. 1:10; 2:6; 4:5; 1 Thess. 2:12; 4:1, 12; contrast Rom. 14:15; 1 Cor. 3:3; 2 Cor. 4:2; 10:2; Eph. 2:2; 4:17; Col. 3:7; 2 Thess. 3:6,11.

7 E.g., 1 Cor. 4:16; 1 Thess. 1:6; 2 Thess. 3:7, 9; cf. Eph. 5:1.

to the inspection of others, so that others may learn from their successes (and likely also their failures) in pursuing Christ.

For many, of whom I have often told you and now tell you even with tears, walk as enemies of the cross of Christ. Their end is destruction, their god is their belly, and they glory in their shame, with minds set on earthly things (3:18-19).
In sharp contrast to the fine instances of Christian living in the previous verse, Paul now reminds his readers that there are many others who serve as wicked paradigms. By implication, their evil performance is to be observed and avoided.

Paul's use of 'many' (*polloi*) people here is likely intentional. Much as Jesus warned of the narrow gate that leads to life, and the wide way that leads to ruin (Matt. 7:13), so we will discover that there are many cases of those who are heading toward spiritual ruin. Paul has warned the Philippians about such dangerous examples before – certainly in this letter (2:15; 3:2; cf. 1:15, 17, 28; 2:20-21), and likely in his personal ministry among them in the past. Yet, Paul does not view them with mere scorn, or even disinterest; rather, the fact that so many are on a destructive road brings him to tears. Likewise, we should share in this apostolic compassion for the lost.

Note the marked contrast with the preceding verse. In verse 17, Paul exhorts the Christians in Philippi to 'walk' in accordance with his example. Here in verse 18, the enemies of Christ also 'walk', but they do so in a way that leads them down the path to destruction. As noted above, the imagery of 'walking' depicts conduct (day-to-day progress through life). One can proceed through life well, but Paul also speaks repeatedly of people marching into evil.[8] Christians once walked according the evil pattern of this world (Eph. 2:2; Col. 3:7) but do so no longer (Eph. 4:17). Paul speaks elsewhere of those who walk in fleshly jealousy and strife (1 Cor. 3:3) or who tread with crafty motives and thus adulterate the Word of God (2 Cor. 4:2). These examples are to be repudiated by Christians.

Paul calls these destructive exemplars 'enemies of the cross of Christ'. Elsewhere he openly acknowledges that before God

---

8 Rom. 14:15; 2 Cor. 10:2; 2 Thess. 3:6,11.

called Christians to salvation, all of us once were 'enemies' of God (Rom. 5:10; Col. 1:21), though now we have been reconciled through Christ back into an intimate relationship with Him. Yet many more people remain His adversaries. Here, however, these foes are explicitly conducting their lives in such a way as to oppose the 'cross of Christ'. Their enmity is especially focused on repudiating Jesus' crucifixion. Paul famously has called the cross foolishness to the Greek and a stumbling block to the Jew (1 Cor. 1:18-25). Jesus' shameful, humiliating death at the hands of oppressors may well have been something that people, who might otherwise desire to associate with Jesus' teachings, would have wished to disparage (or even deny, as many Gnostics did later in the second century). Yet the cross remains absolutely central to Jesus' work and to the salvation found in His name. To oppose the cross is to contest the core of Jesus' ministry and the very essence of the Christian faith. Such opposition makes one an enemy of Christ.

Those who walk as enemies of Christ's cross are described in several ways in verse 19. First, their future is foretold – their end is destruction. Of course, to be an 'enemy' of Christ is to be in grave danger of eternal judgment – a point Paul firmly acknowledges in keeping with Jesus' own warnings against His opponents.[9] 'Destruction' has been juxtaposed with 'salvation' earlier in this letter (Phil. 1:28). And the Greek word for destruction (*apōleia*) is one Paul elsewhere applies to the eternal judgment that awaits anyone apart from Christ.[10]

Second, their false religion is depicted: 'their god is their belly, and they glory in their shame.' The notion of worshipping a belly seems almost laughable, and it is certainly tinged with irony. The 'belly' (*koilia*) here specifically speaks of the stomach (e.g., 1 Cor. 6:13; cf. Matt. 12:40; 15:17), though it can refer to the womb of a pregnant woman (e.g., Luke 1:41-42; Gal. 1:15). In Romans 16:18, Paul warns of heretics who do not serve Christ but who serve their own bellies. Much as itinerant philosophers in antiquity often taught others simply to win their next meal, so these heretics are seeking to feed their faces and care nothing for true service unto Christ. Of

---

9 1 Cor. 15:25; cf. Luke 19:27; and Ps. 110:1 as quoted in Luke 20:43; Acts 2:35.
10 Rom. 9:22; 2 Thess. 2:3; cf. Matt. 7:13; 2 Pet. 3:7; Rev. 17:8.

them, Paul says, 'their glory is their shame.' Combining this with the immediate context, he apparently asserts that their focus remains on shameful, earthly and fleshly things, as opposed to the glorious things of God, and thus they reverse the very purpose of life. They find glory in what they ought to find shameful.

Finally, these opponents of Christ's cross are portrayed as those whose minds are 'set on earthly things'. The Greek here connects us with concepts running throughout this epistle and reads, more literally: 'those who think earthly things.' Paul employed the word 'think' (*phroneō*) earlier, saying the mature are to 'think' as he instructs (3:15), and the church is to 'think' together the same thing (i.e., to unite in focusing on the things of Christ; see 2:2, 5; 4:2). Whereas it is a Christian duty to contemplate Christ and His kingdom, these rivals of Christ think instead about 'earthly things'.

Such a juxtaposition between heavenly and earthly realities was elsewhere highlighted in early Christian teaching;[11] and Paul (using a cognate expression) speaks of putting to death '... what is earthly in you: sexual immorality, impurity, passion, evil desire, and covetousness, which is idolatry' (Col. 3:5). It appears that these are the very kinds of things the opponents of Christ are embracing and glorying in. This is not to say that Paul encourages people to reject all their earthly needs as irrelevant, in some sort of gnostic over-spiritualization of life. God created us as both physical and spiritual beings, and the goal of Christian theology is not the utter denial of the physical in a vain attempt to gain some kind of higher spiritual plane. Yet if all we do is focus on our next meal or glory in earthly achievements and sinful, fleshly desires rather than focusing on Christ, then we have fallen in with those aligned against Christ. All this should be contrasted with the heavenly focus of Christ's followers in the next verse.

It is possible that these few tantalizing comments on the 'enemies of the cross of Christ' can be combined with the scant information about the 'dogs', 'evildoers', and 'mutilators of the flesh' in Philippians 3:2 in order to develop a composite picture of who Paul is opposing (see commentary and Additional

---

11 John 3:12; James 3:15; cf. 1 Cor. 15:40; 2 Cor. 5:1.

Notes on 3:2). The information is so slender, however, that we would have to deem any such reconstruction tentative. It is not even certain that the same figures are in view in 3:2 and 3:19. If we were to attempt a reconstruction, however, then we would assume that these are Judaizing itinerant heretics, who are seeking earthly recompense for their teaching and who oppose Paul's gospel of the crucified Christ.

But our citizenship is in heaven, and from it we await a Savior, the Lord Jesus Christ, who will transform our lowly body to be like his glorious body, by the power that enables him even to subject all things to himself (3:20-21).
Unlike the opponents of Christ's cross, who have their 'minds set on earthly things' (3:19), Christians are to remember that they possess a heavenly citizenship as they look forward to the glorious return of Christ and to their resurrection unto eternal life with Him.

Earlier in Philippians, Paul began his discussion of Christian living by instructing Christians to be worthy citizens of the gospel of Christ (see comments on 1:27). Here he again invokes citizenship language to remind Christians to look beyond this world for their identity in this present life. Remember that Roman citizenship gave people special privileges in antiquity (e.g., Acts 22:26-29) and that Philippi was a Roman colony, which was populated in part by resettled families that had received citizenship through military service. Thus this word 'citizenship' bore a great social significance to Paul's audience. Though many in the ancient world could wish for Roman citizenship or exult in already possessing such social status, Paul points to a much more glorious citizenship in heaven. Such citizenship calls forth notions of allegiances, privileges, and responsibilities. Christians are those whose allegiance is to Christ, whose privileges are vouchsafed by the surety of the Holy Spirit, and so in this life, they are responsible to conduct themselves as good citizens of the kingdom of God.

Jesus presently sits at the right hand of the Father in heaven,[12] and from there he will come to judge the living and

---

12 Phil. 2:9; Rom. 8:34; Eph. 1:20; Col. 3:1; cf. Acts 2:33; 5:31; 7:55-56; Heb. 1:3,13; 8:1; 10:12; 12:2; 1 Pet. 3:22.

the dead.[13] Paul speaks here in Philippians to the positive outcome of that judgment for Christ's followers – resurrection unto life. Paul subtly reminds us that Jesus, who is both the Lord and the Messiah, is also the one responsible for making our eternal hope a reality – He is our Savior, and apart from His salvific work there is no hope of future glory. We live today in light of the confidence we have in that coming glory, and thus we 'wait' eagerly for the coming of the Lord Jesus Christ.

This is what that future holds: glorified resurrection bodies. Many popular images of Christian future hope are governed by a vague notion (evident in cartoons, books, movies and TV) that St Peter will stand at some pearly white gate in heaven and grant wings to good people, who will spend eternity playing their harps while floating in the clouds. This is not at all what this verse teaches. Rather, Christ will come 'from' heaven (3:20), and He will transform our humble bodies to conform to the pattern of His glorious resurrection body. There is a very material, earthy expectation in Paul's words. He does not look to become some sort of ghostly spirit floating around in the world, nor does he mimic a pagan notion of an ephemeral future amid the Elysian Fields, nor does he expect to be bodiless in bliss on some higher spiritual plane. Paul anticipates a body and a physical life in the world to come.

Yet, there is also a change. In Paul's eschatological (i.e., future) expectation, he looks for 'creation' to become 'new creation'.[14] He expects Jesus' reign over His people, though now inaugurated, to be consummated. He expects death to be destroyed, the dead to be raised, sin to be abolished, and the holy worship of Christ to be our continuous joyful duty.[15] He also expects (as here) our bodies to be transformed (1 Cor. 15:35-55): 'Behold! I tell you a mystery. We shall not all sleep, but we shall all be changed, in a moment, in the twinkling of an eye, at the last trumpet. For the trumpet will sound, and the dead will be raised imperishable, and we shall be changed' (1 Cor. 15:51-52).

---

13 2 Tim. 4:1; cf. Matt. 25:31-46; John 5:27-29; 2 Cor. 5:10; Acts 10:42; 17:31; 1 Pet. 4:5; Rev. 19:11.
14 Rom. 8:19-23; cf. Isa. 65:17; 66:22; 2 Pet. 3:13; Rev. 21:1.
15 Phil. 2:10-11; 1 Cor. 15:20-57; 1 Thess. 4:13-18; 5:9-10.

The word in verse 21 for 'transformed' (*metaschēmatizō*) can mean 'disguised' (cf. 2 Cor. 11:13-15), but here it refers to a true change of external form. Paul calls our current bodies 'lowly,' with the Greek here (*tapeinōsis*) referring to the humble state of our present bodily existence (comparable in some ways to an impoverished person in contrast to a wealthy individual). Yet our humble bodies will be transformed into a new pattern – we will share the likeness (*summorphos*) of Christ's glorious body. That which is humble and lowly has been transformed into the same glory (*doxa*) of the body of our resurrected Lord.

The clear theological implication is that Christians should expect to be physically resurrected and live in a new creation. Just as God originally created humanity to be simultaneously physical and spiritual beings who dwell in a physical world – and He called that 'very good' – so we look to the new creation reality to echo Eden in important physical ways. Moreover, if our bodies are to be transformed according to the likeness of Jesus' resurrection body, then we can ponder the gospel accounts of Jesus' resurrection (and the rest of the Scriptures through to the book of Revelation) and begin to anticipate what our future state might look like. Just as Jesus after His resurrection could be touched, could feel, could stand, could eat and drink, could talk, and could be seen and worshipped in person;[16] thus, we too should expect a physical reality in the world to come. Yet Jesus' body was also somehow different[17] – with the most important change being that the mortal has been raised to immortal life.

The reader would certainly benefit from pondering this further: What would it be like to inhabit a resurrection body in the new creation? Yet we should also recognize that Scripture provides only the barest glimpses into that future, and so we must constrain our speculations while nonetheless pondering these deepest expectations.

This hope is sure because it is vouchsafed by Jesus' dominion. Paul says our bodies will be transformed '…by the power that enables him [Jesus] even to subject all things to himself' (Phil. 3:21). In other words, there is a potency that transforms our lowly bodies into resurrection bodies, and

---

16 E.g., Matt. 28:9; Luke 24:30, 38-43; John 20:14, 20, 24-29; 21:23; Acts 1:3.
17 E.g., Luke 24:31, 36-37, 51; John 20:17, 19, 26; Acts 1:9.

this mighty force is according to the same authority that empowers Jesus to submit all things under His rule. Paul has elsewhere taught that all things will be subjected to Jesus.[18] The authority such subjugation entails also promises that Christ will resurrect His followers. The dead in Christ are raised, and Christ will reign over all.

Summary
Paul paints a huge picture for us of our future hope. Our ultimate prize in the race of life is an eternal inheritance with our Lord Jesus. That prize grants us immortal, resurrected bodies while we worship the Messiah as He rules over all things. In light of that future hope, our lives today ought to be lived as racers who strain for that prize, abandoning anything else that would entangle us as we run. Though perfection is not yet ours in this life (even the apostle Paul had not attained it!), yet the mature believer imitates Paul's devotion to running the race. There are others who would derail our focus – those whose minds are set on earthly things and on feeding their own faces. We dare not follow them, for their end is destruction. Yet we are citizens of the most glorious kingdom imaginable, and we should live as Christ's followers today while looking forward to His appearing.

Can you relate to this? Do you sometimes feel that you are in a race, but that you have lost your direction? Do you worry about the earthly matters so often that you forget the heavenly? In the midst of the decay of our earthly bodies, do you long for a body that will be glorious and imperishable? Let us join in imitating Paul's concentration on the prize at the end of the race. A better day is dawning. We know that Christ will surely reign, and with Him, we shall be raised.

Questions for Personal Reflection:
1. Do you find it encouraging when the apostle Paul readily admits that he is not already perfect? What are some of the tensions that we experience as we desire to be holy and perfect in this life, and yet

---

18 Phil. 2:9-11; 1 Cor. 15:27-28; Eph. 1:22.

constantly fall short of that goal? How do you deal with those tensions?

2. When you read Paul's athletic metaphor in 3:13-14, in what ways do you find it helpful as a portrait of Christian living? Are there ways we can take this metaphor too far? How can this metaphor be useful in your life?

3. How would your life be different if you lived consistently as a 'citizen of heaven'? Can one be (as the old saying goes) 'so heavenly minded that one is no earthly good'? What does it look like to live in this world as God's ambassador from His heavenly kingdom? How should this affect your family life, work, relationships with your neighbors, etc.? List some of the many ways we can be involved in transforming this world as agents of God's kingdom.

4. How have you seen heaven portrayed in popular media? What difference does it make if you conceive of your future life with Christ as a bodily resurrection existence rather than as the media often portray heaven? Do you look forward to a resurrection body?

Study Questions:

1. In 3:17 Paul gives us a clue as to why he has included so much autobiographical information in this letter. From the context of this passage (and from elsewhere in Philippians), name some of the areas where Paul encourages the church to imitate him.

2. In an earlier lesson (on 2:19-30) we asked how following other people's Christian examples can be helpful to us in our Christian lives, and also where it can be detrimental. What further thoughts do you have on this?

3. How would your life look different if you were to imitate more fully the Christian walk of the apostle Paul?

4. In 3:12, what does Paul mean by: 'Not that I have already obtained this or am already perfect'? What is the 'this'? What would such 'perfection' (or 'maturity') look like?

5. Does it encourage you in any way that the great apostle Paul openly acknowledged before the church that he was not already perfect? What are some of the tensions that we experience as we desire to be holy and perfect in this life, and yet as we also constantly fall short of that goal? How can we properly deal with those tensions?

6. Paul draws on an athletic metaphor in 3:12-14 to illustrate 'pressing on toward the goal for the prize of the upward call of God in Christ Jesus.' What might be some roughly equivalent metaphors in our contemporary setting? How would our lives look if this goal was constantly in front of us?

7. How does Paul describe the enemies of the cross of Christ (3:18-19)? What emotive language do you see here? How can this serve as a model for us in approaching contemporary opponents of the Christian church?

8. Observe the contrasting elements between 3:20-21 and 3:18-19. How does 3:20-21 contribute to our own sense of identity as Christ's followers?

9. How have you seen heaven portrayed in popular media? What difference does it make if you conceive of your future life with Christ as a bodily resurrection existence rather than as the media often portray heaven? Do you look forward to a resurrection body?

10. How would your life be different if you lived consistently as a 'citizen of heaven'? Can one be (as the old saying goes) 'so heavenly minded that one is no earthly good'? What does it look like to live in this world as God's ambassador from His heavenly kingdom? How should this affect your family life,

work, relationships with your neighbors, etc.? List some of the many ways we can be involved in transforming this world as agents of God's kingdom.

Additional Note:

3:12 The prepositional phrase translated as 'because' in 'because Christ Jesus has made me his own' bears this same causal function elsewhere in Paul (Rom. 5:12; 2 Cor. 5:4; Phil. 4:10).

12

Standing Firm Together in the Lord
(Philippians 4:1-9)

¹Therefore, my brothers, whom I love and long for, my joy and crown, stand firm thus in the Lord, my beloved.

²I entreat Euodia and I entreat Syntyche to agree in the Lord. ³Yes, I ask you also, true companion, help these women, who have labored side by side with me in the gospel together with Clement and the rest of my fellow workers, whose names are in the book of life.

⁴Rejoice in the Lord always; again I will say, Rejoice. ⁵Let your reasonableness be known to everyone. The Lord is at hand; ⁶do not be anxious about anything, but in everything by prayer and supplication with thanksgiving let your requests be made known to God. ⁷And the peace of God, which surpasses all understanding, will guard your hearts and your minds in Christ Jesus.

⁸Finally, brothers, whatever is true, whatever is honorable, whatever is just, whatever is pure, whatever is lovely, whatever is commendable, if there is any excellence, if there is anything worthy of praise, think about these things. ⁹What you have learned and received and heard and seen in me—practice these things, and the God of peace will be with you.

Imagine what it would be like sitting next to the apostle Paul when he was writing this great epistle. The guard stares intently at him as the scribe writes down his every word.

Epaphroditus is eager to head back to Philippi with Paul's letter in hand. The apostle comes toward the conclusion of the letter. And we are all wondering how he will conclude. What will be his final words of exhortation? What last things will he emphasize before he moves on to thanking the church for the gifts they have sent?

These are the words he chose. Though a few verses remain after these – important for the thankfulness they convey and the attitude they model (4:10-23) – these nine verses before us constitute his last major directives to the church in Philippi. So these are going to be important.

In many ways, Paul re-emphasizes material he has already covered: 'stand firm', 'rejoice', 'be of one mind', and imitate the Christian obedience of others. The very fact that Paul reminds his readers again of such matters indicates just how important he holds these to be in the Christian life. Yet, some new themes arise: prayer, peace, and the discipline of the mind. Through all this, we glimpse the apostolic perspective on how we should conduct ourselves amidst this world.

Therefore, my brothers, whom I love and long for, my joy and crown, stand firm thus in the Lord, my beloved (4:1).
Two aspects of this verse most stand out: the admonition to 'stand firm,' and the many endearing terms that display Paul's love for the Philippians. Yet we should begin with the first word, 'therefore.'

How does this passage connect (via this 'therefore') with the preceding material? Most immediately, it relates to the 'heavenly citizenship' of the believer affirmed in 3:20-21 (cf. 1:27). This citizenship comes with the assurance that when the Lord returns, we who long for His appearing will receive resurrection bodies and join together in celebrating His universal reign (cf. 2:9-11; 3:8-11). In light of that promise, we must stand firm in the midst of a world presently opposed to Christ (cf. 3:18-19).

The admonition to 'stand firm' has already resounded in this letter (1:27 – see notes on this verse). In that passage, it appeared within the context of the twin themes of Christian citizenship and church unity. It can hardly be a coincidence that both themes are found in the immediate environs of this verse as well – heavenly citizenship (3:20-21) and Christian unity (4:2-3). To 'stand firm' is not primarily an individual command. Corporately, Christians are to live out their heavenly citizenship in this world by standing together in Christ in the midst of a world opposed to the things of God. Moreover, they stand firm 'in the Lord'; it is by His strength and for His glory that they together hold fast to His gospel.

Perhaps this command to stand firm together serves as an overarching directive, with the following verses (2-9) providing some of the ways that Christians stand firm. Yet even as Paul announces his imperative, he also conveys his great fondness for the church at Philippi. He calls the Christians in Philippi his 'brothers', his 'beloved', whom he 'longs for', and whom he considers his 'joy and crown'. These words also connect us with his previous statements in this letter.

For example, Paul has called them 'brothers' already (1:12; 3:1, 13, 17) and will soon do so again (4:8). He also speaks of Epaphroditus as his brother (2:25), along with other Christians around the world (1:14; 4:21). Earlier, in studying these passages, we noted how the word 'brother' serves as a term of endearment frequently found in the early church. It reminds all church members that they are now adopted into a new family, the family of Christ, in which they are all brothers and sisters in God's economy.

In this verse, Paul especially emphasizes the word 'beloved'. Although the above translation speaks of the Philippians as both those 'whom I love' and 'my beloved', in the original Greek, Paul simply repeats the same word (*agapētoi* – 'beloved, one who is loved'). After the opening depiction of these church members as brothers, he then bookends the other titles he gives them with this word *agapētoi* –'beloved'. This repetition signifies that Paul definitely wanted these Philippians to know his affection for them.

Paul 'longs for' them. He has repeatedly stated his desire to return to the church in Philippi (1:24-26; 2:24). This Greek adjective (*epipothētoi*) is related to the verb *epipotheō* ('yearn for') in Philippians 1:8, where he declares: 'For God is my witness, how I yearn [*epipotheō*] for you all with the affection of Christ Jesus.' Clearly, Paul strongly desires to see them again, and he wishes to make sure that they know this longing stems from his great fondness for them.

Paul also calls them 'my joy and my crown'. Just as he anticipates that at the physical return of Jesus, he will rejoice in their accession to Christ's kingdom, so he, their spiritual father in the faith, knows that the Philippians themselves will be his celestial triumph (his 'crown'; cf. 1 Thess. 2:19). They are one of his greatest sources of 'joy' in the kingdom (both now and in the culmination of the kingdom in Christ's return; cf. comments on 2:16).

I entreat Euodia and I entreat Syntyche to agree in the Lord. Yes, I ask you also, true companion, help these women, who have labored side by side with me in the gospel together with Clement and the rest of my fellow workers, whose names are in the book of life (4:2-3).

It is a sad truth that even the most committed servants of the church can end up in bitter conflict with one another. Paul repeatedly emphasizes in this letter his call for Christian unity. We learn in this verse that he has at least one specific reason to be distressed – Euodia and Syntyche are in conflict.

The individuals named here are unfortunately not certainly identified in any other writings so we do not know how this conflict was resolved. Though a man named Clement is later important in the church at Rome, there is no firm evidence to connect him with the Clement here in Philippi. Polycarp's second-century letter to the Philippians does not directly reference this conflict.

It would be tempting to imagine that such divisiveness could only stem from people who are less than admirable servants of Christ. However, though we might desire to know more about who these women were, it is clear that Paul held both Euodia and Syntyche in high esteem. They had 'labored side by side' with Paul 'in the gospel'. In doing so, they appear among the ranks of others he applauds, such as 'Clement and the rest of my fellow workers'. All of these people, including presumably Euodia and Syntyche, have their 'names' found 'in the book of life'. The reference to the 'book of life' indicates Paul's confidence that they will be listed among Christ's chosen servants, whom our Lord will call into His kingdom at the final judgment.[1]

---

1 Such a 'book' being known elsewhere in early Christianity and from the Old Testament; see Rev. 3:5; 20:15; 21:27; cf. Exod. 32:32; Isa. 4:3; Luke 10:20; Heb. 12:23; also see Ps. 69:28; Rev. 13:8; 17:8; 20:12.

Yet in addition to testifying to Paul's esteem for these Christian servants, these same descriptors also call these two ladies to live up to the apostolic ideal of working cooperatively toward the same end. Just as they have 'labored *side by side*' and have been among Paul's '*fellow* workers,' so they are to return to such collegial co-laboring. The same verb for 'labored side by side' (*sunathleō*) appears in 1:27, where Paul desires to hear that the church in Philippi is standing firm 'with one mind *striving side by side* [*sunathleō*] for the faith of the gospel' (cf. Rom. 15:30; Col. 4:12). And the title 'fellow worker' (*sunergos*) in this epistle was first granted to Epaphroditus (Phil. 2:25). Paul commonly designates as 'fellow workers' those who toil alongside him in collaborative gospel ministry.[2] Thus Paul reminds Euodia and Syntyche (and the whole Philippian church) that ministry is to be a cooperative endeavor, performed by humble servants of Christ who work side by side for His glory.

Paul emphatically repeats the Greek verb 'entreat', perhaps recognizing that any solution to this conflict must result from the active participation of both parties. He 'entreats' both Euodia and Syntyche equally. The verb for 'entreat' refers to exhortation with the goal of encouraging proper Christian virtue (*parakaleō*; e.g., Rom. 15:30; 16:17; Eph. 4:1).

Paul specifically entreats them both 'to agree in the Lord'. It is important here to reiterate a point made earlier in this commentary. The Greek for 'to agree' literally commands them: 'to think the same thing' (*to auto phronein*). Paul addresses the whole church with similar phraseology in Philippians 2:2 ('complete my joy with the result that you *think the same thing* [= *to auto phronēte*]'). Then in Philippians 2:5, Paul portrays Jesus as the exemplar of the kind of humble self-giving that the church is also to live out (where the Christian is literally to '*think this one way* [= *touto phroneite*] among yourselves which also was in Christ'). In other words, Paul's previous calls to Christian unity have been preparing the whole church to receive this specific exhortation now addressed to Euodia and Syntyche.

This 'agreement' stems from a determined, mutual desire to discipline their thought life so that they come to a unity of mind and intent. We might say that they 'think on the same

---

2 Rom. 16:3, 9, 21; 1 Cor. 3:9; 2 Cor. 1:24; 8:23; Col. 4:11; 1 Thess. 3:2; Philem. 1, 24.

page'. It undoubtedly entails compromise for the sake of harmony in the church. It requires humility as each listens to the other and as both come to reciprocally agreeable solutions.

Moreover, their 'agreement' is to be 'in the Lord'. Or, more literally, they are 'to think the same thing in the Lord'. They are not to find just any basis for accord, but their agreement and concord must be founded on their common commitment to Christ. In order to overcome their present divisions, they are being asked to find unity of thought in their mutual devotion to their Lord.

Nonetheless, Paul senses that they may need some outside help. So he calls upon an anonymous 'true companion' to assist them to end their conflict. The Greek *suzugos* ('companion') can refer to 'comrades at arms' or to others who are paired together toward a particular end. Various attempts have been made to identify this person. Some have suggested that this true companion was Epaphroditus, who is Paul's fellow worker depicted in Philippians 2:25-30, but there is no clear link to him in this verse. Since a *suzugos* can be a term used of a spouse, some have actually proposed that this refers to Paul's wife, but we have no reason to assume that Paul was even married (cf. 1 Cor. 7:7; 9:5), let alone that he had left his spouse in Philippi. And some have assumed that the person's actual name was 'Suzugos,' though again with little evidence. In short, we do not know who this person was.

It is certain, however, that this 'true companion' has been called upon to 'help these women'. The verb for 'help' (*sullambanō*) possesses a variety of meanings in different settings, but here, the context invokes the notion of 'help by taking part with someone in an activity' (cf. perhaps Luke 5:7). It implies that this companion is to come alongside these ladies and assist them in their efforts at reconciliation.

Even if this conflict potentially could escalate to generating broader factions in the Philippian church, it is still striking that Paul would care this much about a division between two of his fellow servants. This serves as an excellent reminder to us that we must all be careful to work together in the church and should all remain attentive to reach appropriate compromises for the sake of Christian unity and peace. Sometimes it is even necessary for an outside party to be involved in facilitating the reconciliation of the various sides of a dispute. The goal of Christian life together remains that we all labor side by side in the Good News of Jesus Christ.

Rejoice in the Lord always; again I will say, Rejoice (4:4).
The importance of this command is made evident from its emphatic repetition, from Paul's command at earlier important junctures in the epistle (2:18; 3:1) that the church 'rejoice', and from the manner in which he intentionally models 'joy' and 'rejoicing' throughout this letter.[3] This is not the only epistle in which Paul commands the church to rejoice (e.g., 2 Cor. 13:11; 1 Thess. 5:16), but the repetition of 'joy' vocabulary throughout Philippians indicates that it is an especially important theme here.

As we reflect on Paul's previous remarks about 'joy', it is evident that he is not speaking about a transitory happiness that arises from pleasant circumstances. In fact, Paul often rejoices despite his situation – such as when the gospel is proclaimed by those who desire to inflict harm on him (1:18), or when he is 'poured out like a drink offering upon the sacrificial offering of your faith' (2:17-18). Of course, favorable events can also bring joy to Paul – such as when he remembers the Philippians in prayer (1:4; cf. 4:1), or when the Philippians gather together in Christian unity (2:2), or when they assist him while he is imprisoned (4:10). Yet in both difficult situations and happy events, Paul finds his joy in the Lord. Thus he models the command to 'rejoice in the Lord *always*'.

What then is the secret to such perpetual joy? The key must be found in the phrase '*in the Lord*'. Paul does not advocate merely looking around for things to be happy about (as in the old song 'Keep on the Sunny Side of Life'). This is not some optimistic self-help technique (such as those so popular today). Nor does he simply prompt us to hope that things will get better in our lives somewhere around the bend. Rather, Paul instructs Christians to root their joy in the Lord Himself.

Just as English can convey the *cause* of rejoicing by how we rejoice 'in' something, so also can the Greek expression 'to rejoice in' (*chairein en*).[4] We might 'rejoice in' many

---
3 Phil. 1:4, 18; 2:2, 17; 4:1, 10; cf. 1:25; 2:18, 28-29.
4 Cf. Luke 6:23; 10:20; Phil. 1:18; 3:1; 4:10; also possibly Col. 1:24.

different things throughout our lives. We might rejoice in relatively fleeting items, such as our team winning a sports championship or our day going well. Or we might rejoice in more significant matters such as a new job, or a newborn baby, or our friends, or our family. Paul does not instruct us to abandon such causes of happiness, but he demands that we root our lives in a much more foundational joyful truth – he calls us to find joy 'in the Lord'.

Such a notion Paul likely discerned in his study of the Old Testament. Thus in Habakkuk 3:18-19, even in the midst of horrible circumstances, the author says:

> [18]yet I will rejoice in the LORD;
> I will take joy in the God of my salvation.
> [19]GOD, the Lord, is my strength;
> he makes my feet like the deer's;
> he makes me tread on my high places.

The gospel connects us to an eternal hope founded on the advent of our Lord, on His death and resurrection, and on the surety of His return. As we reflect on our loving Lord Jesus Christ, who voluntarily gave Himself graciously on our behalf and who now reigns on high (cf. Phil. 2:5-11), our spirits are lifted to exult in Him. He remains sovereign over all creation and even over all our days, so we can trust where He will take us. He beckons us on to an eternal inheritance, when our lowly bodies will be transformed to be like His glorious resurrection body (3:20-21). Thus in the midst of the travails of life, our citizenship is not of this world but of the world to come (3:20). Contemplate these truths, and the many other grand realities about our glorious Lord, and we cannot help but be elevated to joy amid the ups and downs of this life.

We might wonder whether this verse (4:4) seems a bit disconnected from its context, as though it were a general proverbial maxim Paul threw in for good measure. Yet earlier, we observed that Paul's previous command to rejoice *in the Lord* (3:1), in addition to being sage advice on Christian living, also served in context as a safeguard against heretical notions of putting confidence elsewhere in life (3:2-4). In 3:1-4, Christians who rejoice in the Lord (and thus focus on Him) do not allow themselves to be captivated by anything less. Here in

4:4, in an analogous fashion to the mention of 'rejoice in the Lord' in 3:1, it is also likely that Paul emphasizes 'rejoicing in the Lord' in keeping with the immediate context. In this context, such a centering of life on the joy of Christ promotes the kind of Christian unity he is begging Euodia and Syntyche to achieve. If they are both seeking their joy 'in the Lord Jesus', then it should be no problem for them to agree 'in the Lord' (Phil. 4:2). In fact, we see Paul's similar emphasis on harmony in the church alongside rejoicing in the Lord in 2 Corinthians 13:11, where he asserts: 'Finally, brothers, rejoice. Aim for restoration, comfort one another, agree with one another, live in peace; and the God of love and peace will be with you.'

Thus, 'rejoicing in the Lord' is not only a natural response to the glorious riches of salvation found in Jesus, it also forms a safeguard for the Christian church. If we rejoice in Christ, then the petty things that might otherwise captivate us throughout our lives hold little appeal. And if we rejoice together 'in the Lord', then it becomes much easier for us to set aside our paltry personal desires, to agree 'in the Lord', and to labor side by side in the Lord's church.

Let your reasonableness be known to everyone. The Lord is at hand (4:5).
If the preceding verse (4:4) continues to connect with the call to Christian unity (4:1-3), so does this passage (4:5). The word translated 'reasonableness' here (*epieikes*) most often conveys the notion of 'gentleness' – in particular a gentle demeanor toward others. One Greek lexicon (BDAG) remarks that this adjective speaks of 'not insisting on every right of letter of law or custom, yielding, gentle, kind, courteous, tolerant,' and this meaning is witnessed elsewhere in the New Testament.[5] Such 'gentleness' is a quality that Christian leaders are to embrace (1 Tim. 3:3). Paul addresses this in another place (Titus 3:2) when he calls on Christians 'to speak evil of no one, to avoid quarreling, *to be gentle*, and to show perfect courtesy toward all people.'

Thus we observe that Christians are to embody a gentle disposition to one another, even yielding to others for the sake

---

5 James 3:17; 1 Pet. 2:18; cf. LXX of Esth. 13:2; 16:9; Ps. 85:5.

of true Christian unity in the Lord. Moreover, Paul does not limit such an attitude toward just those fellow believers whom we like. Rather, our gentle disposition is to be recognizable by 'everyone'. They are all to 'know' our gentle demeanor and are all to experience first-hand how we treat others with gentleness and respect. Certainly, if church members were to behave toward one another in such a kind and courteous manner, this would do much to heal any divisions. Moreover, what a pleasant place the Christian community would be, if we all made our love for one another evident by our desire to yield to one another in the context of mutual joy in the Lord.

This verse continues by reminding everyone that 'the Lord is at hand'. There are two key questions concerning this brief phrase: (1) Does this mean that Jesus is spiritually 'near' Christians now, or does it refer to the imminence of the Lord's return? (2) Does this verse go with the preceding passage(s) to give reason for obedience to Paul's command to be gentle with one another, or is it an introduction to the verses that follow (4:6ff.)? Neither question can be answered with absolute certainty, but both are worth careful consideration.

What does Paul mean when he says, 'the Lord is near'? Certainly, theologically Paul speaks both of his anticipation of the Lord's physical return (e.g., Phil. 3:20-21) and also of Christ's presence in this life with those who are in Christ.[6] In many ways, this conforms with the 'already' and the 'not yet' of the gospel – we are already in the age where the kingdom of God has drawn near (e.g., Luke 10:9), yet we also await the consummation of God's kingdom in the return of Christ. Christians are already in the presence of Christ in this life, yet we long to see Him face to face at His return.

Still, the word 'near' (*engus*) is often associated in the New Testament with the Lord's return,[7] and the most immediate context here in Philippians does indeed look to the reappearance of Christ in judgment and glory (3:20-21). So, it appears that Paul refers here to the Lord returning soon in order to judge the world and to vindicate His people. Though nearly two thousand years have passed since our Lord was raised

---

6 E.g., Phil. 1:1; cf. 2 Cor. 2:10; 8:21; 1 Tim. 5:21; 6:13; 2 Tim. 4:1.
7 Matt. 24:33; Mark 13:29; Luke 21:31; cf. James 5:8; 1 Pet. 4:7; Rom. 13:11-12; Rev. 1:3; 22:10.

from the dead, still the Lord, for whom a thousand years are like a day, is not slow to fulfill his promise – and soon our Lord will appear like a thief in the night (2 Pet. 3:8-10). We cannot know the day and the hour of our Lord's return; therefore, we must live in light of the hope that His advent is near.

Such a reality motivates us to attentive resolve – we could call this 'eschatological urgency'. Does this accord best with the verses preceding (4:1-5a) or those following (4:6ff.)? If the phrase 'the Lord is near' were to have referenced the present reality that Christ is with His people, then that would have favored a parallel with 4:7 (that the 'peace of God' through Christ being present with us would rule our hearts and minds). However, if 'the Lord is near' reminds us of the eschatological urgency that Christ will return soon (as we have already argued), then that might best undergird the need for Christians to rejoice in the knowledge of His return and to act in a proper way toward others in the church (knowing that Christ will soon come to judge and to vindicate). The church should seek even now to attain unity, since we expect the Lord to return soon, and since we desire Him to see that His church has been laboring together to focus on Christ and to rejoice in our Lord. Thus it appears that the main import of these words in 4:5b refers back to the material in 4:1-5a. Still, the reality of the Lord's return might also serve to alleviate earthly anxieties in this life – and to these anxieties Paul turns next.

Do not be anxious about anything, but in everything by prayer and supplication with thanksgiving let your requests be made known to God. And the peace of God, which surpasses all understanding, will guard your hearts and your minds in Christ Jesus (4:6-7).

This strikes me as one of the simplest commands in Scripture (don't be anxious, but pray instead), and yet it is one of the most difficult to live out in our daily lives. It can seem that there is much to be anxious about in this life – our health, finances, standing in society, future, etc. (not to mention similar concerns for others whom we care about). Given such potential for concerns to arise, it is not surprising that we so often drift into anxiety about such matters. When we think about it, a major part of what makes us anxious is that we are truly not in control over such issues, even if at times we are under the illusion that we can attempt to become masters of our fate. The truth is, despite my best efforts, I might tomorrow be diagnosed with a dreadful disease, or I might be 'let go' from my job, or I might accidentally do something stupid and lose the respect of my peers, or my future might take a drastic turn for the worse in some other way. We are not in control, and that makes us nervous. However, the good news is that we know the God who *is* truly sovereign. He is in control.

From where does much of our anxiety originate? I well remember a theology class I took on the Danish Christian philosopher Søren Kierkegaard. In reflecting on his book *The Concept of Anxiety*, we discussed how anxiety is actually a great barometer of how much we are trusting in God versus how much we are relying on ourselves. If we trust in ourselves, then we are bound to become aware of how little in control we are of our future; but if we trust in God, then we are giving ourselves over to a Sovereign who cares for our best. An example of this could be the expert thief who, having drafted his robbery plans in great detail, still spends the evening before his crime wondering about everything that could go wrong. The thief, who clearly is breaking the law of God, cannot reasonably hope that the Lord of justice will make things turn out well for him. Whereas the person who lives in keeping with the gospel can faithfully trust that God loves us so much as to constantly seek our best.

Not that we ourselves always know what is truly best in this fallen world, and sometimes God guides us through difficult places. For example, Paul gives this very instruction to not be anxious while he is imprisoned and awaiting a possible death penalty. Yet, such sufferings and trials in life ultimately can lead us to being refined more fully into the image of Christ, and Paul reminds us that even death itself results in us being brought into the full presence of the Lord (1:23). So God does not always direct us into pleasant places, but He always comforts us in our affliction, refines our character, and enables us to look forward in eternal hope. With that kind of confidence, we can lift our concerns up to God in prayer and receive the peace that comes from knowing that His response, whatever it may be, is indeed best.

The word for 'be anxious' (*merimnaō*) more broadly refers to 'be concerned for'. Not every concern we have in life is misplaced. For example, Paul uses this same word when he describes the admirable 'concern' Timothy has for the Philippians (2:20), and the 'care' believers are to show for one another (1 Cor. 12:25). However, our 'concerns' can often become allied with a lack of trust in God for our future, and thus they become 'anxieties' (cf. Matt. 10:19; Luke 10:41; 12:11; 1 Cor. 7:32-34). Anxiety itself is a complex phenomenon – some anxiety can be good (even necessary in this life), since a fear of death prevents us from getting too close to dangerous situations (e.g., the edge of the cliff) or can motivate us to run from others (e.g., the bear on a hiking path). Anxieties can also have complicated origins; for example, the anxieties some people suffer result (at least in part) from chemical imbalances in the brain that can be treated with medications. Often, however, our daily worries stem from doubts and fears about our future, as if God did not lavish us with His loving provision for our lives.

Famously, Jesus Himself called for His followers to put off anxiety: 'Therefore I tell you, do not be anxious about your life, what you will eat or what you will drink, nor about your body, what you will put on.... Therefore do not be anxious about tomorrow' (Matt. 6:25, 34; cf. Luke 12:22-31). Jesus aptly observes that there is more to life than such concerns ('Is not life more than food, and the body more than clothing?' Matt. 6:25). He remarks that by worrying about such matters, we do not necessarily improve our situation ('Which of you by being anxious can add a single hour to his span of life?' Matt. 6:27). And, most importantly, he reminds us that God cares for us more than we can ever imagine ('But if God so clothes the grass of the field, which today is alive and tomorrow is thrown into the oven, will he not much more clothe you, O you of little faith?' Matt. 6:30). If we worry too much about our own daily possessions and provisions (as if we could control such matters!), then we endanger ourselves by focusing more on mammon (material goods) than on God (Matt. 6:24; cf. Matt. 6:19-23; Luke 12:13-34). Jesus insists that we refocus from such anxieties and entrust ourselves to God ('But seek first the kingdom of God and his righteousness, and all these things will be added to you,' Matt. 6:33).

It is likely Paul had this instruction of Jesus in mind when he penned these words to the Philippians. Similarly, 1 Peter 5:6-7 reads: 'Humble yourselves, therefore, under the mighty hand of God so that at the proper time he may exalt you, casting all your anxieties on him, because he cares for you.'

Note that Paul is quite emphatic when he commands us to 'be anxious for *nothing*'. The Greek word for 'nothing' (*mēden*) appears first in the clause, adding emphasis. Paul desires Christians to have no inappropriate concerns in their lives at all.

Paul's solution to such worries is found in this juxtaposition: rather than worry, we are to pray. Much as Jesus contrasts anxiety with 'seeking first the kingdom of God', so Paul juxtaposes angst with prayerful reliance on God. In addition, the contrast extends to being anxious for 'nothing', but praying about 'everything'.

Paul's words also expand our concept of prayer: 'but in everything by prayer and supplication with thanksgiving let your requests be made known to God.' In this short verse, Paul employs multiple words for interacting with God – prayer, supplication, thanksgiving, requests. 'Prayer' (*proseuchē*) is a general term for engaging in communication with God. 'Supplication' (*deēsis*) often refers to entreating someone for something (in the New Testament, this always involves engaging *God* in prayer). The two words 'prayer and supplication' overlap in meaning but together convey the sense of approaching God to ask for His provision (cf. Eph. 6:18; 1 Tim. 5:5; and many places in the Greek Old Testament – e.g., Ps. 6:9). 'Requests' (*aitēmata*), as the English word implies, denote items that we ask from another. Here, such requests are presented to God in the context of 'thanksgiving' (*eucharistia*). This is a wonderful cue that in the midst of our pleas for God's provision, it is highly important that we remind ourselves of how God has lavished His care on us in the past, and it is fully appropriate that we thank Him for such previous provisions.

We 'make known' our requests to God by means of such prayer and supplication. Here we enter into the great mystery of prayer. How is it that we make known something to the omniscient God? If God already knows what we need, then why must we make Him aware of it? Of course, this verse does not seek to answer such a conundrum, and often the

Biblical rejoinder to 'why pray if God already knows' is simply 'because He commands us to'. Nonetheless, note how in this context, our own anxieties are relieved by knowing that we have communicated with God about our needs. Further, our prayerfulness repeatedly reminds us of our dependence on God, who sovereignly controls all things. Beyond that, we should look on prayer as a divine invitation to engage in personal relationship with the God who loves us. Earthly fathers often already know what their children want (be it for nightly dinner or for their special birthday gift), yet we often still desire our children to ask gratefully for these simple things so as to express their gratitude, dependence, and love. Similarly, our heavenly Father, who cares for us far beyond what any earthly parent can imagine, loves to hear the thankful prayers and supplications of His children.

Paul has delivered a twofold command: do not be anxious but make known your requests to God. That dual command comes with a promise: peace that transcends all understanding. The opposite of fretful worry is indeed peace. That is what we so often long for in this life. This peace '*of* God' specifically comes *from* God. Paul often invokes God's peace on the Christian church.[8] And this peace is truly amazing – it 'surpasses all understanding' and thus exceeds any human imagination.

Such peace serves as a protection in this life. It guards our hearts and minds – with 'hearts and minds' speaking of the two centers of thought and reflection in Greek antiquity. Both are emphasized, since the pronoun 'your' is repeated – 'your hearts and your minds'. While in our sinful nature, our minds are prone to worry and to wander into sinful places. As we engage our God in prayer, we are enveloped in a peace from Him that alleviates anxieties and allows us to contemplate truth, purity and love (4:8-9). Paul emphasizes that this protecting peace comes to us in the context of relationship with Christ – it is 'in Christ Jesus' that this peace flows to us.

We all should take time to reflect about what makes us anxious. And then, we should lift those anxieties up to the Lord in faith, thanking Him for our daily provision in life and allowing His peace to rest on us and guard us from ungodly thoughts.

---

8 E.g., Rom. 1:7; 15:13, 33; 1 Cor. 1:3; Phil. 1:2.

Finally, brothers, whatever is true, whatever is honorable, whatever is just, whatever is pure, whatever is lovely, whatever is commendable, if there is any excellence, if there is anything worthy of praise, think about these things. What you have learned and received and heard and seen in me – practice these things, and the God of peace will be with you (4:8-9).

At the conclusion of verse 7, Paul has already begun to address the thought-life of the believer. It is in the midst of thankful prayer that peace guards our hearts and minds. Now Paul directs our minds and our actions to that which is truly admirable. Two imperatives occur in these two verses: 'think about' and 'practice'. Paul calls here for Christian contemplation and praxis.

On the opening word (i.e., 'finally'), see comments on 3:1. This word serves here to emphasize Paul's next instructions. Perhaps it also indicates that these two verses culminate his advice on the issues he has discussed previously (at least since 4:1). If Christians are to stand firm together, put off dissension, rejoice in the Lord, and put off anxiety through lifting up concerns to the Lord – if they are to do all that – then they need to take their thought-lives captive to praiseworthy thoughts, and they must live out the kind of Christian walk Paul has modeled for them.

Christians are to 'think about' (*logizomai*, 'consider, ponder, reckon') those matters that are virtuous. The list of such virtues here is profound. 'True' (*alēthē*) denotes that which is without falsehood (e.g., Rom. 3:4; 2 Cor. 6:8; Titus 1:13). 'Honorable' (*semna*) signifies that which is worthy of respect (cf. 1 Tim. 3:8, 11; Titus 2:2). 'Just' (*dikaia*) occurs frequently in the New Testament, and concerns those matters that are righteous (e.g., Phil. 1:7; Titus 1:8). The 'pure' (*hagna*) is that which is innocent and undefiled by sin (e.g., 2 Cor. 7:11; 1 Tim. 5:22; Titus 2:5). 'Lovely' (*prosphilē*) speaks of those things that are beloved by God and should be pleasing to sanctified humankind (cf. Esther 15:5; Sir. 4:7; 20:13). 'Commendable' (*euphēma*) references that which should be praised and not condemned (cf. the cognate word in 2 Cor. 6:8). Those things of 'any excellence' employs the Greek term for 'virtue' (*aretē*) – namely, those matters of moral excellence which were publicly commendable and were to be imitated (e.g., 2 Pet. 1:5). Finally, anything 'worthy of praise' (*epainos*) affirms that which is properly lauded and thus is praiseworthy (e.g., Rom. 2:29; 13:3) – with *epainos* often referring to the praise of God Himself (e.g., Phil. 1:11).

These many descriptions should be taken as a whole, and must not be separated into distinct categories. In other words, it is not the case that some items worthy of Christian reflection fit in the category of 'true', while others are 'honorable', and others are 'worthy of praise'. Rather, all these words combine to remind us that all our thoughts should be focused on those matters that God approves because they are true, honorable, just, pure, lovely, commendable, virtuous, and praiseworthy.

That we are commanded to choose to contemplate such laudable virtues reminds us: (1) that God cares about our minds (not just our actions) and (2) that we have volitional control over what we contemplate. As Paul says in Romans 12:2, 'Do not be conformed to this world, but be transformed by the renewal of your mind…' (cf. Col. 3:10). Throughout every day, we are bombarded by thoughts that can imperil our Christian walk. The media constantly barrages us with smooth-sounding words and alluring images, enticing us to buy into the value systems and thought-forms of the world around us. Sophisticated philosophical ideologies, predicated not on the love of God but on some other metaphysical beliefs, can attract us with their intellectual austerity. Heretical religions abound that pretend to furnish true spiritual insight. These and many other dangers infected the world of the Philippians, as they do our own. Paul calls Christians to focus on other, more holy, matters.

We should not assume, however, that this is a call to completely close oneself off from the world. On the contrary, Paul must have studied the heretical notions of his opponents well enough so that he could incisively critique them in the midst of teaching that which is true. Critical engagement with the world around us is necessary if we are to reach out with the gospel to those enraptured with the world's attractions. Yet we must also always keep a close guard over our own thoughts.

As important as our thought-life is, this passage also reminds us that Christian living extends beyond our thoughts to our actions, and Paul calls these believers to good Christian practice. We have previously noted how Paul elsewhere summons Christians to imitate him as he imitates Christ (1 Cor. 11:1; see comments on Phil. 3:17). Indeed throughout this epistle, Paul's autobiographical moments are aimed not merely at apostolic introspection, but they purposefully depict the kind of Christian mindset that Paul wants others to follow (e.g., 1:12-26, 30; 2:17-18; 3:3-17; 4:12-13). Here in verse 4:9, Paul reminds the church in Philippi that he stands as a proper example to them of good Christian praxis. Notice that Paul's verbs express his dual role as teacher and as exemplar of Christian virtue. Paul commands the Philippians to practice what they '...have learned and received and heard and seen in me'. The first two verbs speak of Paul's teaching – the disciples in Philippi have 'learned' from his instruction and have 'received' the apostolic Christian tradition that he has passed down. The second two verbs refer to Paul's example – the disciples have 'heard' and 'seen' in Paul a pattern of Christian living.

We might well think that Paul, as an apostle called by Christ to help establish the foundations of His church in that crucial first generation of Christianity, had an especially strong calling as teacher and exemplar. This is probably true to some degree. Paul also will point, however, to other (non-apostolic) leaders in the church as educators (e.g., 1 Tim. 5:17; Titus 1:9) and as examples (cf. 1 Thess. 2:14). So Paul will place side by side with his example that of others, 'Brothers, join in imitating me, and keep your eyes on those who walk according to the example you have in us' (Phil. 3:17). Indeed, Christian leaders today must recognize that they too bear the responsibility of this dual role – they are not only called to educate others in Christian truth, they are also directed to live out their lives as examples of those saved by grace and alive in the Spirit. This helps explain why the sections in Scripture that address the selection of church leadership all emphasize the importance of examining Christian character before installing potential leaders into positions of recognition within the church (e.g., 1 Tim. 3:1-13; 5:9-10; Titus 1:5-9).

Of course, leaders find this calling to be a daunting task. It is hard enough to teach well and accurately the truths of the faith, but so much more difficult to truly serve as a good example of the Christian life. Still, it is important here to recognize that if our gospel is one of sinners saved by grace, part of being an exemplar requires us to readily admit that we are all fallen people who do not 'have it all together' except by the power of God working to transform us. We are all forgiven sinners who battle daily with the temptations of the world, the flesh, and the devil; and yet we can emerge victorious in that fight because the Father has brought us out of spiritual darkness, Christ has atoned for our iniquity and redeemed us from slavery to sin, and the Spirit of God has empowered us to live out the fruit of Christian life. When we permit people to witness this truth in our lives by humbly acknowledging our moment-by-moment reliance on God, then this kind of 'real life' example can serve as a powerful model in the church, simply because it makes the Triune God the hero (and not the church leader into a superman).

Paul's plea for the Philippians to engage in proper Christian contemplation and praxis comes with a pledge: 'the God of peace will be with you' (4:9). Paul promises them that they are not alone in this world, but God Himself accompanies them through all of life. In particular, the God who brings peace is with them to shower them with peace even in this life. Paul has already mentioned that the peace of God overflows to those who lift up their potentially anxious moments to Him (4:7). Indeed, Paul is pronouncing a kind of benediction over the church, as he often does when he mentions the 'God of peace' (Rom. 15:33; 16:20; 1 Thess. 5:23; cf. Heb. 13:20).

Summary

Throughout this passage, there are motifs that together create a beautiful mosaic portrait of the daily Christian walk: standing firm in Christ, rejoicing in the Lord, lifting our anxieties in prayer to the Lord, contemplating virtuous thoughts, and emulating worthy Christian examples. These come with some wonderful promises of God's direct presence with the believer: the Lord is near, the peace of God will rule Christian hearts and minds, and the God of peace will be with you. In this manifold mosaic, we discern some other key themes.

First, the Christian life is not a solitary undertaking. We are not left to our own devices or to fend for ourselves. Nor do we minister as a series of independent contractors who need not engage in corporate relationship with one another. Christians 'stand firm' as a church body (4:1). Ministry involves people laboring side by side in the Lord (4:3). Moreover, the Lord himself is ever with us in this life as the God of peace makes known His comforting presence (4:7, 9). And we await an even fuller experience of Christ's presence at His return (4:5). We stand 'together' as the people of God who know the nearness of our Lord.

Second (and building on the first), the Christian life requires Christians to work alongside one another in the Lord's presence. It is together that we stand firm (4:1). It is together that we must think the same thing (4:2). It is by rejoicing together *in the Lord* that we jointly begin to share the same aspirations that the Lord will be glorified in our corporate church (4:4). By practicing gentleness with one another (4:5), we prepare the way for humble agreement.

Third, the Christian life involves the whole person. What we *do* matters, and thus we seek to live according to the teaching and example found in Scripture and displayed in the lives of good Christian exemplars (4:9). Yet, what we *think* matters as well, and thus we ought to contemplate that which is praiseworthy (4:8). When we ponder and practice together that which is commendable, undoubtedly we are well on the road to church unity. And all this prepares us to stand firm corporately in the Lord's presence, prepared to encounter the mental, spiritual, and physical assaults that this fallen world throws at us.

People in our world are often overwhelmed by anxieties, frequently long for peace, commonly desire a sense of corporate belonging, and regularly wish that they might stand for something that counts. Here, Paul addresses those deepest desires – peace comes from God, corporate belonging is found in being in unity with His people, and together we stand for that which is true, honorable, just, pure, lovely, commendable, virtuous, and praiseworthy.

Questions for Personal Reflection:

1. Are there situations in your life (or in the life of your church) where you are called to 'stand firm in the Lord'? In those situations, how can we stand firm together more successfully?

2. Reflect on some conflicts you have witnessed among Christians. Was resolution reached? How were these conflicts handled well, and how were they conducted poorly? Were there ways that these conflicts damaged the church or the church's testimony to a watching world? Are you currently in conflict with anyone in the church? Do you know others who are in conflict? What can you do to help everyone 'agree in the Lord'?

3. In verse 4, Paul again commands Christians to rejoice in the Lord. Why do you think Paul emphasizes joy so often in this short letter to this church in Philippi? Are there connections between your situation and the situation of the church in Philippi that makes Paul's imperative to rejoice especially applicable to you?

4. What are some recurring anxieties in your life? How have you dealt with these in the past? Compare and contrast Paul's words (in 4:6-7) to your typical approaches to dealing with the anxieties of life.

5. Read Philippians 4:8 again. How can you put this directive more fully into practice in your life? What particular temptations do you face in your thought life?

Study Questions:

1. Read Philippians 4:1-9. Note how 4:1 begins with 'therefore'. How does this passage relate to the preceding verses? Do you see any inner logic that connects these nine verses together?

2. What does it mean to 'stand firm in the Lord' (4:1)? Are there situations in your life (or in the life of your church) where you have been called to 'stand firm in the Lord'? In those situations, how can we stand firm together more successfully?

3. Quickly skim the commentary on 4:2. Note how the Greek wording for 'agree in the Lord' in this verse is identical to Paul's instructions in 2:2. How does Philippians 2:1-4 apply to this circumstance between

Euodia and Syntyche? What terms does Paul use when he speaks of Euodia and Syntyche? How would you imagine that Paul felt about this situation in Philippi?

4. Reflect on some conflicts you have witnessed among Christians. Was a resolution reached? How were these conflicts handled well, and how were they conducted poorly? Were there ways that these conflicts damaged the church or the church's testimony to a watching world? Are you currently in conflict with anyone in the church? Do you know others who are in conflict? What can you do to help everyone 'agree in the Lord'?

5. In context, what do you think Paul was trying to express with his command to 'rejoice in the Lord always' (4:4)? In your estimation, what are some of the reasons that Paul emphasizes joy so often in this short letter to the Philippians? What might this joy look like in our lives?

6. How should we interpret 'let your reasonableness be known to everyone' (4:5)? How does this imperative apply to today?

7. What are some of the anxieties that we wrestle against in our current lives? How does Paul's admonition in 4:6-7 address such anxieties? Compare and contrast Paul's words with your own usual approaches to dealing with the anxieties of life.

8. Consider Paul's instructions in 4:8. Name some challenges to implementing this command in our lives today. What particular temptations do you face in your thought life? How can you put this directive more fully into practice in your life?

9. Paul again urges the Philippians to practice what he has taught and modeled (4:9). Where else have we met this theme of imitation in this short letter? Why do you think this theme forms such a recurring element in this particular epistle?

13

Of Gifts and Greetings
(Philippians 4:10-23)

[10]I rejoiced in the Lord greatly that now at length you have revived your concern for me. You were indeed concerned for me, but you had no opportunity. [11]Not that I am speaking of being in need, for I have learned in whatever situation I am to be content. [12]I know how to be brought low, and I know how to abound. In any and every circumstance, I have learned the secret of facing plenty and hunger, abundance and need. [13]I can do all things through him who strengthens me.

[14]Yet it was kind of you to share my trouble. [15]And you Philippians yourselves know that in the beginning of the gospel, when I left Macedonia, no church entered into partnership with me in giving and receiving, except you only. [16]Even in Thessalonica you sent me help for my needs once and again. [17]Not that I seek the gift, but I seek the fruit that increases to your credit. [18]I have received full payment, and more. I am well supplied, having received from Epaphroditus the gifts you sent, a fragrant offering, a sacrifice acceptable and pleasing to God. [19]And my God will supply every need of yours according to his riches in glory in Christ Jesus. [20]To our God and Father be glory forever and ever. Amen.

[21]Greet every saint in Christ Jesus. The brothers who are with me greet you. [22]All the saints greet you, especially those of Caesar's household.

[23]The grace of the Lord Jesus Christ be with your spirit.

As Paul concludes his letter, he shares his delight in the Philippian church's support for his needs and his appreciation of their partnership in the gospel. They have helped to supply him with what he requires while he is imprisoned and awaiting trial, and he wishes them to sense his gratitude. Yet Paul, the consummate teacher, still finds a few more moments to instruct his audience and to model the Christian life. Even while expressing his gratefulness, Paul will remind those in Philippi that God strengthens the believer to endure any circumstance, and that the Lord supplies our needs in this life.

I rejoiced in the Lord greatly that now at length you have revived your concern for me. You were indeed concerned for me, but you had no opportunity (4:10).

Paul cannot help but rejoice one more time in this letter – a letter that so often mentions 'joy' (1:4, 18, 25; 2:2, 17, 18, 28, 29; 3:1; 4:1, 4, 10). He stresses the depth of his delight with the emphatic Greek word *megalōs* ('greatly'). It stirred Paul to immense joy when he experienced how the Philippians continued to care for him. As before, this joy is found 'in the Lord' (cf. 3:1; 4:4), and thus the joy Paul expresses ultimately leads to him exulting in the Lord on behalf of the Philippians. Yet his joy also has an earthly basis, stemming from the concern that the Philippians have shown for his welfare.

We might be tempted to read this verse as a backdoor rebuke to the church members who only 'at length' (the NIV even has 'at last'; cf. Rom. 1:10) have finally come around to 'reviving' their concern for Paul. Might Paul somehow be saying, 'Where were you before?' Yet that is not the best way to understand his comments. The whole context speaks of heartfelt commendation for the church, and it relates how the Philippians' generosity made Paul rejoice. Moreover, Paul quickly affirms that the Philippians have all along been concerned to assist him, but earlier they 'had no opportunity' (4:10). They had a long track record of providing financial assistance to Paul's ministry (4:15-16), although there has not been a clear vehicle for them to do so of late. Only now, by observing Paul's need while imprisoned, have they found a tangible way to express their desire to assist the apostle.

The Greek verb for 'revive' (*anathallō*) draws on an agricultural metaphor to indicate that their concern has 'bloomed again'. Just as their generosity had flourished before, now in this season, it has again blossomed. The word for 'concern' is actually a verb that focuses on cognitive activity (*phroneō*)[1] – they had 'thought' about Paul, and then conveyed that thought into lived-out action. There was a time when they 'had no opportunity': the Greek (*akaireomai*) conveys that the season was previously not proper for their concern to bloom. Now that the opportunity has arisen, the Philippians have again found a way to tangibly express their thoughts for their dear apostle.

Not that I am speaking of being in need, for I have learned in whatever situation I am to be content. I know how to be brought low, and I know how to abound. In any and every circumstance, I have learned the secret of facing plenty and hunger, abundance and need (4:11-12).

In the midst of thanking them for their gift, Paul also desires to model contentment in the Lord's provision throughout life. Verse 11 contrasts with verse 14: 'Not that I am speaking of being in need… yet it was kind of you to share my trouble.' The intervening material in verses 11-13 explains what Paul means when he says that he is 'not speaking of being in need'. Paul approaches difficult circumstances by relying on God, and he intends these words to serve as an example for the church in Philippi.

Paul reminds us that he has seen both extremes – he has been 'brought low' and he has 'abounded'. He does not specify the precise biographical events he has in mind, though we can well imagine that his ill-treatment by rulers, his shipwrecks, and his many days and weeks in prison might be numbered among those situations in which he would describe himself as having been 'brought low' (see such a list in 2 Corinthians 11:23–12:10). 'Brought low' (*tapeinoō*) speaks of having been made to become humble, even having been humiliated, in such circumstances. Whereas to 'abound' (*perisseuō*) refers to having more than was necessary. Paul provides other juxta-

---

1 see Phil. 1:7; 2:2, 5; 3:15, 19; 4:2.

posed pairs to show the extremes he has experienced: plenty/hunger and abundance/need.

Yet throughout these extremes, Paul has learned a secret to contentment, though he will keep us waiting until verse 13 before he reveals his cryptic solution. When Paul says he has 'learned the secret' he employs a Greek verb (*mueō*) that was often found in Graeco-Roman mystery religions for the act of initiating someone into the religion – they learned particular secrets in order to become members. Paul, however, is not talking about a mysterious membership in a furtive pagan religion but a secret to life itself. And his secret cannot be found in clandestine pagan societies but in the very faith of Christian believers everywhere.

Even in the pagan first-century world that surrounded the apostle, non-Christians discussed the idea of inner peace in the midst of life's variable circumstances. In fact, Paul's word here for 'to be content' (*autarkēs*; cf. cognate in 2 Cor. 9:8; 1 Tim. 6:6) was a term that Stoic philosophers readily endorsed. Their understanding of 'contentment' demanded a kind of 'self-sufficiency' that allowed the rational person to live the life of the mind despite what was occurring to his or her physical body. We might be tempted to think then that Paul is merely trying to imitate pagan virtues. However, what makes Paul's view particularly distinct is the actual secret to his contentment, which is found in the next verse.

I can do all things through him who strengthens me (4:13).
Most pagan moral philosophers suggested that human contentment lies within the human soul and mind, and that inner peace can be gained by pondering one's own rational inner being. By contrast, Paul frames his experience of contentment in terms of his dependency on God. The Lord strengthens Paul through every circumstance (cf. 2 Tim. 4:17). This exemplary text certainly indicates that all those who are Christians ought to rely on the Lord's power to enable them to persevere joyfully in the midst of any (and all) circumstances.

Paul continues here his first-person references to his own approach to life that began in verses 11-12, when he first introduced, by personal example, his secret to contentment in the Christian life. This verse ought not to be extracted from its context. The 'all things' that Paul has been strengthened to endure are illustrated for us in verse 12. Both in the ups and the downs of life, God has been Paul's resource. Such a reliance on God assumes that the Christian is walking in step with the Lord, and thus following His divine will. No one who is acting outside of the will of God should presume that this verse applies to him or her.

The Greek actually conveys something like, 'I have power for all circumstances through the One who strengthens me.' Notice that the strength that God provides overflows to empower Paul to encounter all such situations. We would naturally assume that Paul especially required God's potency in order to deal with the times when he was in need (especially in light of 4:11). However, we may well contend that those who have 'plenty' and who possess an 'abundance' (4:12) also require God's strength in order not to be sucked into self-sufficiency. It is good for us to remember throughout all of our lives (whether we are in dire need or in great wealth) that God should be the focus of our empowerment to endure.

Yet it was kind of you to share my trouble. And you Philippians yourselves know that in the beginning of the gospel, when I left Macedonia, no church entered into partnership with me in giving and receiving, except you only. Even in Thessalonica you sent me help for my needs once and again (4:14-16).

Though Paul briefly digressed to educate the church on true Christian contentment (4:11-13), he quickly returns to thanking the Philippians for their partnership in his ministry. They have long shown themselves to be aligned with the apostle in his work.

As noted earlier, the opening word of verse 14 ('yet' or 'but'; Greek *plēn*), contrasts with the beginning of verse 11: 'Not that I am speaking of being in need… *yet* it was kind of you to share my trouble.' In verses 11-13, Paul models his God-directed contentment in the midst of his various needs, but by doing so, he does not wish to invalidate the Philippians' kind gift. Thus he returns in verse 14 to express his appreciation.

In fact, he moves beyond simply acknowledging their kindness, for the Greek conveys: 'You did well by fellowshipping with me in my suffering.' They 'did well'. They have performed a good work, properly lauded by others and (more importantly) recognized by God as an abundantly fruitful act (see 4:17). What the Philippians actually did was to live out their fellowship with the apostle. Where the ESV renders 'to share my trouble', the Greek conveys 'fellowshipping with me in my tribulation'. The Greek word for 'share' (*sunkoinōneō*) can convey 'take part in' (cf. Eph. 5:11; Rev. 18:4), but it is also cognate with the noun *sunkoinōnos* ('participant, partner, partaker'), which is found in Philippians 1:7: '…for you are all *partakers* with me of grace, both in my imprisonment and in the defense and confirmation of the gospel' (also cf. Rom. 11:17; 1 Cor. 9:23; Rev. 1:9). These are people who participate in fellowship (*koinōnia*) with Paul in his ministry and assist him in his various tribulations. Such assistance/fellowship can take the form of material support (cf. Rom. 12:13; Heb. 10:33) as well as prayer and unity of purpose. It is possible they might have endangered themselves by aligning themselves with Paul (being connected with his legal situation and his persecutions). Still, Paul does not emphasize their personal risk, but rather, he stresses how he has been encouraged because this church continues to walk alongside him in fellowship during his imprisonment.

Paul gratefully reminds the Philippians that their fellowship with him in his ministry goes back to his very first contact with them. He refers to that moment as 'the beginning of the gospel' in their midst. That was the time when Paul had to leave Macedonia in order to minister to those in Greece (especially in Thessalonica). These events align well with the description in Acts 16:11–17:9. After Paul's brief ministry in Philippi (16:11-34), the city officials coerced him to leave (16:35-40), and he then continued south through Amphipolis and Apollonia until he reached Thessalonica (17:1). Paul remained at least three Sabbaths in Thessalonica, until the Jewish leaders incited a mob to attack his colleagues and bring them to court (17:1-10). This record in Acts is condensed, and we do not know the exact timing of all these events. Here in Philippians 4, it becomes evident that the nascent church in Philippi had so appreciated Paul's mission that, during that early period, its members helped him by supporting his work at least twice ('once and again' being literally 'once and twice'; cf. 1 Thess. 2:18).

Their support came in the form of 'partnership', with the Greek word (*koinōneō* in 4:15) conveying (just like *sunkoinōneō* in 4:14) their firm alignment with Paul's mission. They joined him in the enterprise by engaging in Christian fellowship (cf. *koinōnia* in Phil. 1:5) with his activities.

They partnered with Paul in the matter of giving and receiving – implying their direct financial involvement in his work. Indeed, they sent material support for his needs at least twice during his relatively short stay in Thessalonica. In this work, they stood out among the churches at that time.

Paul reminds them of all this, both to express his appreciation for how they have been supportive of his ministry over many years, and also to encourage them in how such beneficence is praiseworthy before God (as we shall see in the next verse).

Not that I seek the gift, but I seek the fruit that increases to your credit. I have received full payment, and more. I am well supplied, having received from Epaphroditus the gifts you sent, a fragrant offering, a sacrifice acceptable and pleasing to God (4:17-18).

Paul desires to make clear that his purpose in thanking the Philippian church is not self-serving. He does not express his appreciation for their recent support (or for their past participation) as a means of financial gain. Rather, he wants them to abound in fruitfulness before God. Yet he also wants them to know that he is indeed appreciative of their generosity.

Paul contrasts two different goals, both with the word 'seek' (*epizēteō*). He did not seek after their 'gift' for his own sake (i.e., for his own material support), but he seeks for the Philippians to receive 'fruit that increases to your credit'. Elsewhere, Paul employs 'fruit' as a metaphor for the results of righteous Christian living (e.g., Rom. 6:22; Eph. 5:9). Such 'fruit' results from walking in step with the Spirit (Gal. 5:16-24). Paul can also speak of monetary gifts as 'fruit' (Rom. 15:28). The representation of righteousness bringing forth 'fruit' is found in the Old Testament,[2] and Paul's imagery parallels that used by Jesus Himself.[3]

---

2 E.g., Prov. 11:30; 12:14; 31:31; Amos 6:12; Jer. 17:10.
3 E.g., Matt. 7:16-20; 12:33; 21:43; John 15:1-17.

Here, that fruit abounds in such a way that its increase (*pleonazonta*) is recorded and accounted to the Philippians by God. Paul does not define exactly what this 'credit' or 'account' (*logon*) means, or when the Philippians will receive their reward from it – whether in this life or in the coming age. Paul does anticipate Jesus' return in an age to come (2:16; cf. 2 Thess. 1:7-10) as a time in which Christians obtain their rewards (1 Cor. 3:10-15; 2 Cor. 5:10). In this, he follows Jesus' teaching that His disciples should use their wealth in this life to 'lay up treasures in heaven'.[4] Nonetheless, Paul can also speak of Christians in the present 'being enriched in every way for their generosity' (2 Cor. 9:11), so we need not limit to the hereafter the benefit of giving to others who are in need. Basically, Paul assumes that such gifts are pleasing to God, who will, in His own timing, reward the giver.

We learn that the items the Philippians sent came via Epaphroditus, who was previously praised by Paul for his service in 2:25-30, where he was called a 'messenger and minister to my need' (2:25). When Paul speaks of these gifts, he does so in exuberant terms. He has fully received all things (*apechō panta*). Beyond that, he has an abundance (*perisseuō*) from them. Indeed, he has been 'well supplied' or better, 'has been made full' (*peplērōmai*) by what he has received from Epaphroditus. It would be difficult to find stronger terms to express Paul's appreciation any more deeply.

Moreover, Paul views these gifts not merely as contributing to his welfare, but as offerings presented to God Himself. Drawing on Old Testament language, he describes the Philippians' gifts as a 'fragrant offering' made to God – this phrase occurs more than 40 times in the Old Testament in reference to sacrificial offerings.[5] Similarly, the idea that a sacrifice may be deemed 'acceptable' appears repeatedly in the Old Testament (e.g., Lev. 1:3-4; 22:20-21; Isa. 56:7).

Paul motivates Christians by the idea that our actions can be pleasing to God.[6] He elsewhere calls Christians to dedicate themselves as living sacrifices (Rom. 12:1; cf. Heb. 13:16), and

---

4 Matt. 6:19-21; Luke 12:33-34; cf. 1 Tim. 6:18-19.
5 E.g., Gen. 8:21; Exod. 29:18, 41; Lev. 1:9, 13, 17; etc.; cf. Ezek. 20:41; Eph. 5:2; 2 Cor. 5:14-15.
6 Rom. 14:18; 2 Cor. 5:9; Eph. 5:10; Col. 3:20.

earlier in this epistle, he spoke of pouring himself out as such a sacrifice (Phil. 2:17). In short, the Philippians' gifts to Paul have become as sacrificial offerings made to God Himself, and Paul assures them that God is pleased with their contribution to his ministry.

All Christians can learn from this passage the importance of partnering with those whose occupation involves spreading the gospel. Such fellowship (including the financial support that is involved) pleases God when we engage in it with right motives. Also, those who are involved in vocational Christian service and must raise support in order to stay in the field should not be bashful about asking other believers to participate in their ministry – especially since it is a great privilege for others to offer such pleasing and fragrant sacrifices to God.

And my God will supply every need of yours according to his riches in glory in Christ Jesus (4:19).
This verse is clearly connected to the preceding passage by the word 'and' (*de*). Paul writes these words in light of the Philippians' 'fragrant offering' and 'acceptable sacrifice'. In relation to the previous verses, however, it is unclear whether the promise in 4:19 is absolute (God always supplies the needs of His children) or is conditioned on their action (God will respond to their gifts to Paul by meeting the needs of the church in Philippi). Theologically, it more likely that Paul understands God to always be the one who meets the needs of His people, and he reminds the Philippians of this in the midst of the costliness of their sacrificial act performed on Paul's behalf.

In an indication of his relational reliance on the one true God, Paul also previously designated God the Father as 'my God' in 1:3 (see comments on that verse). The Greek verb for 'supply' (*plēroō*) actually indicates to 'fill up' or to 'fulfill,' and thus Paul signals that God will fully meet the Philippians' needs. 'Needs' (*chreia*) frequently refers to the financial necessities of life, especially in contexts of Christian charity toward others.[7] Note, however, that this verse does not speak

---

7 Rom. 12:13; Eph. 4:28; 1 Thess. 4:12; cf. Acts 2:45; 4:35; 28:10.

to receiving everything that the Philippians might desire in life; rather, it asserts that God will grant them their daily necessities.

Paul parallels this promise to the church alongside his own experience from the gift he received from its members. The church sent assistance for Paul's 'needs' (*chreia* in 4:16), and he was 'filled to overflowing' (*plēroō* in 4:18). Similarly, God Himself oversees the church in Philippi by 'filling to overflowing' (*plēroō* in 4:19) their every 'need' (*chreia* in 4:19).

Paul's confidence in God's provision comes in part because God has 'wealth' (*ploutos*). Indeed, as creator of the world, God possesses an unending abundance from which He distributes to all. These riches are located in the 'glory' (*doxa*) that God possesses. Glory is a concept found throughout this epistle.[8] Yet the Father's glory is also found 'in Christ Jesus', who has been glorified (3:21) and who brings glory to the Father (2:11). Elsewhere, Paul often connects glory to Jesus the Messiah.[9]

Jesus taught His followers to rely on God to sustain them through their daily needs, especially in the context of generously giving toward others (e.g., Matt. 6:8, 11, 19-34). Paul ties into that early Christian theme as he assures the churches, even in the midst of their sacrificial giving, that God will continue to look after them throughout their lives.

This verse properly reminds us of the benevolent provision we have from God. We can easily be tempted to credit our daily sustenance solely to the work of our own hands, but we must always remember that it is ultimately God who supplies our daily bread. One proper response to this is thankfulness, along with faith and hope in God's provision. For those who do not have enough, they rightly make their appeal to God; yet as a church, we should also follow the lead of the Philippians and look to where God might have us step in and become His means of providing for others.

You may have seen some ministry leaders construe this verse to read something like: 'Give to my ministry, and God will then meet your needs.' Or even, 'God is not meeting your desires because you are not giving to my ministry.'

---

8 Phil. 1:11; 2:11; 3:19, 21; 4:20 – see especially comments on 2:11.
9 E.g., 2 Cor. 4:4, 6; 8:23; 2 Thess. 2:14; Titus 2:13.

Both of these sentiments (especially the latter) are highly presumptuous – as if their ministry today possesses the same credibility as that of the apostle Paul's, and as if they are certain that their work is so holy and pure that it should be the locus of Christian giving today. We should be wary of such 'leaders'. Those of us involved in Christian ministry should not overly correlate giving to our ministries with reciprocation from God. Nonetheless, when we are asking for people to provide financial support to the work of the church, we do so with confidence that, even in times of sacrificial giving, God does indeed supply the necessities of life to His people in His church.

The focus of this verse should always be on God, for he is the one who provides fully for our needs, and it is in that confidence that we are freed up to give generously to others.

To our God and Father be glory forever and ever. Amen (4:20). As in 4:19, this passage is also tied to its preceding verse by the Greek word *de* ('and'). Having just mentioned God's glory in verse 19, Paul here offers up this doxology to God. Such doxologies (expressions of praise and glory to God) are found commonly in Paul's writings and elsewhere in the New Testament.[10] They often proclaim that glory belongs to God 'forever and ever' (e.g., Gal. 1:5; 2 Tim. 4:18). See Additional Note.

Here God is further identified as 'Father' – a title Paul used first in 1:2 (see comments there). Christians stand in relationship to God as children graciously adopted into His family (Rom. 8:15; Gal. 4:5; Eph. 1:5), and thus we look on Him both as our sovereign God and as our Abba (i.e., our dear Father). The closing word 'Amen' (literally 'it is true' or 'let it be so') calls forth a collective assent to this doxology from Paul and his readers.

This verse invokes the mystery of worship. God already possesses untold glory (4:19), yet Paul calls for glory to be ascribed to Him (4:20). We can debate the function of the implied 'to be' verb in the Greek – whether it is indicative (To God *is* glory) or imperative (To God *be* glory). Nevertheless,

---

10 E.g., Rom. 11:36; Eph. 3:21; 1 Tim. 1:17; cf. Heb. 13:21; 2 Pet. 3:18; Jude 24-25; Rev. 5:13; 7:12; 19:1.

the reality is that Paul's heartfelt cry is that God be recognized as the Glorious One for all eternity. This forms a fitting response in light of God's provision for His people mentioned in verse 19. Moreover, it also represents the proper Christian exaltation of the almighty God of the Universe, and it conveys the heartfelt praise within every Christian act of worship.

Greet every saint in Christ Jesus. The brothers who are with me greet you. All the saints greet you, especially those of Caesar's household (4:21-22).

Following the convention of ancient letters, Paul often concludes with a series of personal greetings.[11] These indicate his personal affection for the congregation, and serve to connect members of the body of Christ with one another.

As in the opening of the letter, Paul refers to the whole church as full of sanctified members ('saints'; see notes on 1:1). These greetings are also performed within the mutual fellowship that comes from being 'in Christ' (see notes on 1:1) – these saints are together incorporated in relationship with Christ as members of His body.

While earlier Paul had expressed some sense of being alone in dramatic hyperbole (see comments on 2:20-21), here he acknowledges that there are indeed fellow Christians with him, and they join Paul in greeting the Philippians. Indeed, Paul's greetings often serve the purpose of linking the Christian churches in disparate locales by passing back and forth salutations and prayers.

In this letter, Paul especially singles out those 'of Caesar's household'. This description may well allude to the praetorian imperial guard in Philippians 1:13, but it certainly shows that Paul's message has been circulating among those who serve in imperial circles. We could wish to know more about who exactly is referenced here, and various stories and legends circulated in later Christianity about Christians in the imperial family, but we simply do not have a reliable list of possible candidates. Still, Paul wishes to encourage the Philippians that even some of those who touch the highest echelons of society have become followers of the Christian gospel.

---

11 Rom. 16:3-16, 21-23; 1 Cor. 16:19-20; 2 Cor. 13:12; Col. 4:10-15; 1 Thess. 5:26; 2 Tim. 4:19, 21; Titus 3:15; Philem. 23.

The grace of the Lord Jesus Christ be with your spirit. (4:23) Having proclaimed a doxology to God, and having passed on greetings to the Philippians, Paul ends this letter much as he began – by invoking grace as a benediction on his recipients (cf. 1:2). Paul always closes his epistles in a similar fashion.[12]

Three other of these closing benedictions invoke Christ's grace to be 'with your spirit' (Gal. 6:18; 2 Tim. 4:22; Philem. 25). Though there are only a limited number of times in which 'your spirit' is mentioned in the New Testament (also cf. 1 Cor. 16:18; Eph. 4:23; 1 Thess. 5:23), there often appear references to 'my spirit' (e.g., Luke 23:46; Rom. 1:9; 1 Cor. 5:4) or to 'his spirit' (e.g., 2 Cor. 7:13). All these expressions draw upon an Old Testament precedent for identifying a person's inner soul with his or her 'spirit' (e.g., Ps. 30:6; Mal. 2:15-16). Here we should not assume that Paul remains unconcerned about the physicality of the Philippians, but he does focus his benediction on their innermost being.

'Grace' again speaks to our need for unmerited favor from the exalted Lord. This grace comes as before (1:2) from Jesus who is both Messiah ('Christ') and Lord. The reader cannot help but be informed at this final stage in the epistle that it is this Jesus who, though He was in the form of God, humbled Himself to the likeness of men and willingly endured His atoning crucifixion death. Yet now Jesus has been raised from the dead and exalted again as Lord. This is the Messiah whom Paul proclaims. It is the grace from this Messiah that he invokes on all his readers. May you, O reader, know that same grace.

Summary

Paul accomplishes several objectives as he concludes the letter: he sets out to thank the Philippians for their generosity, to model a Christian reliance on God, to pass on closing greetings, and to pronounce a doxology to God and a final blessing on the Philippians.

Paul's thanksgiving to the Philippians comes with a sense of his deep appreciation for their partnership in the gospel over the years (esp. v. 14-16, 18), even if there were times

---

12 Rom. 16:20; 1 Cor. 16:23; 2 Cor. 13:14; Gal. 6:18; Eph. 6:24; Col. 4:18; 1 Thess. 5:28; 2 Thess. 3:18; 1 Tim. 6:21; 2 Tim. 4:22; Titus 3:15; Philem. 25.

when they did not have the opportunity to give (v. 10). Their gift, though sent to Paul, was really an offering made to God (v. 17-18). In the midst of such a sacrificial work, the Philippians can take confidence that God is the one who supplies them to overflowing with the necessities of life (v. 19).

As Paul has frequently done in this letter, he shares autobiographical reflections in order to serve as an apostolic example for the Philippians to imitate. Paul has learned how to be content in the Lord at all times because he knows that God is his portion and his strength. So too are all Christians to rejoice in their daily circumstances, in prayerful reliance on God.

Paul seeks to connect the Christian churches of his day by letting them know of their mutual affection for one another. Thus he adds the greetings of other believers to his own when he pens his letters. In the process of doing so here, he skillfully slips in one last reference to the progress of the gospel during his own imprisonment (cf. 1:12-14) – the Good News has even spread to Caesar's household.

Finally, following his typical procedure, Paul concludes this epistle with a dynamic vision of Christian worship. He invites the Philippians to join him in pronouncing that all eternal glory belongs to God. And he beckons Jesus, whom he deems both Lord and Messiah, to pour out his grace on His church. Thus, at the end, the church of Jesus Christ worships the Lord through a life of praise to God and reliance on His grace.

Questions for Personal Reflection:

1. Why do you think Paul was able to say, 'I have learned in whatever situation I am to be content'? How true is this of you (be fully honest)? How can this become more true for you?

2. In what ways is your church involved in supporting the needs of others (including the needs of missionaries)? In what ways are you personally involved?

3. Have you ever been the recipient of such support? How did you respond to the contributors? How did you respond to God?

4. Two phrases that are often quoted from this passage are: 'I can do all things through him who strengthens me' (4:13) and 'My God will supply every need of yours according to his riches in glory in Christ Jesus' (4:19). Relate these verses to their immediate contexts. Have you seen these passages misused in the past? What might be some appropriate applications of these passages today?

5. Why is it fitting for Paul to conclude his letter with these two sentiments: 'To our God and Father be glory forever and ever' (4:20) and 'The grace of the Lord Jesus Christ be with your spirit' (4:23)? How can we appropriate those sentiments in our own lives and in the ways we interact with others?

Study Questions:

1. Read through Philippians 4:10-23 and imagine how these verses would have been received by Paul's friends and spiritual children back in Philippi. How does this function as a fitting conclusion to this letter?

2. In Philippians 4:11-13 Paul speaks of his contentment in every situation. Why do you think he talks about this in the midst of thanking the Philippian church for their gift? What was Paul's 'secret' to contentment? How can we similarly learn to be content in every situation?

3. Philippians 4:13 ('I can do all things through him who strengthens me') is one of the more famous verses from this epistle. What does this verse mean in its context? Have you heard this misused or misquoted before (and if so, how)?

4. How does Paul speak of the Philippians' gifts to his ministry (4:14-19)? How might the Philippian church have been encouraged by these words? What do we learn from these verses about financial giving in the church?

5. Another famous verse from this letter is found in 4:19. What does this mean in its context? What are some reasonable applications of this verse to our lives? Have you heard this verse misapplied before (and if so, how)?
6. In the concluding four verses of the letter (4:20-23) we can discern a good deal about what Paul valued. What do you observe here?
7. As we conclude our study of this epistle, share with the group what you have learned about (select any of the following): God the Father, Jesus Christ the Son, the Holy Spirit, humanity, salvation, our future hope, and Christian living.
8. What have been some of the most memorable moments in this group Bible study for you?
9. Where have you been most encouraged by reading through Philippians? Most challenged?

Additional Notes:
4:20 The form of such doxologies is well known in Second Temple Jewish literature (compare 1 Esdras 5:58; 4 Maccabees 18:24; Baruch 5:1). This custom clearly draws on the long history of Old Testament praise offered to God (see esp. Ps. 104:31), and often issues into the form of 'blessing' made to the divine Name (e.g., Dan. 3:52-53). Paul thus is drawing deep on his Jewish heritage when he makes such pronouncements.

Subject Index

A
Abraham 136, 159, 198, 199-200
Adam 136
Antony 87
anxiety 249-53, 258
Aphrodite 177
approval 51
audience of epistle 7, 12-18
authoritarian suppression 107-8

B
Baal 202
baptism 194
'bellies' 230
Benjamin, tribe of 199
blamelessness 51-2, 54, 158-9
bodily transformation 233-5
Book of Life 23
brotherhood 61, 63, 227, 241
Brutus 87

C
Caesar, Emperor .. 10, 16, 139, 272, 274
Cassius 87
Chalcedonian Creed 129, 141
Christian fellowship 21-3, 25, 98-102,
.... 265-7
Christian life
    challenges to 149-50, 157-8
    and citizenship 85, 88, 93-4, 96n,
    .... 150, 232, 240-1
    and contemplation 254-7
    and contentment 264-5, 274
    and encouragement 98-100, 115-16n
    and 'fruitful labor' 75, 81
    and glory of Christ 81
    and 'good works' 47, 153, 156
    and humility 108-11, 117-20,
    .... 123-5, 132, 141
    instruction on 24-7
    and maturity 223, 226-7, 231
    military metaphors for 178
    and obedience 150-60, 163

race metaphors 221-2, 224-8, 235
standing firm 240-1, 254, 257-8
suffering for Christ 91-3, 212, 215
Christian love 101-2, 105
Christian unity 25, 88-91, 97-8, 100,
.... 103-8, 111-12, 123-5, 240-1,
.... 243, 247-8
Cicero 134
circumcision 14, 17-18, 190-4,
.... 194-9, 219n
citizenship 85-8, 93-4, 96n, 150,
.... 232, 240-1
Clement 242
Corinth 64, 98, 105, 109, 154, 200
crucifixion 133-4
cynicism 70

D
Dating of epistle   7, 10-11
David 34, 137
deacons 36-8
death 73-7, 80-1, 180
destructive forces 229-30
dogs 192-3, 219n

E
Earthquake 15
ecclesiology of epistle 22-4
Egnatian Way 12, 13
elders 36-8
Epaphroditus
    background of 177-8
    illness of 11, 60, 177, 179-82
    ministerial service of 29
    as model of Christian ministry 172,
    .... 177-9, 181-3
    relationship with Paul 177-8, 244
    sent to aid Paul 9-11, 16, 60-1, 268
    sent to Philippi by Paul ... 170, 177-81
Epicureanism 14, 70, 74
eternal life 74
Euodia 25, 98, 104, 242-3, 247
excellence 50-1

277

Subject Index

Factionism 63-5, 98, 104-5, 106-7,
.... 159, 244
fallen world 159-60, 250
false teaching 64
family life 174-5
'flesh' 74, 197-9
'fruit of righteousness' 47, 50, 52, 54,
.... 57n, 103, 267
'fruitful labor' 74-5, 81, 83n, 182

'Gain' 204-5, 211
Gamaliel 201
Garden of Eden 139
Garden of Gethsemane 133
Gentiles 14, 17-18, 190-4, 199, 219n
gentleness 247-8
God
    adoption of Israel 39
    blessing of 38
    call of 225
    as creator 39, 127, 138-9
    deliverance through ... 70-3, 76, 78, 80
    discernment of 50-2
    doxology to 272-3, 276n
    and encouragement 99-100, 102
    enemies of 230
    expectation of 72-3
    family of 23, 39, 271
    as Father 39, 127, 139-40, 271
    fear of 154-5
    form of 126, 130, 146-7n
    gifts to 26, 267-71, 274
    glory of 52, 140-1, 270-2
    grace of 18, 38-9, 48, 153
    guidance of 250
    honoring 73
    image of 126
    kingdom of 118
    knowledge of 50-2
    Law of 96n
    as Lord 139
    love of 50-3, 101-2, 105
    name of 136-7
    obedience to .. 132-3, 135, 150-60, 163
    peace of 18, 38-9, 253, 257-8
    pleasure of 156-7
    power of 154-5
    provision of 250-2, 269-70
    redemption of 194
    rejoicing in 189-90, 214
    reliance on 263-5, 269-70, 273
    requests to 252-3
    reverential awe of 154-5, 165-6
    righteousness from 208-11, 220n
    sacrifices to 163-4, 268-70
    salvation through .. 22, 46-7, 53, 71, 162
    service of 130
    sovereignty of 46-7, 250
    Spirit of 21, 71, 156, 194-6
    standing in 89
    strength from 161, 265
    supplies needs 269-71, 274
    thanksgiving to 44-9, 252
    trust in 250-2
    will of 51, 223
    word of 160
    work of 22, 46-7, 53, 153, 156-7, 162
    wrath of 109
'good works' 47, 153, 156
gospel
    citizenship of 85-8
    defence of 48-9, 53
    faith of 79, 90
    obeying 152, 154
    opposition to 89, 91, 192-3
    and paganism 88
    spread of 45-6, 53-4, 59-65, 93, 274
    walking in 227
grumbling 157-8

Hawthorne, Gerald F. 9
historical context of epistle 12-18
Holy Spirit 21, 23, 71, 78, 80, 89-90,
.... 100, 101-2, 195-6
humility 108-11, 117-20, 123-5,
.... 132, 141
hymns 119, 121-3, 144n

Idolatry 138
Ignatius of Antioch 36
'intermediate state' 77, 80
Israel 33, 39, 136, 160

James 109, 158
Jerusalem 199-200
Jesus Christ
    and anxiety 252
    boasting in 79, 161-2, 196-7
    call of 226
    crucifixion of 20, 133-4, 220n, 230
    and Davidic line 19
    Day of 21, 23-4, 47-8, 51-2, 161-2
    death of 20, 77, 117-18, 120,
.... 132-4
    deity of 19-21, 119-20, 127,
.... 129-30, 132, 135
    'emptying' of 128-32, 135
    encouragement in 99-102, 115-16n
    enemies of 91, 138-40, 226, 229-31
    equality with God 125-7, 137, 141
    exaltation of 118-20, 135-41

Subject Index

faith in 22, 46, 52, 92, 202-3,
....208-11
fellowship in 102
gaining 204-6
glory of................................. 72-3, 270
grace of 273
honoring.................................... 72-3
humanity of 19-21, 125-6, 128-32,
....141
humility of 20, 97, 117-20, 123-5,
..............................132-5, 141, 145-7n
image of 21
imitating............................ 228, 255-6
being 'in'............................205-6, 211
knowing 205, 211-12, 222
and 'light' 160
as Lord 39-40, 127, 136-40, 171
love of 76
as Messiah 19, 34, 273
name of 136-8, 142
nearness of 248-9
obedience of 132-3, 135
and Pharisees............................200-1
pre-existence of 20, 125-7
proclaiming of 63-5, 70
rejoicing in............. 189-90, 214, 245-7,
....258,262
resurrection of 20, 23-4, 77, 120,
..........................190-1, 212-13, 234
return of............ 23, 47-8, 53, 136, 138,
.... 161-2, 242, 248-9, 268
salvation through..............21, 76, 140,
.... 152-4, 191, 196, 233
as servant....................... 126-7, 128-32
slaves of 33-4
Spirit of 21, 71
suffering of........................72, 93, 212
union with........ 35-6, 100, 212-13, 215
worship of 137-9
Job..159
John the Baptist 200
Josephus 200
joy..............26, 45, 66, 70-1, 78-80, 103-4,
.... 165, 181, 189-90, 245-6, 262
Judaism.................... 14-15, 19, 34, 51, 134
Judaizers....................17-18, 190-4, 197-8,
.... 206, 211, 219-20n

K ierkegaard, Søren..........................250

'Loss' 204-5, 211
Luther, Martin 107
Lydia 14-15, 35, 46

M ajority rule 105-6

meaning of life........................ 69-70, 73-4
Moses 127, 128, 139, 155, 207

N ew Covenant 194
Nicene Creed 141

O'Brien, Peter T......................9
Octavian, Emperor......................12, 35, 87
outline of epistle................................ 28-9
overseers... 36-8

P aganism 13-14, 45, 88, 163-4, 264
Parachurch bodies................................107
Paul
    as ambassador of Christ.................72
    appeals his case to Caesar..............10
    authenticity of............................ 6, 8-9
    authorship of epistle...... 6, 7-10, 31-2,
    .... 44, 121-2, 170-1
    autobiographical references 9-10,
    .... 26-7, 198-202, 227, 256
    blamelessness of........................ 202-3
    boasting of 161-2, 196-7
    calling of 256
    casts out demonic spirit 15
    charges against 61
    circumcision of 9, 198-9
    conditionals of ... 98-9, 101-2, 114-15n
    confidence of.........................78, 80, 177, 227
    consistency of 6, 38
    conversion of 188, 202
    converts his jailer 15, 46
    and death....................73-7, 80-1, 180
    deliverance of 70-3, 76, 78, 80
    envy towards 63-4
    ethics of..24-7
    and faith 78-9
    first-person references . 27, 29, 32, 170
    greetings of......................... 31-40, 272
    imitating................... 26-7, 29, 60, 188,
    .... 226-9, 255-6
    imprisonment of 9-11, 16-17, 49,
    .... 59-65, 76, 92
    initial visit to Philippi... 14-15, 17, 35
    Jewish heritage of.....14, 198-202, 207
    labor of............................... 74-5, 163-5
    love for the church.......... 11, 24, 43-5,
    ....48-9, 115n, 151-2, 240-1
    as martyr 59, 76
    persecutes church 9, 201-2
    as Pharisee....................9, 191, 201, 207
    prayers of 45, 49-50, 53, 56-7n, 71
    relational ministry of...... 169-71, 175,
    ....178, 183

Subject Index

relationship with Epaphroditus.... 177-8,
....244
relationship with Timothy......... 31-2,
.... 171-6
religious credentials of. 197-202, 207,
....214
rivals of............................. 63-6, 108-9
as Roman citizen 35, 87
as servant...........................33, 176, 205
as slave.. 33-4
style of.. 119-23
suffering of................72-3, 92-3, 204-5
support of the church.... 262-3, 265-7,
....270
thanksgivings of............ 43-5, 53, 56n
trial of 17, 176
weakness of.......................................17
perfection 223-4, 226
Peter 37
Pharisees..............................191, 200-2, 207
Philip of Macedon..................................12
Philippi 12-14, 25, 35, 87, 232
Philippi, Battle of (42 BC)......................35
Philippian church
and citizenship 86-8
composition of.............................36-7
factions in...... 16, 63-5, 98, 104-5, 244
give glory to Christ 78-80
love for Paul....................... 103, 115n
obedience of 150-2
opposition to................... 17, 217-19n
Pauls love for 11, 24, 43-5, 48-9,
.... 115n, 151-2, 240-1
and return of Epaphroditus... 179-82,
....189
as 'saints' 22, 34-5, 48
suffering of................................... 91-2
support for Paul...... 262-3, 265-7, 270
unity in 88-91, 103-4, 107
Phinehas 201-2
Polycarp..242
praetorian guard 11, 62-3, 272
prayer... 25, 252-3
pretense 65-6
pride 118, 150, 153
Prison Epistles 16-17
purity 51-2, 159-60
purposes of epistle....................... 7, 11-12

Questioning................................ 157-8

Reasonableness..................................247
resurrection of believers..... 23-4, 74-5, 77,
....................................80, 180, 212-13, 222-3,
.... 233-5
righteousness...
and blamelessness................... 51-2, 54

and faith in Christ .. 46, 202-3, 208-11
'fruit of' 47, 50, 52, 54, 57n, 103
and law 202-3, 206-8, 211
Robert's Rules of Order (book).......... 105-6
Roman citizenship 86-7

Sanctification........................22, 47, 108
self-denial...110-11
self-identity 187-8
selfish ambition 109
Seneca 134
servitude..33, 130
Silas 13, 15
slavery....................................33, 130, 176
Solomom, King..............................137, 199
sorrow 180
speech 157-9
Stoicism 14, 70, 264
structure of epistle 7, 27-9
suffering 26
supplication 252-3
Syntyche 25, 98, 104, 242-3, 247

Tarsus...200
temptations of the world 255-7
Ten Commandments 138
The Concept of Anxiety (book)..............250
themes of epistle................................18-27
Timothy
authorship of epistle.... 8, 31-2, 170-1
circumcision of 32
initial visit to Philippi...................35
ministerial service of 29
as model of Christian ministry ... 172-6,
.... 183
relationship with Paul..... 31-2, 171-6
sent to Philippi by Paul........9, 11, 32,
....170-7
as servant of God 33
Titus 154
Torah 200, 207
Trinity ... 21, 71, 115n, 120, 127, 140, 195-6

'Walking'.................................... 227-9
'words of life' 160-1

Zealots... 201-2

Scripture Index

Genesis
1:26-28 ... 126
2:8 ... 40, 139
2:15, 18, 22 ... 139
3:8, 9, 13, 14, 21, 23 ... 139
17:1 ... 159
17:5 ... 136
32:28 ... 136

Exodus
3:4 ... 40, 139
3:7, 15-16 ... 139
20:4 ... 138
20:11 ... 138
20:20 ... 155
31:17 ... 138

Leviticus
1:3-4 ... 268
22:20-21 ... 268

Numbers
4:7 ... 164
25:11 ... 202
28:7 ... 164

Deuteronomy
6:13 ... 196
21:22-23.20 ... 134
30:6 ... 193, 194
32:5 ... 160

1 Samuel
9:16, 21 ... 199
10:20-21 ... 199
14:41 ... 33
23:10 ... 33

1 Kings
1:47 ... 136-7
12:21 ... 199

Ezra
4:17 ... 38
5:7 ... 38
10:9 ... 199

Job
1:1, 8 ... 159
2:3 ... 159

Psalms
16:3 ... 34
22:1-18 ... 133
30:6 ... 273
34:9 ... 34
34:22 ... 33
96:9 ... 135
102:15 ... 137
148:13 ... 137

Proverbs
3:34 ... 135
11:30 ... 52

Ecclesiastes
1:9 ... 70

Isaiah
45:23 ... 139
53:1-12 ... 133
56:5 ... 136
56:7 ... 268

Daniel
7:18 ... 34
9:17 ... 33

Amos
6:12 ... 52

Habakkuk
3:18-19 ... 246

Malachi
2:15-16 ... 273

Matthew
3:7 ... 200
5:20 ... 201
6:19-25 ... 251
6:27, 30, 33, 34 ... 251
7:6 ... 192
7:13 ... 229
11:29 ... 132
15:11 ... 158
18:4 ... 132
19:30 ... 118
20:16 ... 118
20:28 ... 118
23 ... 200
23:2 ... 200-1
23:12 ... 132
26:53-56 ... 134
27:18 ... 64
27:27 ... 11

Mark
2:1-12 ... 127
9:35 ... 118
10:31 ... 118
10:33-34 ... 118
10:45 ... 118
12:40 ... 66
14:62 ... 127
15:10 ... 64
15:34-37 ... 133

Luke
5:7 ... 244
9:45 ... 50
10:9 ... 248
12:36 ... 77
12:50 ... 76
13:30 ... 118
14:11 ... 132
18:14 ... 132
20:47 ... 66
23:46 ... 273

John
- 5:18 ... 126
- 6:63, 68 ... 160
- 10:17-18 ... 129
- 16:20-22 ... 180

Acts
- 5:20 ... 160
- 6:1-7 ... 37
- 8:33 ... 132
- 9:5 ... 202
- 13:21 ... 199
- 15 ... 190
- 15:5 ... 191, 201
- 15:23 ... 38
- 16 ... 17
- 16:1-3 ... 31
- 16:1-4 ... 175
- 16:3 ... 32
- 16:11 ... 12
- 16:11–17:9 ... 266
- 16:12 ... 12
- 16:12-40 ... 14, 35
- 16:23-24 ... 13
- 16:37-38 ... 87
- 17:14-15 ... 32
- 19:17 ... 73
- 20:17 ... 36
- 20:28 ... 36, 37
- 21:27–28:31 ... 10
- 21:37 ... 60
- 21:40 ... 200
- 22:2 ... 200
- 22:3 ... 200, 201, 202
- 22:25-29 ... 87
- 22:26-29 ... 232
- 23:1 ... 86
- 23:6 ... 9, 201
- 23:16, 35 ... 60
- 23:26 ... 38
- 23:27 ... 87
- 23:35 ... 11
- 25:10-12, 18, 25 ... 10
- 26:4-5 ... 200
- 26:5 ... 9
- 26:14 ... 200
- 26:31-32 ... 10
- 27:10, 21 ... 204
- 27:30 ... 66
- 28:16-31 ... 60

Romans
- 1:1 ... 33
- 1:3-6 ... 119
- 1:8 ... 44
- 1:9 ... 273
- 1:10 ... 262
- 1:18–3:20 ... 203
- 1:23 ... 140
- 2:8 ... 109
- 2:18 ... 51
- 2:23 ... 196
- 3:23 ... 140
- 4:2 ... 79
- 5:1 ... 39
- 5:2 ... 140
- 5:2, 11 ... 162
- 5:3-4 ... 174
- 5:10 ... 230
- 6:4 ... 140
- 6:5-11 ... 213
- 6:15-23 ... 33, 156
- 6:22 ... 267
- 7:12 ... 209
- 8:1-11 ... 196
- 8:3 ... 131
- 8:7 ... 209
- 8:9 ... 71
- 8:9-17 ... 156
- 8:15 ... 23, 271
- 8:17 ... 72
- 8:19 ... 72
- 9:2 ... 180
- 9:4, 8 ... 39
- 9:4-5 ... 199
- 9:5 ... 120, 127
- 10:9 ... 140
- 11:1 ... 199
- 11:17 ... 266
- 12:1 ... 102, 196
- 12:2 ... 51, 223, 255
- 12:3 ... 140
- 12:8 ... 99
- 12:13 ... 266
- 12:16 ... 104, 132
- 13:9-10 ... 112
- 14:4 ... 89
- 14:11 ... 137
- 15:4 ... 99
- 15:5 ... 99, 104
- 15:6-7 ... 72
- 15:13 ... 103
- 15:14 ... 103
- 15:16 ... 179
- 15:17, 18, 19 ... 162
- 15:28 ... 267
- 15:30 ... 243
- 15:33 ... 257
- 16:17 ... 243
- 16:18 ... 230
- 16:20 ... 257
- 16:21 ... 32
- 16:23 ... 87

1 Corinthians
- 1:4 ... 44
- 1:10–4:21 ... 65
- 1:11 ... 64
- 1:18-25 ... 230
- 1:23 ... 64, 134
- 1:24-25 ... 134
- 1:26 ... 225
- 1:29 ... 196
- 1:31 ... 196
- 2:7 ... 141
- 2:23 ... 154
- 3:3 ... 64, 229
- 3:10-15 ... 268
- 4:6 ... 27
- 4:17 ... 32
- 4:19 ... 172
- 5:4 ... 273
- 5:6 ... 79
- 7:7 ... 244
- 7:20 ... 225
- 9:5 ... 244
- 9:23 ... 266
- 9:24 ... 225
- 11:1 ... 26, 228
- 11:28 ... 51
- 12:9, 13 ... 90
- 14:3 ... 99
- 15:25 ... 140
- 15:26 ... 180
- 15:35-55 ... 233
- 15:50-57 ... 180
- 15:51-52 ... 233
- 15:58 ... 182
- 16:3 ... 51
- 16:10 ... 32, 182
- 16:13 ... 89
- 16:18 ... 273

2 Corinthians
- 1:1 ... 32
- 1:3 ... 102
- 1:4 ... 99
- 1:12 ... 162
- 1:14 ... 79, 162
- 1:19 ... 32
- 2:9 ... 174
- 3:7-11 ... 140
- 4:2 ... 229
- 4:6 ... 205

Scripture Index

4:17 140
5:10 268
5:12 .... 79, 162
5:14 76
7:4 103
7:13 273
7:15 154
8:1-5 16
8:2 174
8:8 51
8:9 .... 129, 205
8:22 51
9:3 .... 79, 162
9:8 264
9:11 .... 152, 268
9:13 .... 72, 174
10:1–13:10 65
10:3-4 178
11:22 200
11:23–12:10 263
11:4 64
11:7 132
12:20 64
12:21 132
13:3 174
13:11 .... 104, 189, 245, 247
13:13 102

Galatians

1:5 271
1:6-9 191
1:14 201
2:2 162
2:15-16 191
2:20 213
3:1-9 191
3:2-3 196
3:10 191
3:21-28 191
3:24-25 203
4:5 .... 23, 271
4:21 191
5:2-6 191
5:16-24 267
5:16-26 156
5:20 109
6:4 51
6:13 .... 191, 196
6:14 .... 162, 197
6:18 273

Ephesians

1:5 .... 23, 271
1:17 50
1:19 212

2:2 229
2:8-10 .... 153, 154
2:9 .... 1962:14 131
2:18 90
2:19 86
4:1 .... 88, 225, 243
4:1-2 17
4:2 .... 109, 132
4:4 90
4:13 223
4:17 229
4:23 273
4:29 158
5:9 267
5:11 266
6:1-4 175
6:5 154
6:12 91

Colossians

1:1 32
1:7 177
1:9 .... 50, 103
1:10 88
1:15 125
1:17 129
1:21 230
1:22 131
1:24 72
1:28 223
2:8-15 119
2:11-15 194
2:12 213
3:4 213
3:5 231
3:7 229
3:12 .... 102, 132
3:20 175
4:12 177

1 Thessalonians

1:6 27
2:2 .... 15, 92
2:5 66
2:7-8 48
2:12 88
2:14 .... 27, 228, 256
2:18 266
3:2, 6 32
3:8 89
4:1 189
5:16 245
5:23 .... 257, 273

2 Thessalonians

1:6-9 140
1:11 .... 2252:16-17 153
3:1 189
3:7, 9 27

1 Timothy

1:2 175
1:3 32
1:8-9 209
1:18 178
3:1-13 .... 37, 256
3:2 37
3:3 247
3:4-5 37
3:8-13 37
3:16 .... 1254:16 160
5:9-10 256
5:17 .... 37, 256
6:4 64
6:6 264
6:12 92

2 Timothy

1:2 175
1:4 103
1:5 32
1:8 10
2:3-4 178
3:15 32
4:6 164
4:6-8 .... 10, 17
4:9 172
4:16 17
4:17 264
4:18 271
4:22 273

Titus

1:4 175
1:5 36
1:5-9 256
1:7 36
1:9 .... 37, 256
2:13 .... 120, 127
2:14 153
3:2 247
3:9 64

Philemon

1 32
4 44
22 71
25 273

Hebrews
6:12 228
8:2 179
10:33 266
12:2 133
13:7 228
13:23 32

James
1:1 38
3:2 158

3:14, 16 109
4:6 135
4:10 .... 132, 135

1 Peter
3:8 132
5:1-4 37
5:5 37
5:5-6 .... 132, 135
5:6-7 252

2 Peter
3:1 51
3:8-10 249

1 John
1:1 160

Revelation
1:9 266
18:4 266

Abbreviations

Ant.	(Josephus') Antiquities
BDAG	W. Bauer, F. W. Danker, W. F. Arndt, and F. W. Gingrich. *Greek-English Lexicon of the New Testament and Other Early Christian Literature*. 3rd ed. (Chicago, 1999)
cf.	*confer* (= compare)
1 Clem.	1 Clement (First Epistle of Clement)
esp.	especially
ESV	English Standard Version
f.	following verse
ff.	following verses
IEph.	Ignatius' Letter to the Ephesians
IMag.	Ignatius' Letter to the Magnesians
KJV	King James Version
LXX	Septuagint (= Greek Old Testament)
Macc.	Maccabees (e.g., 1 Maccabees, etc.)
NASB	New American Standard Bible
NIV	New International Version
p.	page
pp.	pages
RSV	Revised Standard Version
Sir.	Sirach (= Ecclesiasticus)
s.v.	*sub verbo* (= under the word just cited)
Wisd.	Wisdom of Solomon

Selected Bibliography

This is a short list of other commentaries that I would recommend for further study. For more complete lists of commentaries, monographs, and articles, consult the bibliographies in these commentaries (especially those in O'Brien or Hawthorne/Martin).

Fee, Gordon D. *Paul's Letter to the Philippians*. New International Commentary on the New Testament. Grand Rapids: Eerdmans, 1995.

Hansen, G. Walter. *Letter to the Philippians*. Pillar New Testament Commentary. Grand Rapids: Eerdmans; Nottingham: Apollos Press, 2009.

Hawthorne, Gerald F. *Philippians*. Revised by Ralph Martin. Revised edition. Word Biblical Commentary 43. Nashville: Thomas Nelson, 2004.

Lightfoot, J. B. *Saint Paul's Epistle to the Philippians: A Revised Text, with Introduction, Notes, and Dissertations*. Fourth edition. London: Macmillan, 1913. Subsequently reprinted by Zondervan, Hendrickson, and (in an abridged form) by Crossway Publishers.

O'Brien, Peter T. *The Epistle to the Philippians: A Commentary on the Greek Text*. New International Greek Testament Commentary. Grand Rapids: Eerdmans, 1991.

Silva, Moisés. *Philippians*. Second edition. Baker Exegetical Commentary on the New Testament 11. Grand Rapids: Baker Academic, 2005.

Thielman, Frank. *Philippians*. NIV Application Commentary. Grand Rapids: Zondervan, 1995.

Christian Focus Publications
publishes books for all ages

Our mission statement –

STAYING FAITHFUL
In dependence upon God we seek to impact the world through literature faithful to His infallible Word, the Bible. Our aim is to ensure that the Lord Jesus Christ is presented as the only hope to obtain forgiveness of sin, live a useful life and look forward to heaven with Him.

REACHING OUT
Christ's last command requires us to reach out to our world with His gospel. We seek to help fulfil that by publishing books that point people towards Jesus and help them develop a Christ-like maturity. We aim to equip all levels of readers for life, work, ministry and mission.

Books in our adult range are published in three imprints.

Christian Focus contains popular works including biographies, commentaries, basic doctrine and Christian living. Our children's books are also published in this imprint.

Mentor focuses on books written at a level suitable for Bible College and seminary students, pastors, and other serious readers. The imprint includes commentaries, doctrinal studies, examination of current issues and church history.

Christian Heritage contains classic writings from the past.

Christian Focus Publications, Ltd
Geanies House, Fearn, Ross-shire,
IV20 1TW, Scotland, United Kingdom
info@christianfocus.com

www.christianfocus.com